D0396624

Dec 2013

THE SOCIAL MEDIA MBA IN PRACTICE

THE SOCIAL MEDIA MBA IN PRACTICE

An Essential Collection of Inspirational
Case Studies to Influence Your Social
Media Strategy

Christer Holloman

WILEY

This edition first published 2013
© 2013 John Wiley & Sons, Ltd

Registered office
John Wiley and Sons Ltd, The Atrium, Southern Gate, Chichester, West Sussex, PO19 8SQ, United Kingdom

For details of our global editorial offices, for customer services and for information about how to apply for permission to reuse the copyright material in this book please see our website at www.wiley.com.

All rights reserved. No part of this publication may be reproduced, stored in a retrieval system, or transmitted, in any form or by any means, electronic, mechanical, photocopying, recording or otherwise, except as permitted by the UK Copyright, Designs and Patents Act 1988, without the prior permission of the publisher.

Wiley publishes in a variety of print and electronic formats and by print-on-demand. Some material included with standard print versions of this book may not be included in e-books or in print-on-demand. If this book refers to media such as a CD or DVD that is not included in the version you purchased, you may download this material at http://booksupport.wiley.com. For more information about Wiley products, visit www.wiley.com.

Designations used by companies to distinguish their products are often claimed as trademarks. All brand names and product names used in this book and on its cover are trade names, service marks, trademarks or registered trademarks of their respective owners. The publisher and the book are not associated with any product or vendor mentioned in this book. None of the companies referenced within the book have endorsed the book.

Limit of Liability/Disclaimer of Warranty: While the publisher and author have used their best efforts in preparing this book, they make no representations or warranties with the respect to the accuracy or completeness of the contents of this book and specifically disclaim any implied warranties of merchantability or fitness for a particular purpose. It is sold on the understanding that the publisher is not engaged in rendering professional services and neither the publisher nor the author shall be liable for damages arising herefrom. If professional advice or other expert assistance is required, the services of a competent professional should be sought.

Library of Congress Cataloging-in-Publication Data
Holloman, Christer.
  The social media MBA in practice : an essential collection of inspirational case studies to influence your social media strategy / Christer Holloman.
      pages cm
  Includes index.
  ISBN 978-1-118-52454-1 (hardback)
1. Internet marketing.   2. Social media.   I. Title.
  HF5415.1265.H65436 2013
  658.8'72–dc23   2013018239

A catalogue record for this book is available from the British Library.

ISBN 978-1-118-52454-1 (hardback) ISBN 978-1-118-52452-7 (ebk)
ISBN 978-1-118-52451-0 (ebk)

Cover design: Mackerel Ltd
Set in 10/13pt FF Scala by Toppan Best-set Premedia Limited, Hong Kong
Printed in Great Britain by TJ International Ltd, Padstow, Cornwall, UK

CONTENTS

ACKNOWLEDGEMENTS

Till Elizabeth Holloman och Leif Edlund.

För precis var enda söndagsfrukost tillsammans. Tack för all gröt och alla russin, alla multivitaminer, alla långkalsonger man ska ha på sig hela tiden, alla skogspromenader i I2o skogen, allt färdgodis, alla reklambladsrundor, alla vändor upp och ned Formvägen, alla mellanmål och fikapauser, alla charterresor, alla Legobitar, alla skratt och lite gråt.

För den bästa starten i livet någon kunnat önska sig. Jag ser fram emot den dagen jag kan ge det ni gett mig till någon ny liten direktör, grävmaskinist, läkare eller skådis.

PREFACE

"If social is owned by Marketing, Marketing isn't being very social."

Following the success of *The Social Media MBA* published 18 months ago – an Amazon bestseller that at its peak was one of the 500 most bought books of the 6.2 million on sale in the UK and in the top five within its category for half a year – I've been invited to speak at a number of events around the world.

I usually start my talks by asking the audience what they would like to get out of our session together and nine out of ten times the most frequent request is that I share best practice case studies to inspire the development and delivery of their own social media strategy.

Reading the reviews about the first book, online and in the trade press, it also becomes clear that one of the most appreciated aspects of the first book is the handful of case studies I decided to feature in it.

This book was born because of this feedback, your many requests for more case studies.

I tapped into my global network of social media leaders to capture the most interesting applications of social media in this essential collection of case studies never before shared in public.

Who is this book for?

I made a claim in the first book, suggesting that it was the first in the third and final wave of social media literature that didn't talk about the rise of social or serve as an "ABC"-style guide for how to do the basics, but for the first time targeted companies and practitioners that had used social media for one or two years already and wanted to move it to the next level. This book is also for those that already "get" social but who want to become even more clever about the way they use it or want to validate their current approach.

Traditionally, matters relating to social media have been owned by marketing; but companies that confine social media to one department have missed the trick. Social media is a tool that should be leveraged by every department; sales, HR, product development, legal, facilities, etc. If you work in marketing, evangelize and empower; if you don't work in marketing, don't wait for them, just get on with it and do your own thing.

Whatever your country, industry, company size, current degree of social media adoption or your job title or department, the purpose of this book is to inspire you to see how you can raise the bar further to reap new rewards. It will give you the tools to make a difference to your organization's social media strategy development and delivery going forward.

If you want even more context, read what the social media leaders featured in this book studied first to get to where they are today. I recommend that you also consider taking a look at the *The Social Media MBA*.

How cases were selected

Over the course of a year I have probably heard about a thousand different applications of social media for businesses; maybe 1 in 100 stood out to me as something unique and clever, and those are the ones I decided to feature in this book. Diversity has been a key selection criterion so, even though some cases might address a similar issue, the way it was addressed will differ.

I constantly monitor stories and interesting companies related to social media use around the world. Some I feature on *Sky News*, like the innovative small internet startup Carhoots.com that has managed to get more followers on Pinterest then any other brand in the car industry (at the time of writing) – the even bigger stories I have saved for this book.

As I've alluded to already I spend a lot of my time giving talks, training and providing consultancy services relating to social media and other technology trends to audiences ranging from business students to C-level executives at trade shows, as well as external and internal events for clients such as Microsoft, VISA and ADP. This has helped me grow my network of some of the brightest minds in this industry and a number of them even qualified to have their story included in this book.

When I'm not speaking at conferences, I attend a fair few as a delegate, primarily around the US but also across Europe and the Middle East. It was at events like these that I met the social media leaders at Barclaycard, Honda and giffgaff – all three featured in this book.

Add all of these sources together and you get the collection of cases you now hold in your hand. Cases ranging from a government body and public transport provider to specialized B2B suppliers and mainstream B2C brands we all know.

How the cases where developed

Once I had shortlisted the most interesting cases, I arranged to meet with those behind them in person, or by phone, to discuss their story and the most interesting angles, with respect to all the other cases being considered, to make sure I could present you with the most stimulating content for your benefit.

This was followed up by a lengthy in-depth interview, in some instances involving several stakeholders, to capture the story in the best possibly way. It was important for me to push my interviewees not just to give the overall strategy but the tactical approach, in order to make it easier for you to replicate.

I based the outline of the case template on the Harvard University style to provoke thought, discussion, debate and learning. Michael Netzley PhD, Assistant Professor at the Singapore Management University where he teaches corporate reputation and digital media, worked with me to develop the format and questions that I subjected every brand representative to.

Even though I followed the same template when interviewing, each case will vary slightly. This is because different organizations were able to share different kinds of information and varying amount of detail – and due to the nature of each particular case the focus of each write-up might be different. Some cases are more strategic, others more tactical or more campaign focused. I've also aimed to convey the personal style and tone of my interviewees to make the reading more interesting.

The cases, although grouped under topic areas, are not linked to each other so you can start anywhere you like. I don't know which case will resonate the best with you so read the Executive Summary first to see if it captures your imagination or if you should save it for later. Don't make the mistake of only looking at companies in your industry, or those that are similar; lending inspiration from different verticals and countries is a tried and tested success model.

What's next?

We saw social really coming of age during 2012, with almost every company in the connected world now engaging with it in some shape or form. It's fair to say that we have reached the end of the digital beginning, social media isn't a novelty any longer and as such there will be less room for mistakes as your competitors, and tiny startups we haven't even heard of yet, are getting really social media savvy.

I think we have all had enough of "social media experts" so I let the facts and numbers do the talking instead and I think this is something we should all aspire to do. This is particularly important when discussing social media, as it is still perceived as a "black box" by a lot of people in our organizations. This is even more true when thinking about people outside the marketing function and the organizations' senior leaders. Not even the Chairman of Google, Eric Schmidt, was using his own Google+ when it was rolled out, so how can we expect your boss and their bosses to understand what you're doing and why it is important? This book will definitely give you new references to use when teaching your business about social and its potential impact and help you show that social can be much more than just a marketing campaign.

The notion of "bought, earned and owned media" has now been extended to include "managed media" – providing a consistent, managed, brand experience across channels. One aspect of this, which will affect more organizations than ever going forward, is how you deal with crisis in the multi-channel world.

Jochem van Drimmelen, Online Reputation Manager at KLM, told me about a situation that happened in February 2012. Schiphol Airport, Amsterdam, was faced with major flight disruptions due to severe winter weather conditions. Extra safety precautions, including snow removal, de-icing and limited runway capacity, caused lengthy delays. As a result, dozens of flights were delayed or cancelled, and thousands of passengers were stranded throughout the world.

KLM responded by scaling up their social media and rebooking teams to full capacity around the clock. Additionally, they contacted the pool of volunteers they had recruited for this kind of situation. As soon as they were set, they posted a message on the company web site and distributed flyers to passengers at the airport, inviting them to contact them via Facebook and Twitter should they need any assistance.

Over the course of a few days, this resulted in a 20-fold increase in booking related cases. Because they were prepared, they were able to stay within their one-hour service level agreement (SLA) most of the time.

The winter conditions provided them with new insights, which now help them to anticipate and be even better prepared in the future. They are equipped to handle much larger volumes of passengers, even in multiple languages. They also improved their cooperation with the KLM Operations Control Center by setting up a permanent direct connection, providing the latest updates instantly.

As social media continues to attract additional budgets your pressure to deliver a tangible return for your business in this area will increase. Learning from the best through case studies will save you time and money, so it was indeed a smart move of yours to get this book. I firmly believe the case studies I have outlined here will help you take some of the guesswork out of your own equations and inspire you to go further.

With all that said I think we are now set to commence class, sharpen your pens!

Christer Holloman
London, 2013
@holloman

P.S. Are you a member yet?

There is an alumni network of fellow readers, people around the world that work professionally with social media. It is a great place to exchange ideas, ask questions or perhaps look around for new job openings or recruit a member to your team. Join by visiting http://www.socialmedia-mba.com or search for "The Social Media MBA Alumni" on LinkedIn. It's free of course.

HALL OF FAME

Keep an eye on what's next from the social media practitioners featured in this book:

Christer Holloman
The Social Media MBA

@holloman
@sm_mba

Christine M. Talcott
Vice President
Employer Services Global Sales Operations

ADP
@cmtalcott

Natalie Woods
Digital Marketing Manager

Allianz
@YourCoverUK

Jared Young
Senior Director
Barclaycard Ring

Barclaycard
@JaredEYoung

Jeanette Gibson
Senior Director
Social and Digital Marketing

Cisco
@JeanetteG

Sharon Flaherty
Head of Content

Confused.com
@ConfusedSharon

Richard Margetic
Director
Global Social Media

Dell
@Dell

MaryKay Kopf
Chief Marketing Officer and Senior Vice President

Electrolux
@ElectroluxGroup

Nick Bowman
EMEA Corporate Communications Manager

F5
@nick_bowman

Yvonne Chien
Senior Vice President of Marketing

Getty Images
@GettyImages

Vincent Boon
Chief of Community

giffgaff
@VincentBoon

Samantha Hodder
Group Corporate Affairs Director

Go-Ahead Group
@GoAheadGroup

Prithvi Shergill
Chief Human Resources Officer

HCL
@hcltech

Jenni Bair
Brand Marketing Manager

Hobart
@hobartcorp

Simon Nicholson
Social Media Manager

Honda Europe
@Sikenic

Cristina Astorri
Marketing Manager UK and Ireland

LivingSocial
@ascrissy

Carol Naylor
Social Media and Online Communities Manager

Macmillan
@popplestone

Paul Beadle
Senior Manager, Media Relations

Nationwide
@paulbeadle

Jim Ibister
VP of Facility Administration and General Manager

NHL Minnesota Wild
@mnwild

Craig Hepburn
Global Director of Digital and Social Media

Nokia
@craighepburn

Adam Stewart
Marketing Director

Play.com
@playcom

Norman Lewis
Director, PwC One

PwC
@Norm_Lewis

Alicia Holbrook
Social Media Manager

Rentokil
@aliciajharney

Olle Hagelin
Quality Manager, Field Data Management as part
of Quality and Customer Service

Sony Mobile
@OHagelin

Andy Hill
Web and Social Media Executive
Integrated Marketing Organization

Xerox
@Andy_Hill

Part I
Set-Up

1 Nationwide – Creating Senior Leadership Buy-In

IT'S ALL ABOUT THE CUSTOMER, STUPID!

In the highly regulated, risk-averse environment of financial services, Nationwide Building Society's social media strategy breaks the mould by actively encouraging its customers to share their views.

Executive summary

Overview

As one of the UK's most trusted financial services providers, Nationwide used social media to better understand what its customers wanted to talk about and where they wanted to talk. Rejecting the view that "social is just for marketing", they went back to basics and embraced social media as a customer service channel for a generation of customers.

Key findings

- Getting everyone in the room helps stakeholder buy-in.
- Listen first before you do anything.
- Honesty in the face of a crisis is the best approach.

Recommendations

1. Ask the tough questions first – how will social media make life better for the business and our customers?
2. Get the basics down – business case and governance – it makes life easier in the long run.
3. Listen to lots of people – but be wary of those that call themselves "social media experts".

Background

Interviewee

Paul Beadle started his career as a journalist before moving into PR, specializing in financial services. After three years in South Africa, where he helped create the country's first financial comparison site, he returned to the UK and joined Nationwide, setting up the building society's social media team.

Paul Beadle
@paulbeadle

About Nationwide

Nationwide Building Society are the UK's biggest building society, meaning the organization is owned by their members, not shareholders. They are the UK's second largest savings provider and the third largest provider of mortgages, as well as being a major provider of current accounts, credit cards, loans and general insurance. With 16,000 employees and a branch network of around 700, Nationwide has around 15 million customers and assets of over £2 billion.

Their social media strategy

Nationwide approaches social media in a different way to most other financial services companies in that it doesn't view social media as just another marketing tool or, as is often the case, a customer service headache.

Nationwide sees social media as a channel with lots of different opportunities and requirements, many of which overlap and complement each other, requiring different business areas to get involved.

That's why the overarching strategy is managed by the social media forum, a group of key stakeholders that represents interests across Nationwide ranging from PR and customer experience through to HR and legal. This overarching strategy and management model was put in place by the social media team, who sit within external affairs, the department responsible for promoting, managing and protecting the bank's reputation in PR, media relations and public affairs.

Nationwide recognized that social media plays an increasingly important role in how businesses are perceived by the public and influencers, whether it is comment on the service customers receive or the news stories they read. As guardians of that reputation, the external affairs department had the right experience, insight and set of skills required to handle the implementation and development of social media at Nationwide, minimizing any risks and helping to realize the potential of the channel.

Whilst individual business departments are responsible for managing their own social media strategy and budget, PR, marketing and customer service, for example, the forum is responsible for shaping the strategic direction for the use of social media across Nationwide. For example, the forum will consider the effectiveness of its corporate governance, the impact of regulatory changes, potential new uses for social media or the opportunity offered by new technology or platforms.

The external affairs social media team, working with the internet channels team, formed the project group implementing social media at Nationwide, creating the forum, setting up the overarching strategy, putting in place the governance framework and building the initial assets.

The overarching strategy has three key elements:

- **Boosting customer satisfaction:** using social media to help customers by answering their questions and queries, as well as providing them with useful information such as guides, online Q&As and how-to videos.
- **Reputation management:** monitoring comments and mentions of Nationwide online to understand what their customers and others think of their products and services, enabling them to respond to any issues and use that insight to help shape future developments.
- **Increasing customer engagement:** using social media to engage with customers via content such as hints and tips, polls, feature articles, videos and competitions; as well as encouraging customers to share this content to raise awareness of Nationwide.

The external affairs social media and the internet channels teams also set up Nationwide's first social media assets – Facebook, Customer Twitter, YouTube and LinkedIn – creating the sites and putting in place governance to ensure that they are properly managed. In addition the external affairs social media team also implemented a social media listening tool to monitor Nationwide's own social channels and the wider web.

The case

The problem

Financial services is a complicated industry, full of rules and regulations that control the way that products and services are marketed and sold, as well as setting stringent standards for the way customers are dealt with. As a result, many financial services companies are cautious of using social media, nervous of falling foul of regulations or worried about being overwhelmed by negative customer comments.

Yet the web is where people go to find out about the mortgages, savings products, credit cards and current accounts they need and the best companies to use to get those products – social media is the engine that drives this research, whether by sharing opinions with friends and comments in forums, or by checking out reviews by other users and stories from the media and bloggers.

Nationwide wanted to tap into this network of comment and questions, both in terms of understanding what customers wanted and what they already thought of the organization, and how the bank could inform and influence these discussions.

The issue for Nationwide was how to use social media effectively and appropriately within the framework of regulation and its own governance structure, whilst providing something that people would see as worthwhile and would actually respond to.

At the same time, the project team responsible for bringing social media to Nationwide had to show the business case and demonstrate the benefits, prove that it could be managed properly and show how any risks could be mitigated.

Background

Nationwide launched the UK's first internet banking service back in the 1990s, so it has a tradition of embracing new technology. But social media offered more than just a technological challenge – it had implications around reputation, public perception and the culture of the business, as well as putting the company under the spotlight of scrutiny by customers, financial regulators, competitors and even the government.

Nationwide knew that social media could be a powerful way to serve customers, providing them with help and support or resolving their issues, but it also brought with it massive reputational and operational challenges.

When they started to roll out its social media plan at the end of 2010, the financial sector was in the midst of an economic downturn and was struggling with negative headlines and poor public perception. The bank had navigated its way successfully through this period and had never faced any of the issues that many of its banking competitors had. So the opportunity for Nationwide was to build on this position of strength and use social media to raise awareness of the organization and the difference between it and the banks.

Some of the banks had half-heartedly tried their hands at social media, but it was either an ill-thought out marketing campaign that did not really seek to engage with customers, or it was a corporate Twitter feed designed to pump out marketing and PR messages that quickly became swamped with consumer feedback without any real strategy for how to respond and deal with customer service issues.

The solution

Nationwide's first step into social media came towards the end of 2010 when the external affairs team launched its @NationwidePress Twitter, designed to engage directly with the media. Recognizing that the way journalists found their stories had changed – with more turning to social media for leads, insight or public comment – the external affairs team used @Nationwide-Press to communicate with journalists, provide them with comment from the media relations team and alert them to new products and news stories. This also enabled the team to stay on top of emerging issues and breaking news being discussed by the media.

It was at this point that the external affairs social media team was set up, bringing together experts with traditional media relations experience and people with more in-depth social media background. The new team's remit was to explore the impact of social media on Nationwide, particularly in the area of reputation management, and to put together a plan for how social media could be used to benefit the organization.

The team's first step was to listen.

The @NationwidePress Twitter had already given Nationwide a snapshot of what was being discussed online, but the external affairs social media team wanted a much more in-depth and exhaustive trawl of the web, peeping into all corners to find out what people were talking about in forums, blogs and micro-blogs. The team chose the Sysomos monitoring tool, which not only provided the in-depth search and sentiment feedback it needed, but also delivered hourly buzz alerts via email to flag up any mentions to help the social media team identify emerging issues.

Using the insight the listening process had given them, the social media team next began to map out the opportunities and challenges social media provided: what people were saying, where they were saying it and how best Nationwide could get involved and influence those conversations.

Working with Nationwide's internet channels team, who were responsible for the nationwide.co.uk web site and the digital marketing activity, a project team was formed. Next was the creation of the social media forum, which would act as the heart, conscience and sense-check of the new social media project. Stakeholders from across the bank joined the forum, working on the "in the room" principle – if there wasn't someone in the room who knew the answer to any issue, whether it was the impact of regulation, marketing best practice or how internal customer service procedures should be applied to Twitter, then one of the forum members would know where to find the answer.

The forum was also where requirement gathering took place:

Who wanted to use social media?
What was their objective?
How should existing requirements for data protection and information security be addressed?
Who needed to approve content and how was it recorded?

All these questions and more were asked, answered and approved by the project team working through the forum.

An overarching strategy was agreed and approved by the forum and taken to Nationwide's senior management, along with a road map for how it would be implemented. The strategy had three key elements:

1. Boosting customer satisfaction.
2. Reputation management.
3. Increasing customer engagement.

The road map set out what assets would be put in place and by when, along with a timescale for how they would be developed. The approach was to test and learn – implement the basics and then take the insight and experience to develop activity and make things even better. By the end of 2011 the plan began to roll out.

- **Listening:** the Sysomos monitoring tool was in place and was providing the external affairs social media team with valuable insight, as well as flagging up issues and opportunities. The social media team began actively responding to comments and escalating issues or sentiment feedback to relevant business areas, either to coordinate a response or simply to provide them with feedback on what customers thought.
- **YouTube:** Nationwide took a tactical decision to launch its YouTube channel ahead of its other social media channels in order to help promote its new Carousel advert, the first TV advert for a number of years. YouTube enabled Nationwide to link to the advert and promote it on its main web site, offer the media pre-screenings and provide the public with a destination if they wanted to see more of the advert. A content plan quickly followed and a wide range of videos were produced, ranging from guides to using an ISA to vox pops looking at problems for first time house buyers and raising awareness of Nationwide's digital guides to buying and selling property. These videos were embedded in Nationwide's web site, taken by media sites and eventually used in their own social media channels.
- **LinkedIn:** a Nationwide LinkedIn careers page was created to support Nationwide's recruitment strategy, providing information on the organization, details of the latest jobs and a constant stream of corporate news and information, helping to reinforce their position as a leading player in the financial services market and a great place to work.
- **Facebook and @AskNationwide Twitter:** both channels were launched within weeks of each other in early 2012, but had very different remits. The @AskNationwide Twitter was conceived as a customer service channel from the outset and was built by working very closely with the e-contacts team in Nationwide's direct customer service department. A team of six customer service consultants were trained to use Twitter, ensuring the right tone of voice, whilst the existing customer service procedures were modified to provide an issues-handling process and SLAs for Twitter. The channel quickly became popular with customers who wanted to ask questions or had issues that needed resolving. Facebook was designed to build

a community by providing customers with useful information to help them better manage their money, such as how-to videos and downloadable guides, or hints and tips articles or blogs from Nationwide's money experts. To boost engagement, the page also featured polls, competitions and Talk-ingPoints where visitors could ask questions of Nationwide experts. But there was also a strong customer service element with a "How can we help" section featuring interactive FAQs and contact points.

The external affairs social media team and the internet channels team worked closely with Nationwide's brand team to make sure that all the new channels fitted in with the organization's look and feel. An editorial schedule was created to ensure a steady flow of interesting content that fitted in with Nation-wide's other communications and marketing plans, so promotion around new ISA savings products, for example, would be supported by appropriate guides or TalkingPoints on Facebook and across online and social media.

In the spring of 2012 following a fairly soft launch, the new channels of YouTube, Facebook and Twitter were properly launched to the public, as well as Nationwide staff, outlining the strategy, reinforcing the hard work that had gone in to developing a governance framework and inviting employees to provide their feedback. The response was overwhelmingly positive, especially from social media users and in particular when compared to the guarded social media approach taken by many of Nationwide's banking competitors.

As the social media activity ramped up, cross-channel marketing cam-paigns were designed that would cover traditional PR, print advertising, paid for online advertising and social media.

The journey from the creation of the social media project team to a fully-fledged plan being in place had taken less than 12 months.

Results

The statistics began to mount up fast: nearly 130,000 people viewed videos on the YouTube channel, including almost 32,000 for Nationwide's new "On your side" advert.

The Sysomos monitoring tool regularly picked up almost 3,000 mentions per month, highlighting potential issues and even alerting the bank to cases of possible fraud.

Within weeks the @AskNationwide Twitter was dealing with over a hundred Tweets on a weekly basis, providing customers with help and solving their problems.

LinkedIn rapidly became an important part of Nationwide's recruitment process and was being used to attract and recruit new employees.

The Facebook page racked up a reach of over a million people, helping to raise awareness of Nationwide and providing an opportunity for the organization to start social media marketing campaigns.

In summer 2012, not long after RBS had suffered a catastrophic collapse of it computer systems, Nationwide also experienced their own IT glitch – although not on the massive scale of RBS, a significant number of customers were affected. Nationwide immediately used social media as a way of communicating with customers, responding directly to their concerns on Twitter to reassure them that the issue was being fixed, as well as using Facebook to publish updates on progress, information to help customer with problems, a full apology and finally confirmation that the issue had been fixed within 24 hours.

The use of social media throughout the issue generated positive feedback by customers and the media, including Chris Choi, ITV News Consumer Editor, who said on *Daybreak*: "It has been rather interesting to see just how well Nationwide have gone on to (those) social networks and engaged with individual customers and their fury."

Critical success factors

1. Having a clear vision of what social media really could do for the bank was vital, which is why it was important to start with a listening phase first to understand how their customers were using social media to ensure Nationwide could respond to those needs in the right way.
2. Instead of rushing off to try viral videos or marketing gimmicks that fell flat, what Nationwide recognized was that good social customer service was vital and that people wanted their financial services providers to help and support them, not to try and sell to them or pretend to be something they're not on social networking sites.

Lessons learned

Paul says that the first question any business should ask before embarking on social media is: why? What is the potential benefit? How will this help my business? How will it help my customers? What are the risks and the potential pitfalls?

Don't be lulled by snake-oil salesmen "social" gurus into believing that social media is a must-have silver bullet – if it doesn't work for your business or your customers, or if you can't support it properly, any number of shiny viral videos are not going to make a difference to your bottom line. Not only will you struggle to see the value of social media, it could actually become a reputational nightmare.

Paul's top tips are:

- **Listen:** what are people saying about you and what are they saying about your competitors? How can you use this knowledge to shape the way you do business? And do they really want to engage with you on social media?
- **Get everybody in the room:** everybody in your business will have a different take on social media, whether it is a good or bad thing, whether it should be used to sell or to provide service, and whether it's a huge opportunity or a massive risk. The only way you can air these different views, build a consensus and form a workable plan, is by getting everybody with a stake in social media around a table and talking. You'll soon find that issues can be addressed and enthusiasm is contagious.
- **It's about customer service, stupid:** for most organizations, no matter how great their products are, customer service is the thing that will either drive people away or will turn existing customers into advocates. Social media is just a new approach to good-old-fashioned customer service – listen to your customers, respond and help them out. They will quickly repay you by telling their friends about the good service they got after tweeting you on their smartphone about an issue. Once you have those basics in place, then you can develop whizzier forms of social media to engage with your customers.

Want more? See what has been said about this case or get involved and discuss it with the author and other readers on our LinkedIn group, find it by visiting http://www.socialmedia-mba.com *or search for "The Social Media MBA Alumni".*

2 Honda – Creating a Centre of Excellence

Learn how Honda developed communication and collaboration within the European region to develop their social media capabilities and improve communication with customers.

Executive summary

Overview

Moving from a system of independent social media development, Honda creates a regional structure to refine development and improve efficiencies. From bringing expertise together and improving communications a centre of excellence (CoE) was created.

Key findings

- Communications across a diverse 27-country region is a challenge.
- A people-centric approach to change is effective.
- Technology as a tool for humanizing the management of social media.

Recommendations

1. Define a goal for social media in your organization.
2. Understand your organization and the individual roles in your social media teams.
3. Develop analytics and data from activities from the start to build a foundation for data-led decisions.

What you need to know

Honda Motor Europe looked to move social media management from an independent country structure to one of collaboration across the region. The approach was that of consultation and co-development.

- Honda is a global brand with a diverse range of product divisions.
- Honda Motor Europe social media strategy is focused on developing one-to-one customer relationships and improving communications.
- Honda wished to develop efficiencies and consistencies across the region in the management of social media.
- A structure was created to balance consistency with creativity and localization, based around a communications platform.

Background

Interviewee

Simon Nicholson joined Honda in 2011 as Social Media Manager for Honda Motor Europe, responsible for social media strategy across product divisions in the region. Before the move to Honda he held digital communications roles at SDL and Microsoft.

Simon Nicholson
@Sikenic

About Honda

With the head office based in Toyko, Japan, Honda is a global brand with a reported 24.9 million customers in 2011. Established in 1948, the company has grown to become the world's largest motorcycle manufacturer and one of the leading car manufacturers. Honda develops, manufactures and markets a wide variety of products, ranging from small general-purpose engines and scooters to specialty sports cars.

Racing has had an important connection to Honda's heritage. Honda have been involved in racing throughout their history with the entrance into the Isle of Man TT and Formula 1 and continues to this day in championships such as Moto GP and World Touring Cars.

With a strong company philosophy, Honda strives to create products that enhance mobility and benefit society. This can be seen, in particular, in the development of innovative research technologies such as ASIMO and the UNI-CUB.

Honda has a strong history in Europe, with Honda's first overseas production facility being established in Belgium in 1963. Since then, Honda has invested over £2 billion in European manufacturing facilities and today they make cars, motorcycles and power equipment products throughout the European region. Honda's flagship European production is in Swindon, UK, where there is capacity to build 250,000 cars a year. In 2011, Honda had over 1.5 million customers in Europe.

Their social media strategy

Honda Motor Europe social media strategy is focused on developing one-to-one customer relationships and improving communications. This is in response to two trends: increasing complexity in customer relationships and the digitalization of conversation. It is also intrinsically linked to the company's principle of "the three joys (buying, selling and creating)".

Firstly, look at the complexity of the company–customer relationship and developing one-to-one relationships. As a global brand Honda has customers all across the world, and a range of products. There are many contact points and data sources; consumers in the industries in which Honda operates undergo a complex consideration process for purchase; there is also a requirement for communication with the company during the ownership of the product. All these factors serve to add complexities to the company–customer relationship. However, from the perspective of the individual, the relationship is one-to-one with themselves and the company; it is for the company to overcome the complexity to provide an excellent experience. If customer relationships appear complex from the point of view of the customer it will not be a positive experience. Social media is the company communicating online, so it is an important interaction and relationship to get right for the customer.

To reference "the three joys", the "joy of buying" is essentially the establishment of a relationship with the customer, initiated through the products and continued through the sales and service experience, and is achieved when Honda exceed the needs and expectations of the customer. With the dramatic rise in internet use, and since social networking, you cannot look at the customer experience and ignore online interactions. In this sense the Honda social media strategy is an integrated aspect of the company–customer partnership, as is any interaction the customer may have online or offline with the company.

Secondly, looking at the digitalization of conversation and how Honda can communicate effectively. Mirroring the effect of the rise of the internet and the explosion in digital information, the information itself may not have changed but the way we consume it and the shear amount of it we have access to has changed. Similarly, the ubiquitous ability to publish thoughts and conversation online has created new avenues of communication and connectivity beyond what was possible before. As the environment in which a company communicates changes the company must also adapt. In this aspect of the social media strategy, Honda develops internal mechanisms to adapt in order to communicate effectively. This communication is not limited to messaging by PR and marketing departments to potential customers but also includes reacting to feedback and learning as an organization.

Together, through developing relationships with customers and continuous improvement to communications, Honda wishes to develop towards the vision of a seamless social experience. Simon Nicholson comments:

> Think about a shop in a community run by the owner, and the experience she could give to customers. The knowledge of individual requirements based on years of service, giving the customer an excellent service tailored to them. The owner's perfect knowledge of the company and the principles behind it is the best foundation for communication. The challenge for a company such as ours is recreating this seamless experience with the complexity involved in being a global brand.

At Honda the management of social media is split into two aspects. First, the strategic responsibility is centrally owned in the region and sits with the regional headquarters. Within this the structure and systems are put in place for local operations. Locally, in-country managers run the campaigns and own the conversation. This set up is to ensure Honda's communications are as effective and efficient as possible. The central team is best placed to see where efficiencies can be made across countries and to drive a consistent approach. Locally, within the countries in the region, they are best placed to understand their local stakeholders and tailor communication to ensure its effectiveness. There is also a third aspect where communication and collaboration across the central team and local teams in the region drives the ongoing development of social media.

The case

The problem

Honda manufactures and markets products across the whole of the European region. The product portfolio is divided into three main product divisions: automobiles, motorcycles and power equipment. In addition to its consumer and industry products, Honda also develops R&D products, which are an integral part of the company, such as the humanoid robot, ASIMO. The company is also actively involved in motorsport with manufacturer teams in both car and motorcycle championships globally. With so many topics for communication across many countries, this is a complex environment to manage in social media.

When Simon Nicholson joined Honda Motor Europe in 2011, he was given the broad remit of managing social media in the European region. Honda was already operating in social media in the region, with a central listening function and locally managed social media profiles. The local managers recognized the importance of engaging with fans and managing customer queries, and had developed independently. This of course had led to inconsistencies in the region, not only in terms of structure of social media activities but also in terms of success. However, it was the inconsistencies that revealed the opportunity for the region – with local managers and agencies working within social media in a diverse set of situations, and developing a diverse range of ideas, there was an opportunity to capitalize on this expertise.

As Simon explains:

> The challenge was not content: the heritage and the range of products and activities at Honda is a social media manager's dream. The real challenge is how to create a regional system of management to bring out the best outcome in every country, in short how to create a centre of excellence?

Honda was faced with the challenge of how to manage social media activities across a region in an efficient and consistent way, but also bring out the valuable local expertise needed to be truly effective in the way the company communicates.

Background

Central control and independence would both have a negative effect on creating a CoE. On the one hand, too much central control could stifle local innovation and would gravitate towards catering to the average, rather than localized communication and relationships. On the other hand, too much independence would create individual silos of activity and a CoE in the region requires the input of the whole region.

If Honda was to create a CoE the solution had to marry these seemingly opposing directions to create innovation within an efficient and consistent approach.

The starting point of addressing the challenge for Honda was to look at the problem as a system: what inputs are required to be in the position to succeed? Honda had the goal of making communications more efficient, consistent and effective, whilst also improving customer relationships.

Honda set out to identify the individual needs to the local managers running social media in the countries and build a system around them. The local managers were selected as the central point because of their in-market expertise and understanding, which is difficult to replicate. Honda was fortunate to have a strong group of managers within the company who had been pioneers within their countries to champion social media activities. It was from this point that the approach was discovered, rather than chosen.

The solution

Discovering individual needs

Honda decided that the approach would need to be developed in consultation with the countries. It was noted that the success of any regional initiative to change the way social media was managed would require the participation and support of the managers within the countries.

A council was put together from leading countries in the region in terms of social media adoption, consisting of the UK, France, Germany, Spain, Italy, Netherlands and Poland. It was decided that the council should not extend to the whole region straight away, the consideration being that it would be more effective to build out a core to include additional countries, rather than attempt to scale too early.

The participants were selected from PR and marketing disciplines for a communications focus. From this focus the participants would then coordinate with other parts of the business for specific activities, such as legal, HR and customer service. The central concern was the point of communication, and how Honda as an organization adapts to communicate through these online media. This then integrates with other activities where the core purpose has not changed.

From this council of pioneers within the business, Honda set out to understand the challenges and obstacles they face, in order to properly assess what inputs could be made. According to Simon:

> It was important that we were able to get everyone around a table in person, as this would be the foundation of our future planning we needed to make the most of the time together.

Out of this scoping meeting came the following overlying themes:

- More communication – for the local managers to do their work they required more information. Not just social media data but from across the company.
- More collaboration and local participation – if social media campaigns were to be fed down from above, without the participation of local teams, it was felt that such a campaign would not meet local requirements.
- More central support – with local budget and time restraints, it was not possible to do everything they wanted without support.

Planning the system
1. Communications platform
Given that communication, collaboration and participation were strongly desired across the region it was noted that the structure of managing social media should have communications at its core.

Investigation into the appropriate method of communication showed that a dedicated communications platform (Salesforce Chatter) would be most appropriate for the requirement.

The solution needed to be dynamic, rather than reference-based information. The objective was not simply to publish information but to create a structure that encouraged participation. Another requirement was that it was in real time, in-person meetings and calls were not frequent or transparent enough for this need. It also needed to be flexible, email was found to be too absolute; you either include every stakeholder in each message and everyone receives everything, or you only include those who directly need to know and this information is not accessible to anyone else.

The system was initially rolled out to the council member countries in early 2012. Later in that year the rest of the region joined the core. Utilizing the expertise of over 100 internal and external participants by the end of 2012, the initial pilot demonstrated the demand that was stated in the scoping meeting.

The difficulty with a new communications system comes at the very beginning. There are two types of benefits; one comes from the volume of users and the ability to access this nexus of expertise, the other comes from the information stored within the system. At the start it was important to develop the information benefits of the system whilst the initial user volume was low. This was crucial for participation, as relying on the network benefits straight away will lead to dissatisfaction with the system. As the champions of the system the central team found they had to provide a lot of information themselves at the start to attract others into using the tool.

2. Social data and analytics

At Honda they knew that the analytics and data had great value for each country individually. There was also value in data from all countries. The next stage was to implement a region-wide consolidation of social media data and analytics and to make these data completely transparent between countries. The thinking at Honda was: why learn the same thing twice when they could learn once? By standardizing the data each individual country would be able to learn quicker than they would have been able to with their own information alone.

Simon comments:

> To make informed decisions in social media you need data, and you also need the experience to know what to do with the data. Our plan was to provide the countries with all the information they require as a foundation for their decision making.

Moving to data-based decision making is a difficult and a slow process. It also requires historic information in order to make informed decisions. This is where building a foundation to develop from is crucial, and this was the focus for Honda. It was important to concentrate on developing the capabilities of the present and leave scope for future integration.

Honda migrated to the new listening platform (Radian6) and social media content management system (Adobe) alongside the communications platform implementation; using the platform to inform the region and manage the implementation of the new social media technologies.

3. Social media management

In conjunction with the technology rollout the operations were adapted to maximize the value of collaboration.

Community managers were connected together in the region with the communications platform to share insights. The use of the tools and establishing clear workflows for social media engagement also serves to create efficiencies in operations. It took many months to develop this horizontal thinking. The important aspect of the development was that it was not forced. The approach was to demonstrate value in order to influence change, rather than to dictate. This in itself was a test of this way of working for Honda, as if it could not demonstrate value then it would likely be flawed in its approach.

Applications developed as templates within the content management system based on local country requirements. Then the templates were made available for localization and customization for better local fit.

Social media content was created in an established approach that includes an initial consultation, central creation and delivery, and finally feedback to inform the future creation process.

Results

The primary measure was participation. In creating a structure to benefit the countries in the region it was crucial for all to participate. This was achieved late in 2012, ahead of the projected March 2013.

- The results of the structure are still to be realized. However, some key milestones have already been reached.
- All countries participating in the social media listening roll-out have integrated the data into their local campaigns.

- Facebook application template development began, providing bespoke applications to local managers at a fraction of the cost.
- There was pan-European analytics reporting.

Critical success factors

1. Base your solution and change around people, not technology. This is critical for success; the technology is a tool which helps perform a task. If there is no understanding of the individual tasks that make up your social media management and how that contributes to your goals, then your approach will be flawed and likely come up against resistance.
2. Patience to see through organization change is another key success factor. In a large organization it is not enough just to know what result you want; there will be a process for change, which needs to be managed. When dealing with change across a region, there will be many diverse issues to consider, rushing any implementation at this scale risks undermining the project.

Lessons learned

Simon concludes:

> When you join a new company and you have a project to complete, your first thoughts might be towards social media theory and best practice. It doesn't take long to develop an idea of a solution in your head; many of the changes will seem obvious. However, if managing social media was simply the case of remembering what you've read in a blog somewhere, we'd all be experts! Chances are what you first think of won't work because you've started thinking about solutions before the problem. First, what is your objective? Then look at your organization, understand the business, the people and the customers. Then you can start to look at how to tailor a solution to your organization to achieve your goal. The lesson I learnt as a social media manager is that: you don't know; you find out.

- Time spent gaining understanding is not wasted, and should not be underestimated.

- Taking the time to have a discussion can be more valuable than any report.
- More haste, less speed. Take the time to plan and carefully implement.

Want more? See what has been said about this case or get involved and discuss it with the author and other readers on our LinkedIn group, find it by visiting http://www.socialmedia-mba.com *or search for "The Social Media MBA Alumni".*

3 Cisco – Social Media Center of Excellence

This case study outlines how the Cisco Social Media Center of Excellence was born and how it has evolved in its three years of existence. Learn from Cisco's experience and gather new ideas for your centre of excellence (CoE).

Executive summary

Overview

Imagine a place with many social media practices but no way for practitioners to share their best practices and lessons learned, imagine a place with little cross-segment coordination and imagine a place without advocacy for social media. Cisco was once there. This is the story of how Cisco has transformed social media from the Wild West to an operationalized model.

Key findings

- Cisco has grown its social media practitioner base from a few dozen to over 300 and built an SME programme that now includes over 2,500 social ambassadors globally.
- 5,000 total live and on-demand social media course participants and a social media policy rolled out to the entire employee base.

- Adoption of social media company-wide has significantly increased the quality and quantity of conversations about Cisco. Cisco has grown its conversation volume from 2,500 to 7,000 mentions per day, increased its competitive share of voice to overtake competitors and maintains a combined neutral and positive sentiment of approximately 90 per cent.

Recommendations

1. Build a strong business case – start small and grow in phases.
2. Lead with data – implement social listening to showcase the voice of your customer.
3. Evangelize – embrace being a social champion inside your company and share information regularly at all levels (pilot results, listening data, lessons learned, etc.).

Background

Interviewees

Jeanette Gibson leads the global social and digital marketing team at Cisco. Her team is responsible for the company's global digital brand presence on cisco.com, social web sites and mobile environments. As head of social media, her team is responsible for setting Cisco's social marketing strategy and success metrics and driving alignment, governance and best practice sharing across the company. Jeanette is a 14-year veteran at Cisco and has held several leadership positions in marketing and corporate communications. Prior to joining Cisco in 1998, Jeanette worked for a startup, PointCast, and prior to that she held account management positions at PR agencies. Gibson holds a BA in Communications from the University of California at Santa Barbara.

Jeanette Gibson
@JeanetteG

Petra Neiger leads social business and the digital implementation of Cisco's brand campaign. She is the recipient of several industry awards for social media excellence and was named one of the Top 25 Digital

Petra Neiger
@petra1400

Marketers by *BtoB Magazine* in 2012. She has brought to life many innovative programmes and campaigns, and has helped several groups kick start or advance their own social media practice.

LaSandra Brill is a change agent, social media enthusiast and marketing visionary who was named "2012: 25 Women Who Rock Social Media" by Top Rank Marketing Blog. As senior manager of global social media marketing, LaSandra shapes Cisco's marketing strategy to include a mix of innovative digital, mobile and social media techniques. At Cisco she is known for building and executing the social media strategy of one of the top five product launches in company history and for driving social innovation across Cisco.

LaSandra Brill
@LaSandraBrill

About Cisco

Cisco (NASDAQ: CSCO) is the worldwide leader in IT, helping companies seize the opportunities of tomorrow by proving that amazing things can happen when you connect the previously unconnected. The Cisco vision and strategy is to become their customers' most strategic business partner by delivering intelligent networks and technology, and business architectures built on integrated products, services and software platforms. Fiscal 2012 product sales were $36.3 billion, service revenue was $9.7 billion. Worldwide employee count in Q4 FY12 was 66,639.

Their social media strategy

Cisco encourages the use of social media by its employees and provides the necessary infrastructure, tools, guidelines and best practices to help widen and deepen social media knowledge and comfort level inside the company. Cisco's social media strategy is to encourage engagement with the brand online by empowering its employees, customers, partners, shareholders and the public to interact with Cisco and each other in an open and transparent way. In addition, Cisco uses social media to listen and respond with customers, share thought leadership about business issues and challenges and offer support and assistance. Social media is planned and executed on multiple levels.

Corporate level

The charter of corporate social media is twofold. On one hand, it is responsible for the Cisco brand in social media and on the other hand, it drives social business for the company.

Social brand management includes the delivery of content, innovations and interactions on Cisco's various social media properties across the owned, paid and earned spectrum. In addition, social brand management encompasses the planning and execution of corporate-level social media initiatives and campaigns.

Social business management helps ensure that practitioners across the company have the necessary infrastructure and know how to effectively engage in the social web. Training and enablement, consulting, tool and vendor management, social media governance and other social media programmes to encourage, guide and reward participation are critical components of social business management.

Business segment or functional level

Cisco's business segments and functions create and drive their own social media strategy based on the infrastructure, tools, branding, training and enablement resources, consulting and governance put in place by the corporate effort. Not only does this approach help ensure consistency between corporate and segment-level execution but it also enables scale across the organization while maintaining integration opportunities across corporate and segment-level efforts for greater impact.

Individual level

The company believes in the power of its employees regardless of whether they are individual contributors, managers or executives. Several initiatives have been implemented to identify and activate employees to help spread the word, answer questions and otherwise engage with Cisco customers, partners and influencers online. In general, Cisco calls those employees that choose to participate in social media for business purposes social ambassadors.

Cisco's digital and social framework

The company has created a digital and social framework to speak about its strategy. This approach has five pillars: intelligence, engagement, measurement and advocacy, all underlined by enablement. Take a look at the case for more information.

Cisco's Digital & Social Framework

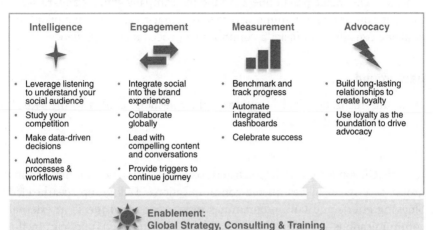

Intelligence	Engagement	Measurement	Advocacy
• Leverage listening to understand your social audience • Study your competition • Make data-driven decisions • Automate processes & workflows	• Integrate social into the brand experience • Collaborate globally • Lead with compelling content and conversations • Provide triggers to continue journey	• Benchmark and track progress • Automate integrated dashboards • Celebrate success	• Build long-lasting relationships to create loyalty • Use loyalty as the foundation to drive advocacy

Enablement:
Global Strategy, Consulting & Training

Governance I Training & Certification I Strategy & Consultation I Social Ambassadors

The case

The problem

Rewind the clock to 2009 and you will find yourself in a company where social media was used in very powerful but disparate ways. Cisco started blogging in 2005 and by 2009 had built a well-established group of over 600 bloggers, thousands of customers participating in technical communities and several groups dabbling in emerging social media such as gaming, crowd-sourcing and virtual worlds. While Cisco had many early successes in social media, it lacked consistent governance and coordinated planning, which resulted in duplicative efforts and a fragmented vendor and tool landscape.

As adoption of social media increased across the company, two issues became apparent:

a) education and training needed to be a priority in order to mitigate risk to the company; and
b) the proliferation of tools warranted the need for a common infrastructure to reduce cost, ensure integration with existing systems and create consistent measures of success.

This reinforced the need to create a central team and build a CoE in order to provide social media practitioners around the company with a standard set of tools, an education programme, access to best practices, innovation pilots and strategic consulting to foster a community of social media excellence.

Background

Once this realization had been made, the questions shifted to the "who", "what", "how" and "where".

The "who"

Jeanette Gibson led the social media efforts in the corporate communications group, as director of new media communications. This group spearheaded blogging efforts and built programmes to leverage social media in external communications by actively using Facebook, Twitter, YouTube, etc. In the period up to 2009, Jeanette and her team helped drive a 70 per cent shift in external communications efforts from traditional means using press releases and posting stories on the company's online newsroom, to using blogs and video blogs as the main communications channel. While this transformation was occurring in the communications organization, there were similar efforts in the marketing organization that realized signification ROI from social media such as reducing product launch costs by 75 per cent and increasing customer engagement by 150 per cent. This inspired a small group of self-identified social media aficionados to seek leadership buy-in for a new dedicated social media team with the hopes of increasing the role of social media across marketing and driving change in the traditional marketing mix. With these two organizations leading the way for positive ROI with social media, it became clear that a new central team was needed to operationalize and scale social media.

Soon, with the buy-in and support of the head of communications and the head of corporate marketing, a business plan advocating the creation of a central social media unit was starting to take shape. An evangelism tour began inside the company with decision makers and influencers to secure buy-in for this new team. The plan for the dedicated social media marketing team was ultimately presented to and approved by the chief marketing officer, and the new CoE was born. Jeanette Gibson was appointed leader of this new team as director of social media marketing, reporting to the SVP of corporate marketing. Jeanette created her founding team by recruiting four social media experts from other teams including solutions marketing, event marketing, corporate communications and corporate marketing.

The "what"

Behind the plan was a detailed *discovery process* to uncover opportunities for improvement. Before any recommendations were put onto paper, the team evaluated the existing social media landscape and audited the company's existing social media activities and channels, their business purposes, audiences and maturity levels. All these findings were documented. This exercise enabled Cisco to understand the lay of the land, suggest improvements and set priorities and benchmarks.

The outputs of this report were key to the planning process and to the plan itself. These findings became the building blocks of the business case for the centralized team. Upon the CMO's blessing of the plan, attention shifted to the definition of this new team's roles and responsibilities, the CoE structure and the group's near-term and long-term deliverables.

The "how"

The next chapter of Cisco's journey was centred around how the CoE should be operationalized. At the time, the idea of a CoE was fairly new and, therefore, not too many companies to model such a team after. Cisco looked at examples from other industries, used the results of its social media landscape analysis and applied a predictive approach to anticipate what was next. Flexibility, consistency and scalability have been sewn into the fabric of this organization.

Scalability is the holy grail when an organization first establishes a CoE. Cisco has employed (and continues to employ) the following variety of tactics to make social media participation scalable:

- **Infrastructure:** the basic premise behind any of Cisco's infrastructure and related innovations is that it needs to be scalable and repeatable. This helps not only recover investments faster but also to ensure consistency in management and reporting.
- **Online community:** at the time of its inception, it was a web site that housed social media governance, best practices and other useful information for all Cisco social media practitioners. Since then this web site has become an internal community with contributions by the larger social community, not just the core team.
- **Virtual training and enablement:** Cisco thinks of training in the larger context of enablement. A formal social media training and certification programme was put in place early on but was complemented with quickly producible enablement programmes. In general, Cisco's social training and enablement programmes are delivered virtually (over the internet) with on-demand post-session resources and discussion forums in the online

community. When you think of scalability, consider asking your advanced practitioners, vendors and other companies to provide best practices and lessons learned to the rest of your company instead of you having to create all of these deliverables all the time. What Cisco realized is that there is much knowledge out there and, sometimes, it is enough to connect people with each other to facilitate learning. The centralized team doesn't always need to be the group creating content.

- **Ambassadors:** Cisco encourages employee participation in social media, which in return can help individual business segments scale and generate authentic conversations.

The "where"

Based on the landscape analysis, the company's social media initiatives and defined direction of the group, the decision was made to create the CoE within corporate marketing. Although the CoE resides in the marketing organization, it has formed strong bonds with other parts of the company such as corporate communications and customer support, to name just a few.

The solution

Roles and responsibilities within the CoE were based on the pillars of Cisco's social media strategy. At the time the CoE was created, Cisco defined its social strategy as follows: listening, planning, engagement and measurement. By the end of its first year, the team had just about ten people (contractors included) to implement this strategy.

Listening: the CoE assessed the various business segments' listening efforts, where there was one, and used these insights to establish a robust, centralized social media listening practice. The CoE standardized on listening tools and vendors, and managed brand-level listening activities. In addition, it started a listening evangelism tour to show the value and possibilities of social listening to executives and various business segments. Interest from various parts of the organization started peaking and soon a network of business segments with a listening practice was formed. To help accelerate adoption, the CoE provided setup, training and consulting services to the participating business units.

Listening continues to be a key strategic pillar for Cisco. At the time of writing this book, Cisco had a formal Social Media Listening Center (SMLC). The early version of the SMLC was a one-screen display outside of the CMO's office, which has grown into a multi-screen tool that enables the instant, customized visualizations of conversations and hence encourages the company to take action. The SMLC comes in the following multiple flavours:

- **Primary display:** this multi-screen unit lives in the home of the digital and social media marketing team and features a variety of easily swappable topic profiles. The conversations are regularly monitored and addressed as needed. The primary display was the first of the multi-screen tools that was brought to life.
- **Executive Briefing Center (EBC) display:** this special setup features conversations relevant to Cisco partners and customers, and any other Cisco visitors in the EBC. This multi-screen unit is placed in a well-trafficked area within the EBC.
- **Mobile display:** as the official network infrastructure supporter, Cisco created a pop-up version of its Social Media Listening Center in the Cisco House at the London 2012 Olympic Games. The multi-screen mobile display allowed Cisco to monitor sentiment, manage crisis and effectively respond to ambush marketing.

Cisco Social Media Listening Center installation in the company's executive briefing centre in San Jose, CA

Planning: the CoE assessed the company's social media maturity level and put in place the following tools and resources to help practitioners with the planning and execution of their social media programmes:

- **Governance:** before any Cisco employee can engage in social media, they must read and accept the Cisco Global Social Media Policy. This policy comes with additional guidelines on requirements and expectations of the social practitioner. All governance-related resources are available on the online community to anyone with a Cisco ID. This policy and the resources are reviewed annually and social practitioners are required to sign this policy each year electronically. The social policy has been integrated into several other tools to give more exposure to employees, such as Code of Business Conduct (COBC) and new hire portal, just to name a couple. It is also a foundational course in Cisco's multi-level social media training and certification programme.
- **Consulting:** in the beginning, consulting was a key role of the CoE because the interest in social media participation was growing but the social media resource library was limited. Consulting was a natural way for the CoE to engage with practitioners while team members were diligently crafting self-service resources. With the availability of more on-demand resources, training and other knowledge-sharing opportunities, the need for consulting hours declined, thus freeing up CoE resources for other business-critical activities.
- **Self-service resources:** the first step towards self service was the creation of a social media web site, which since then has evolved into a social media community. This community features templates, frameworks, short "how-to" videos and check lists, mini case studies and other useful resources to help build foundational knowledge in a repeatable fashion and demystify social media.
- **Social media training and certification:** the early training and certification programme focused on the basic know hows of social media. As social media usage started to proliferate and mature, the central team realized the need for new content. Based on research and analysis, the CoE redesigned and reinvigorated the training and certification programme. At the time of writing this book, the Cisco Social Media Training and Certification programme is a virtual, multi-track and multi-level programme that encourages social media aficionados to progress through various levels of learning regardless of where they are located in the organization. In addition, it offers specialized tracks for certain interest groups, such as Cisco executives.

- **Networking programmes:** in addition to the training programme, formal and informal networking opportunities were put in place to connect practitioners and those that were interested in social media with best practice resources. These programmes included best practices sessions with fellow practitioners inside and outside of the organization, third party experts and even certain Cisco social media partners.
- **Approved resources:** it is in the planning phase that practitioners think about the infrastructure, vendors and tools to use for their social media engagement. Shortly after it was formed, the central team initiated a year-long process to vet and streamline the infrastructure it wanted to build the company's long-term presence on and interviewed a myriad of social media vendors to decide which ones aligned more closely to Cisco's objectives. These vendors became Cisco's preferred social media partners and the company standardized on the use of their technologies and tools. This helped practitioners tap into already existing resources and save time and cost rather than reinvent the wheel.

Engagement: As described earlier, the central team assumes responsibility for brand management but each segment or function drives its own social media activities. For the CoE, this means two fundamental things:

- enabling the segments via the needed infrastructure, education, resources and tools is critical to the success of a segment's engagement; and
- the CoE has an opportunity to lead by example through its brand management efforts:
  - **Infrastructure-driven engagement:** the on-going management of Cisco's social media infrastructure falls on the central team. Since the central team manages the infrastructure, it is in a unique position to drive innovations on these platforms to increase social engagement. The CoE also partners with related organizations, such as the Cisco.com web team to implement social capabilities on Cisco's web site as well.
  - **Content-driven engagement:** the CoE has the opportunity to create consistent branding across Cisco's multiple channels, show the ropes to other teams and pilot new ideas and approaches, which – if successful – can be expanded to the rest of the organization.

Making the CoE an entity that delivers social media programmes not only helps increase the team's value and credibility, it also brings more attention to social media internally and externally.

Measurement: The CoE created a holistic measurement framework and provided standardized metrics for practitioners. The framework classified metrics into three main buckets: market perception, community health and metrics with a direct correlation to dollars. This framework is the foundation for how Cisco talks about measurement and is a key consideration in the goal-setting process.

As the CoE has matured so has Cisco's social strategy. The foundation that was laid when the central team was born is still there but the team has evolved Cisco's social strategy. This evolution includes the shift from a pure listening programme to intelligence, which includes social listening, social competitive analysis and social CRM. Planning and enablement became a foundational discipline and the advocacy pillar was introduced in the new model, signalling a shift in focus towards loyalty.

Results

Since the centralized social media marketing organization was formed in 2009 Cisco has successfully trained a large number of employees to engage with customers and partners in social media. Cisco has been recognized in the industry numerous times including being named #1 B2B company on Twitter via ComScore and being awarded Forrester's Groundswell award for best B2B social media, among many others. The creation of a CoE has brought about many positive changes at Cisco. Some of the benefits are:

- **Consistency:** the CoE has created consistency in the tools, infrastructure and vendors it uses and in the branding of the company's various social media channels. Besides consistency, the existence of pre-approved infrastructure and tools helps the company manage costs, and the clear branding provides an improved customer experience.
- **Integration:** partnerships with different marketing and non-marketing groups across the company place the CoE in a unique position to help connect people and initiatives, both at the segment and brand level. This allows for greater integration between brand- and segment-level programmes.
- **Innovation:** the CoE takes on innovation pilots to test and prove concepts. Sometimes pilots are managed solely by the CoE and sometimes they are delivered in partnership with a business segment. This helps introduce new ideas and ways of doing social media while minimizing risk.
- **Shared learning:** the pace of learning has accelerated since the inception of the CoE due to the availability of a one-stop online community, consulting,

a formal training and certification programme and other enablement programmes. All were designed to encourage not only CoE-to-practitioner but
also peer-to-peer and external presenter-to-Cisco best practices sharing in
easily digestible formats.

- **Efficiency:** investment in a scalable and flexible infrastructure, availability
  of proven practices and tools coupled with an innovative and collaborative
  mindset have contributed to Cisco's increased efficiency in social media,
  from the time it takes to get a campaign out the door to rolling out new
  social features on web and other properties.

Critical success factors

The success of a social media CoE can be attributed to several factors:

1. **Do your homework first:** start with a landscape analysis and gather input
   from different sources to gain a comprehensive view of your social media
   activities.
2. **Use data to build a business case and make decisions:** the outcome of the
   analysis should inform your business plan. Keep an open mind and detach
   from the outcome. Yes, you want to create a CoE but let the research drive
   the "how" and "where".
3. **Find an executive champion:** executive buy-in is critical. Partnering with
   an executive to help build and sell the case with you is priceless.
4. **Evangelize:** share the vision with as many decision makers and influencers
   as possible. Listen to their feedback, address their concerns and follow up.
5. **Follow through:** once you have the green light, follow through on your plan.
   Keep your stakeholders appraised of your progress and keep the lines of
   communication open.

Lessons learned

There are many organizations today with a social media CoE and several of
them are evolving to the next level. These stories can be used as benchmarks
for any organization. If there are any question marks, smart experimentation
can open up new doors. The key behind experimentation is to know when to
move on if it's not working.

Cisco's success with its CoE is largely due to the fact that it is flexible,
inclusive and owns social media deliverables.

Flexible: Cisco has evolved (and continues to evolve) its CoE as social maturity increases within the CoE as well as across the company. Recognizing that the CoE charter may change over time and following through these changes are important.

Inclusive: the central team realized early on that calling on advanced social practitioners inside and outside the company can help scale its efforts as well as create a community of practitioners inside the company. Members of this community can help each other with social media best practices and lessons learned and can also act as brand ambassadors in the social web.

Owner: setting up a CoE exclusively as a consulting arm could lead to challenges. Having members of the central social media team be "real practitioners" will help increase credibility and creativity.

Want more? See what has been said about this case or get involved and discuss it with the author and other readers on our LinkedIn group, find it by visiting http://www.socialmedia-mba.com *or search for "The Social Media MBA Alumni".*

Part II

Social Media Strategy

4 Nokia – Delivering Social Media Strategy

NOKIA
诺基亚

This is an account of Nokia's global strategic approach to social media, and the principles Nokia have chosen to guide their efforts. There are elements in this case, challenges and opportunities, that are specifically about Nokia, but there is also a great deal that any organization, of any size, in any sector, can identify with.

Executive summary

Overview

In this case we cover Nokia's six guiding principles for their current and future activity in social media. For each principle we will describe the organization's ambition, the way they should play out in their behaviour and marketing approach, some best-practice guidance from Nokia's marketing teams and some illustrative examples of the ways in which Nokia is already using each principle:

- Consider the social opportunity in everything we do.
- Engage in better conversations with more consumers.
- Deliver personal experiences (be authentic) and earn trust.

- Sharing is more important than control.
- Define clear objectives from the outset.
- Invest and commit to social presences.

Key findings

For all of the uncertainty and noise about social media there are a number of things we can be sure of:

- A new set of consumer behaviours have emerged and are here to stay.
- Social media usage is growing and will likely continue to do so.
- Influence is shifting from organizations into networks and crowds.

Recommendations

1. Listen to what people are saying about your brand, and be efficient, creative and authentic in your response.
2. Don't go looking for new fans, look for ways you can encourage people to engage with your brand instead of just following it.
3. Employ people that are passionate about achieving your goals, as well as those of the wider organization.

What you need to know

Consumer behaviour has fundamentally changed, requiring Nokia to change as well.

Background

Interviewee

Craig Hepburn is responsible for leading the digital and social media strategy and a world class team of highly skilled experts to bring it to life.

Craig joined Nokia from Open Text where as Director of Social Media Strategy he advised and consulted on social media and Enterprise 2.0 strategies

Craig Hepburn
@craighepburn

for some of the world's largest organizations including T-Mobile, Novartis, SAP, RIM, Motorola and the Canadian government.

About Nokia

As a company Nokia has been around since 1865 – a whole decade before Alexander Graham Bell was awarded a US patent for the telephone.

Back then the organization made pulp at a mill in south western Finland in a place called Nokia. Today, Nokia is a global leader in mobile communications, selling 13 phones every second, with over 100,000 employees in 120 countries and annual revenues of around €38 billion.

Their social media strategy

Nokia try to look at social media in terms that make sense to non-marketing specialists.

When the jargon and technical language of marketing and the web are stripped away there are three things they talk about:

Stories: the elaboration of the large and small ways in which Nokia and their products and services are changing people's lives. Content assets, insights, folklore, the scattered matter that makes up what the brand means both for employees and customers.

Conversations: the connections with customers and other influencers online; the dialogue that keeps Nokia open and honest; the conversations between customers that the company can learn from.

Numbers: the data and insights that flow from Nokia into the social web and vice versa; the measures and evaluation methods to understand what is happening and how decisions can be made.

These three are a loose but useful construct with which to think about social media and the value it can deliver.

Craig is responsible for aligning social media activities across the business and leading his team of highly skilled experts whose goal is to take social media beyond marketing so that they can transform the whole organization into a "social business".

This is an account of Nokia's global strategic approach to social media, and the principles they have chosen to guide their efforts. There are Nokia-specific elements here, but there is also a great deal that any organization, of any size, in any sector, can identify with.

The case

The problem

At its simplest, the challenge everyone faces with social media in marketing is that Nokia need to re-learn their trade. Being expert in one-to-many marketing is not enough. Nokia, like many organizations, needs to re-think their planning, investment, execution and measurement in order to succeed. This is because companies are all now operating in a world where many-to-many communication is increasingly important. Nokia's efforts in social media need to be addressed at a systemic level. Nokia need to rethink how they do marketing, centring their focus on the things that have changed.

Look at the marketing element of Nokia's business – like so many other major brands – and you might be convinced that this business was basically "advertising plus support". Paid messages dominate budgets, thinking and strategy for everything from brand building to specific product promotion, and everything in between.

If social media is simply thought of as "media", a replacement or a helper of existing paid media marketing systems, Nokia, and others, will miss a bigger opportunity: to understand how the world is changing, how consumers are changing and how the business can change too.

Background

Consumer behaviour has fundamentally changed, requiring Nokia to change as well. For all of the uncertainty and noise about social media, according to Craig, there are a few of things we can be sure of:

- A new set of consumer behaviours have emerged and are here to stay.
- Social media usage is growing and will likely continue to do so.
- Influence is shifting from organizations into networks and crowds.

Nokia need to structure their marketing efforts, treating every touch-point with the consumer – from the first brand message they see to contacting support staff – as an opportunity to reinforce the Nokia brand, and foster more attachment to their product and services.

Perhaps most of all, the opportunity lay in the role social media can play in "advocacy" – people who have positive experiences with Nokia products and services and want to share that enjoyment and satisfaction with others. For Nokia to have these kinds of connections with consumers greatly expands the opportunity for word-of-mouth messages to spread further and faster.

Marketers have under-valued and, therefore, under-invested in activity that will encourage, facilitate and spread consumer advocacy. Social media marketing can provide Nokia with tools that can help redress this imbalance.

Eventually social media will be so much a part of everything Nokia does that their employees won't need to think about it, it will run through every conversation and function of the business. For now, however, social media represents a shift – a shift in media, commerce and society – that demands a bold and ambitious response.

The solution

Principle 1 – Consider the social opportunity in everything we do

Social media should never be an afterthought in any marketing activity – it needs to be a consideration from the outset. Right at the start of the planning phase, marketers need to ask what they can learn about their consumers from social media, what role the social web will play at each stage of their experience of the brand and what are they trying to achieve by way of brand or product and service awareness, consideration or preference.

This means that:

- Nokia's employees need to understand how to initiate relevant conversations with consumers rather than broadcast, or speak at them.
- Nokia's products and services can often be inherently social, enabling people, through technology, to have conversations, share stories among their networks of friends, colleagues and families.
- Nokia's employees need to understand social as a mindset – authentic, useful conversations with consumers – not simply as platforms.

Example: Nokia's Tron sponsorship

In 2010 Nokia sponsored the Disney box-office smash *Tron* with Nokia devices featured in the movie (a sequel to the cult 1980s classic). Nokia made the very most of their sponsorship through point-of-sale, digital and ATL (above the line) promotions but they also put social right at the heart of the project. For example, Nokia's access to exclusive content, such as a Nokia version of the trailer, was used to inspire a "takeover" of key Nokia social presences (Facebook, Twitter and blog) by the fictional Encom business that features in the movie. Users from the target gaming audience were challenged to solve clues left in binary and Konami code (appealing to the movie's fans) to unlock the exclusive content.

The activity not only drove over 150 per cent increase in daily activity on Nokia's Facebook page, it also attracted a new audience: 70 per cent of those engaged in the *Tron* campaign on Facebook had never spoken about Nokia before. There were over 80,000 participants in this conversation during a single day at the height of activity.

Principle 2 – Engage in better conversations with more consumers

Important elements of the consumer's experience with Nokia take place within social media, which is why Nokia are starting to empower their employees to participate in conversations, to maximize the value of those direct interactions for both the communities and the business itself.

Education and support are the key, which is why Nokia have begun the roll-out of Socializer, a system using listening tools to provide a real-time action framework for marketing, Agora, a 6 plasma-screen installation showing visualizations of real-time conversations on the social web, and powerful reporting and analytics tools.

It's also a system to help Nokia listen and respond to consumers quickly. It focuses on the most significant conversations about a variety of hot topics – for example, battery life – and brings it to the attention of the right people within the organization, in real time, so they can respond and react.

By putting Agora in open spaces around the company, such as in the cafeteria area at the headquarters in Espoo, Finland, Nokia are giving a public demonstration of their willingness to listen, and signalling to their employees that this is something that is encouraged within the business's culture.

Example: Nokia Tweetsender app

In December 2012, Nokia launched a Twitter app called the Tweetsender. This app helped the organization to solve the problem of sending device or location-specific messages on Twitter to their large pool of followers.

Followers of @Nokia on Twitter can sign up to receive personalized messages, based on their device and location, about upgrade information, software updates and apps to their Direct Messages inbox. This allows Nokia to provide their followers with relevant information they actually want, and turn the company's marketing efforts on Twitter into a more meaningful exchange between the brand and Nokia fans.

Principle 3 – Deliver personal experiences (be authentic) and earn trust

The tone and mode of communication that comes from being personal, from acting with a genuine desire to earn trust, is a subtle art. It's not about "big splashes" and peaks of activity. In this new, personalized world of communication, the ideal approach is made in small consistent moves, adding up to a greater shift overall.

Within Nokia's marketing community, the organization regularly connects with around 5,000 influencers in their online network already. On an individual consumer and product level, Nokia has begun to deliver personalized experiences too. Nokia has a community management team who are focused on engaging directly with consumers. They also have the Nokia connect team who are working to engage in conversations with influencers around the world.

Example: Nokia Follow Friday

Follow Friday is a tradition among Twitter users where (each Friday) people recommend people to follow, attaching the #FF tag to their tweets. The first special Nokia Follow Friday (#FF) stemmed from a social media team day out in Espoo, Finland. The planned activity was to spend a day learning to become graffiti artists. There was an opportunity to share this experience with a larger group than the social media team itself. The team created a huge, visually engaging graffiti art mural and included the Twitter names of a few dedicated and engaged Nokia advocates on Twitter. A photo of the mural was posted on Twitter to mark the first official Nokia Follow Friday.

The response from those who were tagged in this way was extremely positive. It is estimated that the reach of the conversation around this activity on Twitter was one million interactions. The cost of this activity was zero – since it was content generated as part of a team day that had already been organized. Since then, similar Follow Friday stunts in the real world – FF word games, FF sticky note art – have been used to generate digital content and conversations with much success.

This is a simple and authentic way for Nokia to show their appreciation to fans, build stronger relationships and show them that there is more to Nokia than a global corporation.

Principle 4 – Sharing is more important than control

Making sharing a part of its culture, in marketing and more broadly within the company, means developing it as a skill, an instinct, a kind of digital literacy. Nokia's employees must develop an approach to sharing that makes them say "what are we not going to share?", rather than "what can we share?" This is about a shift in mindset, and not everyone in Nokia understands this yet. Those leading the culture shift at Nokia require the support of the leadership team to help make change possible.

When Stephen Elop became CEO of Nokia, he used the organization's internal microblogging platform, Socialcast, to begin a conversation with employees. The platform had not been widely used up until this point. His public endorsement of the tool – and his open and honest conversation within it – sent a clear signal to everyone in the business. Usage doubled in the month following his first post.

Example: Nokia #Switchhub
The best example of sharing, rather than controlling, content can be seen on Nokia's homepage. Instead of broadcasting brand messages, a social tool was built that allows them to pull videos, tweets and reviews of Nokia products and services from real people in the social space. This means that all the content, opinions and reviews the visitors see are authentic and real time and has resulted in increased interaction with the page and a lower bounce rate.

Principle 5 – Define clear objectives from the outset
Nokia's success in social media is underpinned by two things: setting clear objectives and understanding how to measure results.

Craig finds that a useful way to shake out the cobwebs and preconceptions about measurement is to take a look at how academics think about the whole subject of measurement. He quotes Margaret A. Miller of the University of Virginia, offering the following insight:

> Every time we quote a statistic we are validating the choices made by those that created them, choices that reflect values and beliefs that we may or may not share. Measurement systems are undisputedly useful.

First: they permit us to compare . . . performance.
Second: they help us identify good practice and progress.
Third: quantification results in a common currency . . . within a system.
Fourth: numbers are a way to tell a complicated story succinctly.

Many marketers have become entranced with the number of Facebook "likes" their brand or product page has. In fact, unless there is interaction with consumers on the page, a high number of likes can be next to meaningless. The value lies with the quality of conversations and engagement with consumers above the reach.

On the web, everything is connected. There are two billion users of the web: meaning the potential reach of anything you post anywhere on the web – be it on a social network or a common web site – is two billion. Engagement, conversation, connections and actual reach, these are the things that you need to value and measure.

Example: Nokia's success with social commerce
Nokia has always been dissatisfied with the idea that ROI for social media activity is hard to measure. For example, Nokia's work to generate referral traffic to commercial domains directly from Facebook has proved that ROI is tangible and measurable.

For example, Nokia's Facebook page has specific objectives:

- Building awareness – measured by traffic.
- Engagement – measured, for example, by the number of downloads of an app.
- Sales – measured, for example, by the number of pre-orders for a new phone.

Results are encouraging: the promotions tab is the most popular after the Wall (the main page) itself. The average click-through rate for a promotion on the Nokia global Facebook page is 13 per cent and the Lumia's The X Factor/One Direction promotion generated a 37 per cent click-through rate. In comparison, a typical banner ad click-through rate is 0.1 per cent.

Principle 6 – Invest and commit to social presences

Social media is far from free. It requires different models of investment and measurement of return than paid. When social media is not fully understood by marketers, they sometimes see it as free or at least very low cost. Presence requires commitment. That means planning to sustain a blog, social network profile or community presence, often over long periods. That may not be expensive, but it is certainly not free. Nokia acknowledges that the shift to social demands presence and long-term commitment. It invests accordingly. Currently there is investment in the tools and infrastructure that will shift the culture and approach within the organization significantly and permanently.

Examples include the Socializer system, local community management teams around the world and a global social media team.

Example: @NokiaConnects advocacy activity on Twitter
One example of investing for the long term, which is currently happening at Nokia, can be seen in the global Nokia connects programme. As part of this

strand of work, Nokia's global team of community managers are monitoring Twitter to look for opportunities to open up conversations with existing and potential advocates. In one case, an influential blogger in India tweeted to his followers that he was fed up with his new phone, which was prone to break. As a former Nokia consumer he wondered aloud to his followers whether he should think about switching back his loyalties. The @NokiaConnects team spotted this and contacted him, asking him if he would like to trial a new Nokia phone for a couple weeks, no strings attached. This single contact generated a very positive outcome. The blogger himself was delighted to have been contacted. He liked the new phone and wrote several blog posts about it. His authentic, earned advocacy reached a wide group of people online – people that Nokia wouldn't or couldn't have reached directly itself.

Lessons learned

Social media, social technology, will continue to evolve, mutate and bring new opportunities and risks to companies like Nokia. There is no option but to take the risks and carefully observe and learn from failures in as transparent a manner as is possible for a large organization.

Nokia have three factors at work that may lead to significant success in adapting their marketing approach to social media:

- Social media is a priority in their marketing and is building a business case for more investment.
- Getting the right support from relevant stakeholders is vital to help marketers understand the importance of social media (and its earned media partner disciplines, content strategy, word-of-mouth marketing and search engine optimization).
- Guiding principles: the articulation and adoption of the six principles outlined in this case will help guide decision making and strategy around the world.

Want more? See what has been said about this case or get involved and discuss it with the author and other readers on our LinkedIn group, find it by visiting http://www.socialmedia-mba.com *or search for "The Social Media MBA Alumni".*

5 LivingSocial – Getting Social in B2B

SOCIAL INITIATIVES THAT GROW ENGAGEMENT AND BUILD
THOUGHT LEADERSHIP AGENDAS WITH B2B AUDIENCES

Understanding the social media needs of your target audience is key to developing truly engaging campaigns. LivingSocial is an example of an organization using interactive social media methodologies to build relationships with business customers.

Executive summary

Overview

By shifting their focus from growth of their social media communities, to more specific engagement campaigns, centred on the needs of LivingSocial's customers in the local business community, the organization has demonstrated its commitment to extending wide-ranging business support to their local businesses partners across the UK and Ireland with business advice, social media support and case studies of same-sector business success stories.

Key findings

- Focus in the social media space is rapidly moving away from an acquisition focus. Follower and community numbers are increasingly less significant, with emphasis shifting to understanding and engaging the audience on their own terms, creating an appealing, engaging community and facilitating the exchange of ideas.

- Interactivity drives engagement, and strategies to identify and utilize the 1 per cent of influencers in your user base will pay real long-term dividends.
- With resources limited for many brands in the social media space, experimentation, innovation and consistent testing prove key. Acquiring and implementing feedback after each Google Hangout ensures consistent improvement.

Recommendations

1. Start small and stay focused on understanding the audience need, in order to provide compelling content in an engaging environment that will inspire conversation and the sharing of ideas.
2. Feedback from key influencers within your audience is invaluable – developing bespoke, segment-appropriate methods of gathering user insights, and incorporating these into future strategies, will allow your brand to build a social media environment that fits your objectives.
3. Interactivity drives engagement and the ability to converse; learning from and engaging with other clients in similar sectors adds great value in a B2B environment, providing a powerful driver of engagement.

Background

Interviewee

In this role, Cristina Astorri's duties include oversight of all brand marketing initiatives for the UK and Irish markets, social media, advertising, research, online and offline campaigns, B2B relationships and much more. Prior to her current position, Cristina has gained experience in the fields of marketing, research, PR and TV journalism in the international sphere. She holds a double Masters in Marketing Communications from ESCEM Business School and London Metropolitan University.

Cristina Astorri
@LivingSocialUK

About LivingSocial

LivingSocial is a local marketplace to buy and share the best things to do in your city.

With unique and diverse offerings each day, they aim to inspire members to discover everything from weekend excursions to one-of-a-kind events and experiences, to exclusive gourmet dinners and luxury spa experiences, to family day trips to the aquarium, spectacular sky diving experiences and more.

They set out to help local businesses grow by introducing them to high-quality new customers and give merchants the tools to make the LivingSocial members their regulars.

Today they have over 70 million registered users around the world.

The case

The problem

With flourishing consumer-centric social media platforms and rapid follower growth, in 2012, LivingSocial opted to shift its strategic focus to extending its marketing consultancy services for the local business community it serves, using social media channels. When compiling their social media strategy for the UK and Irish markets, the organization centred their thinking on key questions, such as how to increase engagement with their past, current and potential clients online and add value to their business plans from a long-term, strategic viewpoint.

With thousands of business clients in local markets across the UK and Ireland, LivingSocial's business model is built around successfully connecting the local businesses it partners with to engaged, appropriate, local customers. Connectivity, therefore, was another key issue considered when looking at the strategic direction, and the organization challenged itself to explore ways of helping client businesses not only improve their marketing plans but also connect more easily with their future regular customers.

Finding solutions to both of these questions was key in the social media planning process.

Cristina Astorri explained:

> With supporting local enterprise key to the LivingSocial mission, and social media intrinsic to our modus operandi, connecting the two

seemed the next natural step in the evolution of our social media presence in the UK and Ireland. The problem-solving approach we take to strategy development – ensuring each initiative we launch answers a specific question or need on behalf of our audience or our brand – helps us focus on key activities that genuinely help move the needle.

Background

Founded in 2007 in Washington DC, LivingSocial is the local marketplace for discovering exciting things to do and experience in the local area, connecting local businesses with customers. The company forms part of the social commerce industry, partnering with local businesses around the world.

Having grown from a startup to a global enterprise employing over 4,000 talented individuals in over 20 countries in just five years, LivingSocial pride themselves on putting innovation and customer focus at the heart of their social media strategy.

With a global presence and social media thinking at the core of their business model, the organization have significant social media interaction with their millions of customers worldwide.

During 2012, the organization focused their UK social media initiatives on four main platforms, building a strong presence across Facebook, Twitter and Pinterest, with a growing presence on Google+.

The solution

LivingSocial nurtures strong relationships with some of the best local businesses in the UK and Irish markets, offering a fantastic resource for interactive content; a resource they were keen to utilize, centralizing their outreach on small group conversations, covering varying business sectors and allowing business owners to share experiences, successes and learnings in a round table style environment.

The LivingSocial's team have set their strategic direction with the objective of maximizing the value of social media outreach for local business clients. Cristina explained:

> Working ever more closely with local businesses is core to our strategy, and one of the areas we are most excited about exploring is the capacity of our social media platforms to underpin, develop and reinforce these relationships.

To achieve these goals, a layered strategy was agreed, with the following key components:

- A comprehensive, user-friendly and regularly changing Google+ page with an engaged audience of business owners and consumers alike.
- Regular Google Hangouts with unique content from the LivingSocial UK and Ireland executive team, interactive participation for existing Living-Social business partners and live feed capacity ensuring maximum reach through LivingSocial's owned social platforms.
- Additional supporting initiatives through online and offline channels, targeting an integrated approach.

This strategy requires only in-house resource, but relies strongly on the relationships with local business owners, and the strong engaged consumer base already inherent in the LivingSocial UK and Ireland social media platforms; as well as participant feedback to meet the campaign goals of increasing business-consumer connectivity and continuous improvement.

Results

Following the initial tests a flourishing Google+ community targeting the local business community, and the execution of three successful Google Hangouts, the first reports of this strategic direction show good results.

Engagement levels and contribution rates amongst client businesses show promising initial growth rates and lend themselves well to continued growth in this area of LivingSocial's social media outreach.

Critical success factors

The ability to listen to feedback from clients, customers and your social media community and drive that feedback into the ongoing strategy will be crucial to refining activity. After each Google Hangout, LivingSocial asked for participant feedback and, after analyzing key trends in client feedback, committed to continuous improvement before each new initiative.

Lessons learned

As with any new strategic initiatives, learnings came as a matter of course. LivingSocial prided itself on driving these improvements into each new initiative and found an ethos of continuous improvement to be key in the success of its B2B social media outreach.

Key areas of learning included:

- **Contingency planning:** with Google Hangouts running as live-streamed, real time sessions with participants from multiple businesses in diverse geographic locations, logistical management of both technology challenges and participant queries required considerable time and people resources to ensure smooth running of sessions.
- **Tonality:** with social media interactions being conversational in nature, striking the right tone to constructively drive communications forward and maximize the benefits of interactivity and learning opportunities for all brands involved requires a strong understanding of the aims of each party involved, coupled with a strong strategic vision to guide content.
- **Content:** providing engaging, unique, actionable content that inspires business owners to rethink and revitalize their marketing strategy was a core aim for the project. Sharing new market-specific research, consumer psychology insights and insights from a different member of the executive team for each Hangout provides a great mix of content, builds the company's thought leadership profile and offers a unique "behind the scenes" experience for participating clients and online viewers.

Want more? See what has been said about this case or get involved and discuss it with the author and other readers on our LinkedIn group, find it by visiting http://www.socialmedia-mba.com *or search for "The Social Media MBA Alumni".*

Part III
Social by Department

Across Departments

6 Macmillan – Social Beyond Marketing

WE ARE MACMILLAN. CANCER SUPPORT

Your audience decides how it wants to communicate with you and what it wants to talk about. So, to be effective, social media cannot be the exclusive domain of one department. It needs to be a core competency for all staff, especially those who are public facing.

Executive summary

Overview

Embedding social media within an organization means addressing a lot of preconceptions held by staff and working to change how people think about their organization, their responsibilities to their audience and their own professional reputations.

Key findings

Social media needs to be a business-as-usual activity not a campaign-specific one. Your employees know their audiences best, they just need the tools to engage with them.

- Staff needs to know what success should look like but for many employees this is a new medium and their apprehension is a natural response. Therefore demonstrate best practices but also be patient and supportive.
- Be holistic. Staff uses the same social media channels privately as well as professionally and all of your employees' activity can reflect on your organization. So do not confine training to purely work-related issues. Address concerns about the personal/private question and present your social media training as a personal development opportunity as well as a professional one.

Recommendations

1. Be flexible – technologies are changing constantly and you cannot anticipate everything. Make sure you keep ahead of what your staff members are learning but use their experiences to shape your policies and planning.
2. Remember that there is strength and safety in numbers. Giving your organization many voices online will not dilute a message but spread it more widely. It will also allow you to engage more deeply on specific topics with target audiences.
3. Don't be too prescriptive. Give employees guidelines to keep them safe but treat them as professionals not children.

What you need to now

Embedding social media within an organization requires more buy-in and support than many other projects. For some staff this is a bewildering new discipline while others may be apprehensive about professional exposure on a channel they had regarded as being for personal use only. You cannot impose social media use and be successful; you need to win hearts as well as minds and you can only accomplish this by taking your staff on the social media adventure with you.

Training: start with a core group and make them your evangelists.
Support: provide as much support as your staff demands and let employees decide how that is delivered. Don't confine it to professional issues only.
Learn as an organization: make sure your training, support and policies reflect your experience as an organization. Celebrate successes but also be ready to learn from bad experience.

Put the right staff on the right channels at the right time – make sure teams know what their options are but let them find the right channels for their needs. Then help them to use those channels realistically and to engage fully with their target audiences.

Background

Interviewee

Carol Naylor and her team are responsible for maintaining Macmillan Cancer Support's online communities including 65,000 members of Macmillan's own online community and over 130,000 followers on Facebook. They also support the staff behind Macmillan's 30 regional and fundraising Facebook pages as well as over 50 Twitter accounts. Carol has been involved in medical communications and online communities for over 20 years.

Carol Naylor
@popplestone

About Macmillan

Macmillan Cancer Support are one of the largest British charities, providing specialist healthcare, information and financial support to people affected by cancer.

As well as helping with the medical needs of people affected by cancer, Macmillan also looks at the social, emotional and practical impact cancer can have, and campaigns for better cancer care. Macmillan's goal is to reach and improve the lives of everyone living with cancer in the UK.

The case

The problem

For over 100 years Macmillan has been working to improve the lives of everyone affected by cancer. That's currently about two million people in the UK living with a cancer diagnosis and an additional six million family, friends, carers and employers. Macmillan has calculated that number will double over the next 20 years.

So how can you support four million people? That was the question facing Macmillan's executive in 2010. Doubling the size of the organization was not the answer; they had to find ways to work differently, be more effective and inspire others to help. Reaching out via social media was an obvious option: but what was the best way to use it?

Background

Macmillan looked at what other charities were doing. They found that even two years ago many organizations only regarded social media as a broadcast channel. Social media was generally handled by the PR departments via single accounts on each of the main social media networks. But with so much to accomplish, that wasn't enough for Macmillan. They needed it to do more to meet their interconnected needs – to inform, support, inspire, campaign, raise funds, etc. – and that wouldn't be possible through a single department or channel.

The solution

Their logo reads "We are Macmillan Cancer Support" and they realized this meant they needed to speak out with many voices, not just one. So Macmillan adopted a much broader approach. They'd treat social media communication like email or the telephone – EVERYONE needed to understand how to use it – from the newest intern right up to its CEO.

Looking ahead, they thought it was likely that within five years, many organizations including Macmillan would be recruiting for social media skills as a core competency in much the same way an understanding of MS Office is expected today. However, they needed those skills now, not in five years. So they had to equip staff with those skills themselves.

Planting the first seeds

At the heart of their strategy was an ambassador programme. Macmillan worked with social media consultants to interview staff and identify those with a natural aptitude for using social media. Together with other staff who needed to use social media strategically, this group totalled just over 100; about 10 per cent of Macmillan's workforce at the time.

Together with the consultants, Macmillan's community and social media team arranged a series of one-day workshops for employees, breaking them into groups of five to eight people with common interests, e.g. marketing or fundraising. Each participant completed a survey beforehand to establish their specific interests and ability.

The workshops were customized accordingly but broadly they all covered the same key topics:

- What is Macmillan's social media strategy and where do the ambassadors fit in?
- An overview of the main channels and how Macmillan wants to use them.
- How to use social media professionally to influence and inspire others.
- Building your own networks.
- Best practice tips and examples of how other organizations are using social media.

On a broader scale Macmillan introduced an internal structure, which gave individuals, teams, departments and regions some autonomy to use social media in the way that worked best for them. However, strategy and support were managed centrally through the social media team providing information and insight, keeping everyone moving in the same direction and ensuring that cross-departmental projects could be handled efficiently. Carol Naylor found herself describing her team's role as being:

> like a social media security blanket . . . with attitude. We had to do a lot of reassurance but we also had to drive and inspire staff to use the channels effectively.

All managers were encouraged to make social media part of their business-as-usual plans rather than a project-specific activity. There was no point building a new network every time Macmillan launched an event or a campaign. So, they aimed to build networks of supporters who could be kept engaged on a regular basis and really mobilized when needed.

Some staff and teams who didn't work directly with Macmillan supporters were unsure how useful they could be in this area. But the social media team weren't just thinking about connecting with established Macmillan audiences online – they wanted to raise awareness in new ones as well. Macmillan's staff and supporters include a huge range of professional specialists from programmers to lawyers and designers to statisticians. Many are well known in their own professional fields. What Macmillan was asking them to do was extend that engagement online and, where appropriate, help raise awareness of Macmillan's work among audiences who otherwise might never hear of the charity.

In common with many charity workers, a lot of Macmillan's staff members are recent graduates who already use social media in their private lives. The social media team figured they just had to show staff how to apply that skill professionally.

In practice they found that most people fell into one of three groups:

- Staff who'd already worked out they could use social media to develop their careers.
- Staff who'd never used social media before.
- Staff who were using it personally and were very uncomfortable at the prospect of having their "private" lives invaded by a load of professional contacts.

The first two groups were the easiest to train. Those who were already using social media professionally were obviously very keen to learn more and improve their performance. They embraced the programme enthusiastically. The second group were naturally wary but willing to try once they'd grasped the advantages of what they would be doing. Macmillan had to spend more time teaching them the mechanics of the various channels but they benefited from being "clean sheets" with no preconceptions or any worries regarding their prior use of the medium. They also appreciated that Macmillan was investing in their personal development by giving them a very portable new skill.

The final group presented the most interesting challenges. In truth, none of them really had skeletons in their online closets but there wasn't a single workshop where the private/professional question wasn't raised.

The 140-character solution

To answer this, Macmillan looked at the various platforms. Everyone agreed pretty quickly that Facebook wasn't the best place to develop a professional network. The transmission of messages was too reliant on the cooperation of others and, without a large existing network, reaching new people was too labour intensive. Strategically they decided Facebook was best used by "official" pages run at a national and regional level and by various fundraising teams. LinkedIn was a professional network from the outset so that only left the question of how to balance professional and personal lives on Twitter.

Carol found herself regularly saying to people:

> You need to start thinking about your online activity in terms of your own reputation as well as Macmillan's. The security of any content is only as reliable as the people seeing it. If one of them decides to share it with others there's nothing you can do about it. So if you want to keep it private, don't post it.

And she continued:

> You also need to accept that the lines between professional and personal are getting increasingly blurred online. If one of your contacts Googles your name, you're not going to be standing by the results screen to explain "Oh ignore that photo, I don't drink that much any more . . . and I don't use language like that either, not really." The only way you can deal with any older, negative content is by making sure you produce far more recent, positive content to counteract it (and appear higher in the search rankings).

All of the groups also had some shared apprehensions, the most common being "What if I make a mistake and post something I shouldn't?" There were two responses Carol would give to this:

> Most of the time you won't make a mistake, but if you do there's safety in numbers. If you slip up on the sole account of a multinational corporation you can expect trouble but here you're one voice in a chorus of many other well-respected ones. Your followers aren't looking to trip you up. Own up, fix the mistake and they'll see human error for what it is and nothing more.

If that didn't work, this never failed:

> Hands up, who has ever accidentally posted a private message on a work account?

Invariably, Carol explains, hers was the only hand raised. After pointing out that she had not been struck by the wrath of God or the CEO as a result, everyone relaxed a bit.

After the workshops, the ambassadors discussed with their line managers which social media activity would be most useful to try and reported to the social media team the objectives they'd set. This was then followed up with practical support and suggestions.

Fostering the uptake

Updated information and insights are vital since trends and platforms change so quickly. Even while running the workshops (over a period of four months) Macmillan noticed the channels they'd focussed on at the beginning – Facebook, Twitter and LinkedIn – were being sidelined by questions from ambassadors about Pinterest, Instagram and Storify by the end. It was vital to keep up to date.

Keeping everyone supported and motivated was one of their biggest challenges and they tried several different approaches before they found one that worked. Peer-to-peer support on a secure message board was not really popular; neither was posting updates on their intranet. They blogged, they Storified, they Scoop.it'd, they Paper.li'd but eventually they found that good old-fashioned weekly newsletters worked for them.

However, Macmillan maintained the content curation sites and the blogs. They have wider uses – Carol says, "My team have their own professional networks to nourish after all."

They let the ambassadors practice and experiment for about three months before reviewing what everyone had learned. These lessons were then fed into social media guidelines for the entire organization. One of the most valuable lessons was that Macmillan could trust staff to show common sense online, so the guidelines did not have to be too prescriptive or complicated. A lot of behaviour was already covered in employment contracts so the social media guidelines came down to process descriptions and eight guiding principles for staff:

- Remember what it says in your contract – do not bring Macmillan into disrepute.
- Be sensible – if you think your post sounds foolish, it probably is.
- Be interesting – social media is an opt-in activity; supporters won't stick around if they're bored.
- Be human – you are not an official spokesperson or making a speech. Other people are interested in you because you're like them. So it's okay to talk and act like a human being.
- Be transparent – when it's relevant to a discussion, admit that you work for Macmillan from the outset.

- Remember your mother can read it all – if you wouldn't say it in front of her, then don't say it online.
- "Google has a long memory" – if it was ever visible to another person, then subsequently hiding, deleting or protecting it will make no difference. The only way to keep something private is not to post it in the first place.
- When in doubt, ASK.

Any individual was welcome to use their own Twitter accounts but Macmillan were more strict about Facebook pages and Twitter for branded or "official" accounts. Teams who wanted to start these needed to produce a rough content plan to cover the first six months and demonstrate they had allocated resources to manage the account. It was a practical way of giving them a reality check and helped to filter out any unrealistic plans.

Wherever possible, processes such as customer management, handling complaints and even crisis management were tied into existing processes already laid down within Macmillan. The only difference emphasized was timeframe. People contacting Macmillan online expected a faster response than they would to an offline enquiry. Apart from that, the aim was to make the Macmillan experience as seamless as possible for everyone who contacted them. Therefore, it would be counterproductive to run parallel systems. Ultimately Macmillan is aiming to integrate its social media monitoring with its CRM system.

What it should look like

For Macmillan this should be the ideal customer experience: someone contacts their support line via Facebook for information about their cancer type, the support line realizes this person could also benefit from talking to other people affected by cancer and so directs them to Macmillan's online community. Their details have been added to the CRM so administrators are able to help them set up a community account immediately and recommend some suitable peer support groups in the community. Finally, Macmillan's single sign-on system (launched in October 2012) allows them to engage more easily with other Macmillan services, take online courses in managing their condition and even sign up for fundraising events.

Spreading Macmillan's voice widely has proved unexpectedly useful. Not long after they started the ambassador training, Macmillan got caught in some political crossfire. Figures in a report on welfare reform produced by its policy team were used by the opposition to attack the government. Unable to rebut their argument, several Tory bloggers were forced to try discrediting the source (chiefly Macmillan) with the result that Macmillan had to deal with several emailed complaints, some irate phone calls, a few dozen negative tweets and a lot of enquiries from political journalists.

If Macmillan's main Twitter account had been its only voice, this could have been a problem. At the time they had over 12,000 Twitter followers, all of whom were far more occupied by the issue of welfare reform than any political sniping. Macmillan needed to respond to journalists asking about the criticisms but didn't want to distract its supporters from the real issue. However, since the journalists all followed their contacts on Macmillan's PR team via Twitter, this wasn't a problem. The PR team used its own networks to handle enquiries without forcing Macmillan to split the attention on its main channel. By the following morning one in four of the population had heard or read about Macmillan's campaign on welfare reform. Considerably fewer were swayed by the negative blog comments.

Despite their obvious value, Macmillan isn't possessive about personal networks. If a member of staff leaves and their network goes with them, then Macmillan will recruit someone who can build an equally useful network. If a staff member attracts a network of followers it's probably because that individual offers them value. Carol says:

> We hope, through that staff member, those followers find Macmillan also offers them value and they'll follow us too.

Similarly Macmillan isn't too prescriptive about where conversations between staff can take place. Its values include "We are open", so there is very little talk of internal and external networks. Macmillan only stipulates that everyone behaves professionally, discloses where they work from the outset and doesn't get too cliquey. So occasionally tweeting about the cute window cleaners in the office is fine but bitching about your co-workers is not. In fact Macmillan staff members are relentlessly enthusiastic and often funny; it's second nature for them to welcome everyone to "#teammacmillan". As a result its supporters get to see a bit of Macmillan's world sometimes, and they generally enjoy it. Macmillan counts it as a win whenever anyone comments on a post "I wish I worked for Macmillan" – and it happens often.

One of the advantages of equipping many staff with social media skills is that you can put the right people in the right place when you need them. Macmillan's social media ambassadors include several staff from HR. They discovered those staff members were already using LinkedIn as a recruitment channel, so after the workshops the social media team asked them to take over the supervision of Macmillan's LinkedIn group, since they were the ones using it most often.

Results

About 25 per cent of Macmillan employees now use Twitter professionally and personally, helping to spread Macmillan's messages to about 12 million tweeters a month. Macmillan's fundraising departments support their teams (cyclists, runners, hikers, swimmers) on dedicated Facebook pages and get high levels of commitment from them as a result.

Carol explained:

> It's been especially rewarding to watch departments and staff develop their own voices online. The creative team love to share the amazing design ideas they find on the internet and their work is respected by other organizations' design teams who follow them because of it.

Similarly, Macmillan's cancer information team embraced Twitter whole-heartedly, gleefully impressing everyone with their cheeky but effective opportunism: "Happy St Patrick's Day! Did you know we have information on benefits in Northern Ireland on our web site?" Social media is helping Macmillan cover a huge number of audiences.

Carol knows nobody can be all things to all people but she'll settle for supporting four million.

Want more? See what has been said about this case or get involved and discuss it with the author and other readers on our LinkedIn group, find it by visiting http://www.socialmedia-mba.com *or search for "The Social Media MBA Alumni".*

7 F5 – Social Across Departments

Not all companies start social media as an all-encompassing greenfield project. This case study is a reflection of reality: social media adopted for specific reasons to serve tactical purposes, developed into an essential communications channel.

Executive summary

Overview

F5 is a B2B tech company that adopted social media as an essential tool in various different ways, for different reasons and at different times. This case study spans three departments and several years, examines success factors and looks at logical points of convergence that can and should apply to other similar organizations.

Key findings

- Members of F5's community have at least 10 per cent higher product satisfaction than non-members.

- Net Promoter Score for customers that are community members is 100 per cent higher than for non-members.
- LinkedIn has yielded over 100 on-boarded employees for F5 in 2011/2012.

Recommendations

1. Find out if social media is being used elsewhere in your organization; examine why, learn from it and apply it to your efforts.
2. "Scale" does not equal "quality". Advocates are much more effective than gaining thousands of Twitter followers.
3. Content is incredibly important, and that starts with knowledgeable people. Don't do anything that requires multi-language expert content without commitment from these people.

What you need to know

- Social media started in 2004 for F5 as a way of connecting global expertise in F5's developer community.
- HR have migrated from a recruitment agency-led model to one based on LinkedIn's Recruiter license.
- Examines why Twitter and LinkedIn are – currently – the "right" social media tools for F5.
- Looks at the background needed to evaluate the usefulness and propose funding of social media.
- Examines how a complex technology proposition makes a social media strategy an attractive option.
- Details why creating – or hiring people with – a social media mindset is essential.
- Postulates what the future might hold in terms of cross-functional convergence of social media and its usefulness at executive level.

Background

Nick is a corporate communications professional who has worked in the IT industry at reseller and vendor level since 1996. He spent several years at McAfee, the security software company, before joining application delivery vendor F5 in 2007.

Nick Bowman
@nick_bowman

About F5

F5 is a $1.3 billion IT organization with circa 3,000 employees (as at 30 September 2012) that operates on a global basis. Best known for its BIG-IP product line, F5 helps integrate disparate networking technologies to provide greater control of the IT infrastructure, improve application delivery and give users secure, seamless and accelerated access to applications from corporate desktops and smart devices. F5 numbers most of the world's largest banks, service providers and ecommerce operations amongst its customer base.

The case

The problem

How do you manage social media across multiple departments? Over a period of six years, social media has become an essential tool for three functions within F5: DevCentral (F5's technical community web site), EMEA marketing (corporate communications primarily), and HR. It also examines areas of convergence and potential convergence. Each of these functions uses social media for different things.

Background

External communication

Firstly, a word on what DevCentral is and why it came to be. DevCentral was built and launched in 2004 because F5 had some very smart APIs which were very young, and the existing support services were not designed to support this new, emergent business for F5 and the surprisingly rapid growth amongst their users.

DevCentral began as a way of connecting the global expertise that existed in F5's customer base. The reason that a forum was chosen as the go-to-market was that the value people get from APIs is not supported by immediate revenue for a publically quoted organization. It is hard to deliver very good developer support that scales while the business develops revenue momentum.

A forum also reflects preferred communication methods for application developers. Like going to the dentist, calling support – for a developer – takes a long time and can be painful. The right way to deliver developer assistance is via a community site as it provides an ideal mix between one-to-one and one-to-many communication.

DevCentral uses social media to engage with and help F5's community to do more than they thought possible with F5 technology; to enable through technical articles and tools, and assist them if they experience challenges. When social media became a reality, the DevCentral team saw it as something that could really drive engagement within what was then a new community. The DevCentral team is currently over 110,000 members strong and sees social media as a way to attract more users, develop rapport and reputation on a larger scale and develop an earned advantage versus one only gained by spending more marketing budget.

Internal communication

For EMEA corporate communications, social media is used as a method of advertising UK and German market-focused content hosted on F5's Dev-Central site: ultimately, to educate customers and influencers about how F5 technology fits into wider industry spending patterns and trends. It's important to stress that this content is a departure from the main content on DevCentral, for reasons that are covered in the section "The approach".

In blogging terms, the site is organized by individual rather than by mini-blog or section, so that a person writing for the German market has his or her posts linked to directly and automatically via social media outreach. Country-specific content is also aggregated into specific country pages, but the main focus for outreach is individual posts rather than the page itself. To help make social media a seamless extension of this type of content marketing, DevCentral has built custom integration between its blogs, RSS and syndication points for social media to maximize reach for every author contributing posts.

F5 has agencies in the UK and Germany (and to a lesser extent in other countries) that handle identifying influencers, building a relationship with them, and, related but separately, drive people back to F5 content on DevCentral. Total spend with the agencies is in the (very) low five figures per quarter, and is weighted towards topic and influencer identification and outreach vs. site management or content creation. Once again, this is a very leveraged approach to engaging the right influencers, building a positive reputation and nurturing that relationship over time to create a wide network of extended promoters of F5's value for specific market sectors.

HR

HR use a combination of products with LinkedIn. Initially, paid "inmails" were used to reach out to people directly through the network. When LinkedIn launched their "Recruiter" product, HR jumped on it, viewing the Recruiter license as a great corporate tool.

The solution

Social media has been a central part of the go-to-market for B2C for some years now. In B2B environments – even in tech – that has not been the case until relatively recently. That is to say, there was no shortage of individuals engaged in social media, but for the most part they were participating as individuals, and not in a programmatic fashion with specific company-related goals in mind. This is a premise that holds true for each of the different functions that adopted social media as an essential tool within F5.

For DevCentral, social media per se has never been a strategy – more an essential tool. Other than for certain individuals or consumer brands on Twitter and Facebook, social media in itself does not create a wake that people will follow. DevCentral never viewed social media as a method of delivering on a marketing strategy but simply as an aspect of marketing that needed to be considered in context. Twitter is the primary social media tool used, as it is the most tech-friendly and represents the most flexible and tuneable channel for the widest audience.

In the marketing and corporate communications context, the task for F5 was to extend the communications channels to encompass the facts that:

- There is a significant and growing influencer base for F5 that exists more or less solely online.
- F5's customer base uses the internet as a major knowledge source.
- There was a need, then, to insert the organization into the conversation online.
- Social media in the B2B tech market at the time had all the characteristics of a challenging, nascent market:
  - volatile;
  - fragmented; and
  - bound to old media in terms of activity drivers (like events or major report or product launches).

F5 wanted to augment their connectivity to customers by embracing online channels. F5 are not one of the world's biggest brands, and the company does not have the easiest technology in the world to understand, even though it is critical to everyday lives. If you've taken out money from an ATM, logged on to Facebook, used an online bank or your mobile phone to access corporate applications, then your activity has likely passed through and benefitted from a faster, safer and more reliable experience via the F5 platform.

Social media is a medium by which one-to-one relationships can be formed and developed, and it is a way of bringing people back to specific pieces of content that explain F5's value, one aspect at a time. Ignoring online means that F5 would have been ignoring the need to educate customers and influencers about where the company's technology fits into their picture.

For HR, the decision to examine LinkedIn as an essential tool in the recruitment mix was an easy one. As an aggressively growing company without the people resources to cover a global market of candidates nor the budget to pay exorbitant recruitment agency fees, social tools made tremendous sense. No other online tool has the global professional reach of LinkedIn. Given its local market dominance, Xing in Germany must be considered, but it was not seen as a functional equivalent of LinkedIn.

Competitively, it was clear that other vendors are using this approach. Budgetary reasons would have driven LinkedIn adoption at some point in any case, but, more pertinently, it was seen as a way to target the best people more effectively. It is better from F5's point of view that people are recruited directly from the company. Response rates are better from this direct targeting, it makes HR more effective and, given that these are the type of metrics that get reported to F5's executive team, this is crucial. Further, F5 has developed internal programmes that drive candidate referral, which further amplify the value of social networking.

The approach

Social media for DevCentral started (and continues) with an engagement mindset amongst DevCentral team members. The primary aim of the team is not to "do" social media, it is to keep the community running – but not run it. The team employs people that want to have a connection to the wider world, especially people with a similar mindset.

Reflecting the various customer types within organizations that F5 serves, the DevCentral team have backgrounds that encompass application development, IT architecture, systems, security and network professionals.

The DevCentral community is important to F5 for many reasons, not least because it puts different functions within large organizations – that may not actually collaborate in their own companies normally – in touch with each other. This in turn creates addressable market expansion for F5 as enterprises shift how they look at building and deploying new applications.

Everyone on the DevCentral team has a Twitter account and everyone understands the need to share important pieces of knowledge amongst the community. This has led to an interesting "signal to noise" challenge with social media. It is clearly possible to use automation tools like RSS to save time by sharing any updates to the DevCentral site: a change to a Wiki, a new post or new tech article, a key media event like a Guru Panel or a new code sample.

Automated posting of every new event from DevCentral in this sense would have led to 300–400 new updates per day via RSS, Twitter, LinkedIn or Facebook, to name just some. Twitter and the like are or can be repeaters, but only in certain situations. However, the risk is that this significant traffic would look like noise – or worse, social media "spam" – and turn followers away.

There is a responsibility to the use of social media that goes beyond the type of language used, subject matter or tone. If you have gained the trust of people enough that they sign up to your syndication, don't let the noise-to-signal ratio become outrageous. DevCentral handles this by making sure that human eyes look at everything that goes out. Without transmitting value, the view was that their community becomes less valuable. Value is the education provided.

Within the EMEA corporate communications function, the social of social media began with some scoping research commissioned and delivered in 2010. It examined the three major economies in EMEA in terms of having enough influencers online to make it "worth" putting in place a programme to develop relationships with them, and – crucially – examined whether F5 had the necessary resources in-country to serve this population with original, regular and expert comment, in local language, reflecting the local environment. The UK and Germany were the only two countries that fitted these criteria initially. The research, then, covered the following:

- Created a snapshot of the social media landscape per country: parameters and characteristics.
- Identified F5's share of voice across tiered sites.
- Profiled relevant blogs, forums and communities.
- Profiled relevant online influencers.

Unsurprisingly, the initial findings were that most conversations online were ineffectual; that a few very large events or topics dominated discussion; and that the only tech brands that were making a consistent impact were those that had significant consumer audiences – Sony and Microsoft for instance.

Amongst the companies that F5 consider competitors, profiling them in terms of their own communities plus channels they had a presence in (e.g. YouTube, Facebook, LinkedIn, Twitter) revealed a very mixed bag, but broadly in line with the size of the company. Cisco, for instance, was highly developed in terms of online profile across all channels, and BlueCoat was at the other end of the scale.

The most time-consuming factor in the roll-out was to decide and commit to where the content would live. The logical place for business and technical content that is trend-related, like cloud computing, rather than involved in the nitty-gritty of how F5's products work in a network or data centre environment, is the company's corporate property, f5.com.

That said, DevCentral has been the hub of all blog-type content since its inception in 2004. It had the necessary functionality already in place, and it would take a strategic and funding shift within F5 to allow blog content on f5.com, so DevCentral became home for the UK and German focused bloggers and blog sites.

Over time, as the overall web strategy evolves, DevCentral will probably become what it was at its inception, that is to say a community site for developers, architects and network professionals using F5, while F5.com will become the home for industry trend-focused and business content.

So, once the "home" was decided, what was left was content development, framework and guidelines for content creators, outreach and influencer targets. The latter in particular was an interesting exercise, in that there is no shortage of people with a voice online, especially in the technology sector.

In an ideal world every one of them would be targeted with a tailored message, but resources rarely allow this unless what you're selling is the same to everyone and is of global or national significance. What F5's research agency – Loudhouse, in the UK – came up with was a kind of influencer top trumps: influencers categorized by industry focus, F5 focus, social media presence on a number of metrics and, finally, an overall score that allowed F5 to build a top 20 list for both the UK and Germany to target for relationships and education.

Ultimately, F5 as a business cares about ROI. Do F5's online engagements create ROI? That's very hard to prove currently. Requiring end-user details before downloading a white paper enables a contact point to be recognized on the CRM system. Reading a blog post about cloud computing in the context of UK government IT directives does not mean the reader is recognized and accounted for. However, there are tools F5 continue to evaluate that more passively – and most important, unobtrusively – help the company learn more about users and the content they view and how it ultimately leads to business.

F5 HR's Recruiter license allows the user to find any other user in the entire LinkedIn network. The search feature is enhanced with very slick filters around keywords as well as location, employer name, job title, education institution and so on. The license includes inmails to contact people, but also the ability to create project folders to save profiles to and for better management of communication with candidates. A useful feature of this license from a corporate perspective is that all inmails for bank users are pooled, so the inmails are used more effectively by the entire team.

Another benefit is that project folders are shared, meaning the HR team can see each other's notes and candidate communication. Thus, candidates are not reached out to multiple times unnecessarily.

A final benefit of the Recruiter license is that the relationships are owned by F5 as opposed to a specific HR team member. Hundreds of hours of relationship building are not therefore lost when a team member moves on.

The landing page also has content such as videos and technology or office information as well as job listings, tailored to the profile of the LinkedIn user viewing the page. The fact that LinkedIn users are able to see people in their network that work at F5 and are given suggested contacts helps F5 to improve engagement with them and increases the chance that they will decide to pursue a job with F5. Dynamic job postings allow the organization to advertise 100 positions at any given time.

On a larger scale, social media is a symptom of wider sentiments about companies and topics. From the perspective of a dissatisfied user, social media is a last resort channel of complaint. A company may have made a promise they couldn't keep or not answered the technical support phone line. Most people try "normal" methods of voicing their displeasure before using social media as a very useful amplifier.

Evolution in how social media is used within F5 may involve efforts to recognize and react to macro type factors like sentiment. Social media is a great indicator of what is happening in the wider world. Sentiment analysis tools are costly and relatively unreliable now for many companies – factors like language conversation density means 50 per cent accuracy might be the best you can hope for.

The future is convergence, both of social media across function, and of how the Big Data that is online conversations is amalgamated into decision-making. Global indicators, presented at an executive level, of how people feel about a given company, month to month, taking into account world events or correlatory factors like an important press release, will become important strategy drivers or early warning systems where big losses can be averted and gains made quickly.

Results

DevCentral's longevity and community engagement has made for some truly impressive results. Of most significance, F5 has determined that customers who are members of DevCentral have at least 10 per cent higher overall product satisfaction (when compared to co-workers not participating). Further, the Net Promoter Score (NPS) for customers who are members is 100 per cent higher than those not registered. The effect community has – and social strategies for engaging and nurturing membership – is to drive greater customer happiness and word-of-mouth promotion. This in turn drives revenue and thus marketing budgets increase, thereby creating a virtuous circle.

For corporate communications, social media has been an essential way of driving customers and influencers to F5 content. The three months ending 31 December 2012 saw around 5,000 visits to UK and German blog properties, and this continues to increase at around 20–25 per cent per quarter, and around 800 vetted individuals are followers of the main Twitter accounts associated with these properties.

HR have used LinkedIn very successfully to draw the right people into F5. It has made prospecting more efficient and has allowed an effective pipeline of employees to be developed. The tool has yielded well over 100 onboarded employees for F5 per year in a two-year period.

F5's LinkedIn "followers" receive periodic announcements and news feeds and can receive targeted job postings results too. F5 now have over 15,000 people following the company – a powerful audience – and that number grew over 50 per cent in just one year.

Lessons learned

From the DevCentral perspective especially, social media is an important element of the marketing mix, but requires care in its use. From the DevCentral community perspective, industrial scale usage of social media would be absolutely the wrong approach. The same is true to an extent for the corporate communication function – it is more important to build meaningful relationships than to build a massive number of followers on Twitter. Advocates are more valuable to the company.

Expertise is even more important than content. Thus, engagement internally is incredibly important. The people that F5 connect with online – customers and influencers – tend to be technical. In common with most EMEA marketing organizations in tech – outside of companies that are truly big and therefore have "corporate" type functions like product marketing managers and technical marketing managers – F5's marketing in EMEA is predominantly field-facing, to support the sales and technical field organizations.

This is changing over time with growth, but until this happens there is a need to be able to create content that demonstrates subject matter expertise. This means being able to engage the support of those personnel with technical knowledge, often in multiple languages. Given that these people will usually be outside the marketing organization and therefore not paid to interact online, this can be a significant hurdle that must be overcome in advance of funding a social media programme.

Want more? See what has been said about this case or get involved and discuss it with the author and other readers on our LinkedIn group, find it by visiting http://www.socialmedia-mba.com *or search for "The Social Media MBA Alumni".*

PR and Marketing

8 Israel Foreign Office – Social in Hostile Environments

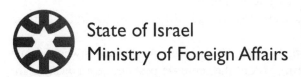 **State of Israel Ministry of Foreign Affairs** The case of Arabic public diplomacy in Israel's Ministry of Foreign Affairs Digital Diplomacy Department is a unique example of an official attempt to bridge the gap of information that exists in the Arab world concerning Israel. A key tool of that effort is the Ministry's Facebook page.

Executive summary

Overview

The Ministry's Arabic public diplomacy copes with the image created for Israel by presenting a full picture of what Israel really is. Through a combination of "soft" materials that involve issues of the Israeli experience, the innovations that are being created in Israel and political materials, the public diplomacy in this Facebook page manages to bring together more than 260,000 people from a hostile environment to read contents posted by the state of Israel in order for them to make up their own mind.

Key findings

The page has currently more than 260,000 fans (members). The total amount of those fans' friends is close to 42 million.

Few of the leading newspapers and communication channels of the Arab world, including *Al-Hayat* (London), *Al-Akhbar* (Lebanon), *Al-Watan* (Kuwait), Alarabiya television channel and more have written about Israel's Ministry of Foreign Affairs Facebook page in Arabic.

During its first 18-month period the page published some 7,200 answers to questions and comments appearing on it and about 1,800 posts.

Recommendations

1. Writing answers to questions and comments on your post is the best way to show your page members that you care about what they have written and about the mere fact that they clicked on "like". People know to evaluate the fact that the page doesn't only publish posts but is also making an effort to conduct a sincere dialogue with them.
2. Among all the ways to convey a message, just speaking the truth clearly is always the best way.
3. An attractive short title together with an attractive picture is what usually stands between entering to read the complete post and just quickly scanning the visible first few sentences on the news feed.

What you need to know

Israel's Ministry of Foreign Affairs Facebook page in Arabic is a way to have a "virtual embassy" in the hostile Arab world until that part of the world is open enough to let Israel in. After years of blocking Israeli web sites, social media enables the Ministry to convey the Israeli experience, its innovative side, its policies and its messages directly to any Arab-speaking person who is interested to learn more about it, and allows anyone who wishes to do so to conduct a dialogue and interact with an official, authorized Israeli source of information.

Despite experience of a high level of hostility by some parts of the Arabic speaking audiences toward the state of Israel, the page manages time and again to bring more citizens of the Arab world around to changing their perspective about Israel.

Background

Interviewee

The Ministry's Media and Public Affairs division and the Digital Diplomacy Department are running an Arabic public affairs branch, which is managing the Arabic internet channels for the Ministry of Foreign Affairs. The branch manages the Arabic channels on Facebook, YouTube and Twitter (@israelarabic) as well as a web site and additional channels of communication.

About the Arabic Public Diplomacy channels of the Israel Ministry of Foreign Affairs

The Ministry's channels operate in the public diplomacy internet arena of the Arabic-speaking world. After managing a standard web site for several years, social media opened new opportunities to reach wide audiences in the Arab world, who use social media to get updates and to communicate with friends.

The Ministry's Facebook page, www.facebook.com/israelarabic, is considered to be the main channel of communication. The Ministry synchronizes information from this Facebook page with the equivalent Twitter account so that every Facebook post also reaches the Twitter channel's followers. Additional tweets are tweeted, to communicate any further information, when required. Different videos produced by the Ministry specifically for the Arab-speaking audience are uploaded to the YouTube channel, www.YouTube.com/israelmfaarabic.

The Arabic public affairs branch sends a weekly newsletter to its subscribers and answers their emails on a regular basis.

Two employees are running the Arabic public affairs branch. Different services are being outsourced, such as translations, video news magazine and subtitles for films.

Their social media strategy

The aim of the channels in the Arabic language is to attract audiences belonging to the Arabic-speaking world, and mainly the Arab world. This is done through the sharing of information in a wide range of topics about the state of Israel.

Due to the severe lack of information about Israel in the Arab media, and the systematic tarnishing of the Israeli image in both the Arab media and the official regimes' propaganda, the Ministry's strategy is to supply Arabic-speaking people with information about what Israel really is. This is done by sharing articles and news covering a wide range of Israeli issues from the following fields: science, medicine, agriculture, education, coexistence, art and history (and much more). Beside the non-political issues, the Ministry publishes articles, quotes from Israeli leaders and announcements by the Ministry's spokesperson, which present Israel's policies.

The channels convey statements made by the prime minister, the foreign minister, his deputy and various other ministers and officials. The Media and Public Affairs Division holds that the combination between "soft" issues, which aren't policy related, and ones which are political, helps to attract the Arab reader most. Hence, the administrator believes that if the Ministry's Public Affairs Division handled only non-political or only political issues, then the chances are that many fans would lose interest and leave.

The Ministry ascribes much importance to the visual side of its posts along with the verbal one. Pictures attract people to pay attention. Also, a short, strong and clear title and sub-title are given much importance as something that can attract the reader to continue reading.

The case

The problem

Israel's Ministry of Foreign Affairs had been addressing the Arab-speaking world with the "traditional" way of conveying its messages and information through the Ministry's Arabic web site. That web site faces huge difficulties penetrating the Arab world because many internet suppliers in the Arab countries block it, as well as many other Israeli web sites, and that is despite the fact that the Ministry's site ends in .com.

The Arabic citizen doesn't have any way of receiving Israeli radio or television transmission and also doesn't have the opportunity to refer questions to or conduct a dialogue with any official Israeli factor.

In this reality the knowledge that the average Arab citizen has about Israel is limited to his or her government's propaganda and to the Arab-owned communication channels. Since the web site is blocked in many countries and since Israel has diplomatic relations only with Egypt and Jordan, then the Ministry had chosen to reach out to Arab citizens through social media channels, which can't be blocked.

The Ministry had opened Twitter channels and Facebook pages at the beginning of 2011, during the eruption of the upheavals of what is called The Arab Spring. The Arab Spring gave social media in the Arab world a great push and the Ministry realized that this trend could be used to promote Arab citizens' knowledge about Israel. The Facebook, Twitter and YouTube pages enable them to reach a huge target group, the majority of whom weren't yet exposed to the basic facts about Israel, but the Arab media only. The Ministry's channels are about the only official source that addresses the Arab world with a wide range of information on a daily basis. The Ministry dedicate great importance to the level of the Arabic language used, providing the very highest lingual level. The only "old" information brought is historic facts; other than that, every item published includes information that brings news, whether this information concerns Israel's policies or general information about the Israeli experience and the innovative achievements of the state.

Background

For Israel's Ministry of Foreign Affairs the work in social media channels in Arabic is work in a generally "hostile environment". The "likes" on the Facebook page, http://www.Facebook.com/israelarabic, can be widely divided into three groups:

- People who support Israel. This group is a minority for the page, but it is noticeable that many of this group's members are eager to write comments and to show affection, support and appreciation.
- People who recognize Israel's right to exist, support reaching peace between Israel and the Arab world, including the Palestinians, but criticize Israel's government and its policies.
- People who don't recognize Israel's right to exist, in any case not as a Jewish state.
- It can be assumed that some portion of the members in the third group do actually recognize Israel's right to exist, but post hateful comments in order to take part in the trend to negate Israel.

One of the major challenges facing the Facebook page, as well as the YouTube channel, is monitoring the curses and comments, which include hate speeches, posted on these channels by some users.

Israel's Ministry of Foreign Affairs can't allow a situation where violent, offensive comments appear on its official channels. The Facebook page administrator continuously checks all the comments and erases the inappropriate ones. Repeat offenders who use curses, insults and hateful speech are being systematically banned from the page.

The page also confronts the prejudices held by some citizens of Arab countries by replying to their comments and enabling a true ongoing dialogue with them. This dialogue is also aimed at breaking the perceived image that many Arabs have about Israel as being arrogant and not interested in a dialogue with them.

Due to this unfortunate background, there exist many myths and incorrect perceptions of Israel as a state and of many historical occasions in its history. Social media enables the Ministry to supply the members and followers with answers to any question and to shatter the inaccurate perceptions.

The solution

The page administrator practices the following methods of conduct when addressing the target audience:

- **Variation:** the more diversified the topics are, the more interest the readers will find in the page and the longer it will be able to prolong its "rating". The page administrator noticed that even eager fans of Israel, who used to write positive comments on almost each of the posts, became less and less involved as time progressed. Variation exists in the featuring of different topics and the use of different methods to share information (pictures, links, notes).
- **Political and non-political:** it is given that a page belonging to a Ministry of Foreign Affairs must allow room for political decisions, statements and policies. It is known that many of the Arab citizens who clicked "like" on this page, and read the page's posts, originally joined due to a political reason. Obviously the misdirected notion of Israel stems from a political background. However, the administrator discovered through reading the comments of page fans that some of them have thanked the page administration for publishing non-political issues that shed light on subjects such as Israel's medical, scientific and agricultural breakthroughs, in addition to songs, cultural trends, coexistence initiatives and even recipes for traditional dishes. The conclusion is that a reasonable combination and variety

of topics is what enables the page to preserve its position as an interesting, attractive source of information.

- **Dialogue:** as mentioned already, conducting a dialogue and answering questions are in themselves a matter of value that can be viewed as a "virtual embassy" of Israel to the Arab world. The administrator is confident that some of the page's reputation in the eyes of its subscribers has to do with the fact that the page supplies detailed, clear and accurate responses. The very nature of social media gives the administrator an opportunity to address and discuss the most fundamental issues of the Arab–Israeli conflict. They ask – the page answers: between 60 to 120 such answers every week.

- **Language:** Arabic speakers usually understand and value the clear and precise articulation of their language. If the page were to use weak language, not to mention make mistakes, then in the context of an Israeli official page addressing the Arab environment, which is generally hostile, the page administrator may be not taken seriously. The fact that the page uses clear high-level Arabic wins it points even from opponents of Israel.

The other aspect of the manner of delivery is the way in which the page supplies answers to members' comments that belittle, make false accusations, or includes empty statements such as "this isn't your land", "go back to where you came from", "you stole Palestine", "you kill children and women", etc. The page administrator always keeps an official, kind and explanatory tone, and never sinks down to the low level of those kinds of comment. The administrator has noticed that this manner is helpful in ensuring the page's good reputation in the eyes of different types of readers. Moreover, this approach has, in various instances, led to some page members asking others to abandon offensive commenting, while encouraging them to learn from the administrator's articulation.

- **Image:** obviously this official page pays close attention to being factual and ensures the content is as accurate as possible. The mere fact that the page addresses an often hostile group demands that the administrators do not write anything that could be used against the state of Israel.

Given the existing image of Israel in the majority of the Arab world, that has fed on decades of blackening and distortion of what Israel really is, the page, as well as the other public diplomacy channels, aims to convey the message that Israel is at the forefront of the world progress in many fields. Israeli achievements don't just involve scientific cutting-edge developments, but also achievements in fields such as archaeology, desert agriculture (which is relevant for and of interest to many Arab countries), education, municipal services and more.

- **Writing to the target group:** the page makes an effort to tailor the content to the Arab-speaking target group. For example, articles that handle complex scientific issues, which can be hard for any non-expert to digest, are articulated clearly, are non-intricate and refrain from using technical expressions. The topics are chosen because they are of interest to the target group. There is much attention given to the formulation of the title and the subtitle, and to the pictures that accompany the articles or news items.
- **Asking questions:** in some of the posts, the administrator asks the members to share their views with the page or to share what they think with the page's community. It is clear that such an approach encourages more people to comment and hence to read the post's content, and also to contribute to the assimilation of information through rising post "shares". At one time, the page addressed its members experimentally, asking them in what ways they find this page contributes to their knowledge about Israel and how it has helped them change their view towards it. There were over 600 comments on that post, with people actually sharing what they had gone through in response to the questions.

Results

The page administrator measures its activity according to the following criteria:

- number of likes, comments, shares and impressions;
- content of comments;
- echoing of Israeli public affairs in Arabic in the Arabic media.

One of the Ministry's targets concerning the Arab world is that the Arab media will write about its activities and share items that have been published on it.

The Digital Diplomacy Department, which is in charge of the Arabic internet public diplomacy, collects details about achievements from the administrator once a week and is supervising the Arabic branch activities.

Critical success factors

1. A team of two full-time employees.
2. A budget that will be sufficient enough to cover all costs, such as translations, editing of subtitles to films, video productions, etc.
3. Learning new developments of Facebook itself.

Lessons learned

If the administrator had to build the Facebook page from scratch again, they wouldn't change anything. What could be done, however, is work inside the Ministry of Foreign Affairs to achieve bigger budgets for promoting the page. Promotion of the page has been carried out successfully, hence it is felt that such a move is necessary for boosting the page.

After originally making five to six posts a day, the page's administrator has learned that it is preferable to reduce the number of posts to about three a day. The larger the number of posts the less information the page's members seem to take in.

Want more? See what has been said about this case or get involved and discuss it with the author and other readers on our LinkedIn group, find it by visiting http://www.socialmedia-mba.com *or search for "The Social Media MBA Alumni".*

9 Confused.com – From Content to Profit

A great salesman might be able to sell ice to Eskimos, but getting that Eskimo to tweet about it is a bit more challenging. This is a story of how even a boring product can go viral.

Executive summary

Overview

One evening in the office, a simple Google search for driving in heels led to one of the most successful social media campaigns for Confused.com in terms of ROI for the whole of 2012. The case focuses on a company that came late to the social media party, but when it did, it came with style, being one of the company's biggest success stories of 2012.

Key findings

- The video received 51,926 views, there were 1,500 tweets about the campaign, 70 Pinterest pins, 21 video embeds, a 33.6 per cent uplift in Facebook fans and 113 links to Confused.com.
- The month long campaign brought 46,064 new visitors to the Confused.com web site.
- It takes just one success for the company to believe in social media.

Recommendations

1. Jump on new social platforms or changes when they emerge, it will get you guaranteed coverage and noise for your brand.
2. Build an in-house content team with social expertise and work with agencies to add value, but don't be reliant on external knowledge.
3. Don't assume you have to spend a lot to get good results, simple ideas can work better than those that come with high cost.

What you need to know

Confused.com were late starters when it comes to social media, really digging their teeth into it in 2012. But the company hit it with full force and on limited budget and have seen exciting results. Who would have thought a simple campaign about driving in heels could have been responsible for such a strong return on investment, but it shows that sometimes simple ideas carried out on a limited budget are the best.

Social content is a direct and entertaining way of reaching an audience you may not, as a company, traditionally attract – but because you dared to try something new and step out of the fray you may just get a piece of their time.

When selecting driving in heels Confused.com wanted to produce an engaging and shareable campaign, which would support their SEO (search engine optimization) position for car insurance through gaining links and video embeds and place Confused.com as the authoritative voice in car insurance and related motoring issues.

The campaign (over just a one-month period) attracted 46,064 new visitors to the Confused.com web site.

Marketing Magazine in Australia highlighted the driving in heels campaign as among the "Top ten uses of Pinterest by brands", alongside Barack Obama's presidential election campaign.

The background

Interviewee

During her time at the company, Sharon Flaherty has pioneered a branded content strategy. Taking her journalism background to the brand, she has introduced an editorial content strategy from scratch with multiple successes. Her award-winning teams drive exceptional engagement for the brand with editorial and social content and are always looking at ways to innovate. Previously she was a journalist at the *Financial Times*.

Sharon Flaherty
@ConfusedSharon

About Confused.com

In 2002, Confused.com launched the first online car insurance price comparison web site, and in doing so spawned a market revolution. Confused.com flourished because it simplified the process of finding people car insurance quotes that suited their budget.

Before Confused.com came along, drivers had to obtain their car insurance through high street brokers, broker web sites or directly through an insurer's web site. If customers wanted to compare deals, it meant hours filling in forms just to retrieve quotes.

Home insurance followed in 2005, and today Confused.com is the comparison site of choice for millions of online shoppers looking for all kinds of insurance – including car, home, travel, life, motorbike, van, pet and caravan, to name just a handful.

Confused.com is also the place to find cheaper gas and electricity, and other household services such as TV and broadband packages. Plus they've branched out into the financial services market. It's now possible to compare credit cards, annuities, savings accounts, mortgages and loans. And the list of products available is ever expanding.

Most recently, Confused.com has launched some handy apps. Their MotorMate app scores users on the safety of their driving, with an aim to reducing the risk they present as motorists. This will hopefully ultimately lead to reductions in premiums, and safer roads. There is also a parking app, which allows users to search and compare prices for car parks using GPS, postcode or the destination's address.

In short, Confused.com exists to make everyone's life easier, with a primary focus on motorists. And if Confused.com can save their customers into the bargain, then all the better.

Their social media strategy

In the second quarter of 2012, Confused.com launched its first social media strategy to build on its existing content strategy. There was no budget for social media in 2012 and social activity had to be absorbed in the traditional content budget that luckily Confused.com had the foresight to have. Dipping their toes into social media this year, the spend was minimal, not exceeding £50,000, but the return on this small investment was huge – not to mention the learnings. The initial strategy saw the company focus on building Facebook fans and Twitter followers, using content as currency. Alongside this was a focus on YouTube to push out Confused.com's video strategy and new social media channel Pinterest as a trial.

The strategy was about being innovative and bold for financial services, a sector which is traditionally seen as more conservative and slower to adopt new technologies. The company took advantage of trends, to try to be the first to experiment in its sector. This saw Confused.com launch video campaigns such as the five second talent show using the new feature YouTube Slam. They also launched zombie videos, a controversial video mockumentary of a cross-dressing rugby player to highlight an important insurance issue, which attracted over 500,000 views, and the public were invited to be burglars for the day. These are just some of the campaigns, but you see the variety.

Although potentially seemingly random, the key theme underpinning the social media strategy is innovation. Confused.com want to reach as many audiences as possible. More than this though, the strategy is about developing a new communication channel that the company believes will become dominant in the future, just like TV has.

Digging deeper into the strategy, SEO is a key driver of performance for the company and content is the medium used to drive this. In a nutshell, for Confused.com, the more high quality links there are to their web site or particular page, the higher it will rank in search engines. Content is the best way to drive interest, engagement, natural links and traffic and this is one reason for their use of it. On top of this, good content is the mark of a good, respected, trusted brand, and good content allows the company to "socialize" with its audience, which in turn will attract views, shares, likes, retweets, fans and create that social buzz and noise that also ultimately supports SEO and drives traffic to the web site.

One more thing, good social stories and social content also attract press coverage, which in turn builds brand awareness at a snip of the cost of TV advertising, something that is becoming more important as companies look to attract and retain new customers or audiences through "new" or alternative media.

Above all though, social content is a direct, entertaining, informative way of reaching an audience you may not, as a company, traditionally attract but because you dared to try something new and step out of the fray you may just get a piece of their time. Sharon adds, "social media is not a fad as some traditional marketers still say, it *is* here to stay".

The case

The problem

Car insurance is perhaps not the most interesting topic in the world but it's the core product of Confused.com's business and, as such, the promotion of it is a priority for the marketing department.

Confused.com, just like other online businesses, has a natural search or SEO strategy that is important to their success. Being high in the rankings for key search terms is a core business goal that is embedded in the objectives of all of the online teams. As such, when launching any through-the-line marketing campaigns SEO has to be considered. With this in mind, the Confused.com content team set about trying to deliver an interesting piece of content that talks around the topic of car insurance – one of their core products – and the subject of motoring, and delivers on the content team values of producing interesting, engaging and quality content that has a buzz, but also on the SEO objectives of driving natural links too. No mean feat at all.

From research, the Confused.com content team found a lot of search traffic for terms related to driving in heels and designed a quirky campaign underpinned by a serious safety message.

Background

Great content is vital to our business strategy, and to satisfy this demand the content team that carries out social media at Confused.com has to be constantly producing good content of all types from infographics to videos, to apps, to blogs or guides. The Confused.com web site is hungry for traffic and the company's social campaigns play a large role in driving traffic. It's no easy feat though, and the campaigns must be engaging, easy to relate to but also generate backlinks to Confused.com as well as social conversations. Achieving these things for each campaign needs, at times, the content to be controversial, but a line has to be established with what sits well with the brand and what doesn't. The content has to be interesting enough to make a splash and hit all the metrics we want, such as shares, likes, retweets, links, social chatter and buzz but not make people so shocked or disgusted that they boycott the brand.

The challenge doesn't stop there. With more investment in social media come the inevitable questions from those guarding the purse strings, such as the value of a Facebook fan or the worth of a video view. Once you've "tinkered" with social, the performance of it has to stand up – why else are you doing it? It's *continued* worth has to be proven. It's no good saying "we got 25 thousand views on our video" this is simply not enough. What needs to be said is "we got 25 thousand views on the video, x amount of those views then came to x page on the web site. X views came from this referrer, x views from this link, this translated into x sales", by way of example. Over time, the tracking should improve too with the learnings you get from each campaign.

Being measured in your output will help put to bed doubt, though don't expect it to remove it completely as there is still a focus on paid media rather than earned, albeit this is changing.

As an advocate and lover of all things content, Sharon believes the value of social media will shock people in the future as we continue to shape our lives around it, but at times there may need to be an acceptance that slow and steady is the route forward with social, for some companies, but one way to speed up the process is to remove constraints.

For example, in the second quarter of 2012, Confused.com brought video production in-house. This was so Sharon was not reliant on agencies to produce video or video concepts, removing the barrier of the time lag that brought. Having an in-house multi-media producer resulted in big changes to the content team as it really brought the content they were already doing to life and gave them the speed they needed to have the desired conversations with their audiences. In fact this step-change really got the company excited about what content was doing for them and could do.

In terms of competition, Confused.com operate in a fiercely competitive market and Sharon feels it isn't long before a competitor is looking to mimic your strategy. But it's not just the direct competitors that need to be considered, it's also the publishing industry as a whole; as brands are now publishers, it is important to keep on top of trends in publishing too.

The solution

The team set out to raise awareness of the dangers of driving in unsuitable footwear, and doing other potentially dangerous things behind the wheel, and to, in a light-hearted way, get people to be more aware of driving safely by:

- Producing an engaging and shareable campaign, which would support the SEO position of Confused.com for car insurance through gaining links and video embeds.
- Positioning Confused.com as the authoritative voice in car insurance and related motoring issues.

The story

A survey commissioned by price comparison web site Confused.com found that 40 per cent of women drive in heels; 39 per cent of women wear flip flops whilst driving and 24 per cent take to the road in bare feet.

Sixteen per cent also confess to driving in slippers and just 34 per cent claim to always wear sensible shoes. The survey also found that one in ten women apply make-up at the wheel and 15 per cent of men shave whilst driving.

The approach

The driving in heels campaign allowed the company to look at driver behaviour. Confused.com wanted to explore what habits many of us have inside the car and which of those could be risky. Earlier in the year they had begun to work with Brake, the road safety charity, and so experts were at hand. The brainstorming began by thinking about the bad habits that as drivers ourselves we know we are "guilty" of and should really avoid. Cue lots of confessions from the team, and a few red faces. The girls admitted to driving in high heels and we agreed this was potentially dangerous. Confused.com spoke to experts at Brake and their car insurance team and they agreed that stilettos should be ditched behind the wheel. So the company commissioned research among 2,000 drivers to find out if the team were alone in their naughty behaviour or if many other drivers would admit to this, and other misdemeanours. Other habits were also included, such as men who pick their noses at the wheel (girls: we would simply not admit to this) and fashion faux-pas like wearing flip-flops or pyjamas. This was not all about safety, it was also about sharing funny stories and getting under the skin (or behind the wheel) of drivers just like those in the team.

The results of the survey proved the hypothesis that behind the wheel of the UK's cars there are a horde of pyjama-clad, nose-picking flip-flop wearers and, most worryingly, 40 per cent of women have worn high heels to drive.

Innovative

The social media experts in the team immediately saw the potential of video and online activity as a way of sharing the findings and also the safety messages. They recommended using a relatively new social medium, Pinterest, as a space where women drivers who love their shoes could share photos of their favourite high heels. This recommendation was grounded in the fact that 68.2 per cent (source: Mashable) of Pinterest users are women, and so the female-focussed aspect of the campaign would appeal to them especially.

The campaign was not about "telling off" drivers for their behaviour, it was about raising awareness of the dangers of driving in unsuitable footwear. So, to ensure people engaged with the message and took the point on board, Confused.com identified a way to reward drivers for admitting their faults and to help with getting them back on the right track. The marketing teams of several footwear companies were contacted and pairs of Butterfly Twists (flat women's shoes) and Vans trainers were successfully procured. These would form part of a give-away and already the team had begun to make a video to promote the planned Pinterest competition aimed at the female audience giving away the Butterfly Twists.

The amusing short film made in-house shows a woman being "checked out" as she struts through Cardiff City Centre in skyscraper heels, only to stall – literally – as she tries to drive her car, losing the respect of her admirers. The call-to-action for women is to enter the Pinterest competition, sharing your unsuitable shoes for the chance to win some more practical footwear.

Shareable

Confused.com's Pinterest and YouTube accounts both had a part to play in sharing the video and competition, with the winners being chosen for the bets pins on the Confused.com Pinterest board.

The campaign captured the imagination of the desired audience (motorists) and the company's innovation was picked up on by several influential technology web sites, including Mashable who commented on the use of the relatively new picture-sharing site Pinterest and shared the video in their media coverage of the campaign: http://mashable.com/2012/04/13/pinterest-contest-driving-in-heels/.

Why is this exciting? Well, Mashable has 20 million monthly unique visitors and 4 million social media followers, it's a must-read site for those connected online and it syndicates its content to top publications including ABC News, CNN, *Metro* and Yahoo! News. It means Confused. com had reached the influencers. The organization was also praised by a number of media web sites for their use of Pinterest and for being early adopters.

The tools used to communicate their message were as follows: Facebook, Twitter, Pinterest, YouTube, Video-onsite, Onsite content, email, competition/giveaway, press release, infographic, pictures and radio (earned).

Cost

The estimated cost of the campaign was just £1,800, including PR outreach, omnibus research, an infographic, actress, short film and competition.

ROI

The campaign was a success in several respects:

- It was a very low-cost campaign, which punched above its weight not just in the UK but also worldwide (Australia and America).
- It exceeded Confused.com's objectives in terms of making social noise and getting links. The company always aims to break-even on campaign spend. However, this far exceeded this target and many other metrics.
- It raised a serious safety message.
- The social noise on Facebook alone saw a 33.6 per cent uplift in fans over the period of the campaign.
- The campaign returned 13 links and 21 video embeds coming in at a value of £18,500 if this were to be bought media, proving earned marketing is financially better than paid for marketing.

Results

The driving in heels safety message was successfully spread, evidenced by the following results.

Coverage

In media coverage terms, the press campaign generated 83 pieces of media coverage including *The Sun, Daily Express, Daily Star, Metro* newspapers and their web sites and on the web site of the *Daily Mail,* which has more than 45 million readers (source: comScore, Jan 2012). This online chatter about the campaign led to Confused.com being contacted by radio stations wanting to cover the story, including Sky News Radio (which syndicates to Magic FM and other commercial stations) and several BBC stations including BBC Radio Humberside, BBC Radio Leeds, BBC Radio Northern Ireland and BBC Surrey/Sussex.

Links

In terms of SEO, Confused.com had 13 links to the driving in heels campaign and 21 video embeds, and over 100 inbound links from other sites to the infographic. The estimated value of buying these links and embeds by the SEO agency was over £18,000 alone, without factoring in the earned radio and online media.

Site traffic

Visits to Confused.com on the driving in heels campaign totalled (5 April–1 May 2012) 46,064 with 144 comments posted on an article, highlighting the engagement with the campaign. Looking at unique visitors to the site via the campaign, we saw that over 65 per cent of visitors were new, demonstrating that the message had reached a new audience as well as the existing audience.

Facebook

Over the life of the campaign Confused.com saw a 33.6 per cent uplift in Facebook fans.

Twitter

After posting the campaign on Twitter via the Confused.com Twitter account, the organization had more than 1,500 tweets about the driving in heels campaign.

YouTube

The driving in heels video has been watched over 45,000 times. On top of this, during the time of the Pinterest competitions (5 April–1 May 2012) the Confused.com YouTube channel had 51,926 views, compared with 6,739 in the same period the previous year. The channel also gained 15 subscribers, 97 likes and 24 shares (YouTube).

Critical success factors

The success of social media campaigns at Confused.com rests simply on one question: did the message get out there? If so, where did it go? For example, was the video shared on Twitter, did their Facebook fans share it with their friends? Did they make it into the viral video charts on YouTube? Did they get any/many shares? Did it get discovered naturally by marketing, social media press and blogs? Did it get linked to? And did it drive traffic from other or new sources as a result of that content being out there? Were there new referrers of traffic? – these are crucial as it means your business is being placed in front of new eyes, essential for business growth.

So, if the social media campaigns are hitting these boxes then the Confused.com content team count it as a success; if not, they will be very disappointed and investigate what went wrong.

Lessons learned

- You do not always have to spend a lot of money to produce a good campaign.
- You get a lot of satisfaction from high success and a small spend.
- It takes just one success for the company to believe in social media.
- Tie up social media, editorial content and online PR to gain efficiencies.

The driving in heels campaign involved tying a lot of strands together, from sourcing the shoes, managing the competition, working with compliance over the terms and conditions, trying to do something new on Pinterest and learning the ropes of the platform, as well as pushing the campaign out through as many channels as possible. Sharon's biggest piece of advice from what she has learnt is to try new channels, find out what works for you and your audiences. If it is coverage and recognition you are after, being one of the first to play with and trial out a new platform is going to attract talk about your brand. So don't wait and watch, jump early, give it a go and create your own noise.

Want more? See what has been said about this case or get involved and discuss it with the author and other readers on our LinkedIn group, find it by visiting http://www.socialmedia-mba.com *or search for "The Social Media MBA Alumni".*

10 Xerox – Help Clients go Social

SHARING SOCIAL MEDIA EXPERTISE WITH CUSTOMERS AT
A TRADE SHOW IS A WIN-WIN

Taking social media to industry trade shows is now widely practiced. Xerox recently extended the role of this tool by using their own social media practitioners to help potential customers.

Executive summary

Overview

At the 2012 drupa print trade show Xerox created a physical social media space for visitors who wanted to learn how social media could help their business. The space provided a place where visitors could converse, ask questions and see opportunities demonstrated in a relaxed and confidential manner. Helping customers with their social media strategy inspired customers, and got them thinking about how to use social media marketing to profit their own businesses.

Key findings

Sharing best social media practices at industry trade shows is a great way to attract and help potential customers. Many show visitors were unfamiliar with social media channels. One-to-one consultations with Xerox social media experts helped build relationships and enabled visitors to ask questions that they would have been uncomfortable raising in a public forum.

Creating photo opportunities, in and around the exhibitor stand, is fundamental to achieving real-time audience interaction and increasing social media profile during a trade show.

Recommendations

1. It is essential for the venue to have good Wi-Fi access. In order for visitors to participate, they must be able to practice social media on the show floor, not when they go back to the hotel.
2. The discussion around social media should be free flowing. Sessions should not be limited to a specific time.
3. Focus efforts on particular social media channels. Xerox analysed a host of social media activity from the drupa show, finding that Twitter was by far the most used channel when compared to Foursquare, Facebook, LinkedIn, YouTube and Instagram.

What you need to know

Begin at smaller shows, with a modest budget, and learn from your experience. This provides the confidence to go to the next level, and eventually to major events such as drupa.

As with every other customer relationship channel, content must be credible and of clear value. At an industry trade show, letting visitors know what is going on, where and what you are offering is key.

Background

Interviewee

Andy Hill joined Xerox in April 1991 and, since 1998, has held a variety of roles in marketing. In 2005 he moved from product management to digital marketing where he ran Xerox's European channel partner extranet. With the creation of a new digital marketing team in July 2011, Andy jumped at the chance to manage the implementation of social media activity

Andy Hill
@Andy_Hill

across Xerox Europe. He describes this as his dream job where he has established a reputation for delivering results.

About Xerox

With sales approaching $23 billion, Xerox is the world's leading enterprise for business process and document management. Its technology, expertise and services enable workplaces – from small businesses to large global enterprises – to simplify the way work gets done so they operate more effectively and focus more on what matters most: their real business. Headquartered in Norwalk, Connecticut, USA, Xerox offers business process outsourcing and IT outsourcing services, including data processing, healthcare solutions, HR benefits management, finance support, transportation solutions and customer relationship management services for commercial and government organizations worldwide. The company also provides extensive leading-edge document technology, services, software and genuine Xerox supplies for graphic communication and office printing environments of any size. The 140,000 people of Xerox serve clients in more than 160 countries.

Their social media strategy

In their stakeholder engagement model, the need to build advocacy is key to everything Xerox do and everything they say, every day. And, social is increasingly the fundamental driver of how the organization informs and engages stakeholders and in how they in turn express their advocacy for Xerox.

To ensure that Xerox is taking full advantage of everything social offers, they strengthened their social marketing competency in 2012 by giving it new leadership, focus and resources as a shared service for the company.

Xerox recently appointed a head of global social marketing, reporting to the chief marketing officer, who has built a global team responsible for:

- Social media strategies that integrate with other marketing campaign elements.
- Social platform expertise.
- Corporate social platforms, like @XeroxCorp and the Xerox Facebook and LinkedIn pages.
- Listening tools, trends and analytics.
- Search engine optimization strategies to increase engagement on social platforms.
- Codes of conduct, training, certification and social-related policies.

- Trend spotting and education in social environments, deployment of new technology to simplify management of social platforms.
- Integrating social content with paid media and complementing other areas of earned and owned media.

Creating buzz at the biggest trade show in your industry is no easy task. Faced with attending a show with 1,850 other exhibitors, Xerox added a new twist to their social media plan by giving out free advice. The approach drove traffic to the Xerox exhibition stand and scored points with potential customers.

The case

The problem

In the printing industry, one trade show stands above all the others. Held every four years for a fortnight in Düsseldorf, Germany, drupa is not only the largest but also the most anticipated of all print exhibitions across Europe.

Xerox did not have the biggest exhibition stand at the show, but it aimed to attract 100,000 of the 320,000 show visitors, create more buzz than other exhibitors and strengthen its association with social media.

The solution

Xerox drew on two levers to attract visitors to its stand – a new proposition called "Freedom to Focus on What Matters Most" and its sponsorship of Canadian circus troupe Cirque du Soleil, which performed three times a day on the Xerox stand.

Darrell Minards, Xerox Europe's head of marketing communications, explained:

> Our main focus at the show was on helping our customers' businesses grow, so we judged everything we did against that primary objective.

Using the two attractions, Xerox set out to achieve high visibility within all social media searches for the drupa event. But the social media plan did not end there, the company also intended to provide "best practice" advice about social media to show visitors.

Social media manager Andy Hill was tasked with creating an integrated social experience to meet these aims. Of the options he explored, two stood out: a social media café and social media clinics, both of which would use the special Cirque du Soleil performances to help attract traffic.

Andy explains:

> With the café, our idea was to create an informal setting where you could relax, have a coffee and learn more about social media and Xerox . . . To help initiate those conversations we had a social media "tweet wall", which was a 72-inch plasma screen with engaging and colourful content capturing all the Twitter conversations (as well as those on YouTube, Facebook and Foursquare) about Xerox and drupa.

Andy said the team also chose to use a social media visualizer – a live info-graphic showing all the conversations on Twitter that mentioned the word drupa, and created a tag cloud, highlighting the most popular drupa related topics.

The social media clinics were relaxed one-to-one sessions where show visitors (typically, print providers) could get help from Xerox social media practitioners on using social media and understanding its business value. To support the conversations, Xerox created guides on simple processes such as "taking your first steps in social media" and "how to set up accounts".

Andy had experimented with a tweet wall at a closed Xerox customer event the year before, and was impressed by how well received it had been. At drupa he wanted to take it to the next level; he explained:

> The potential of the tweet wall was clear for us to see, and with thousands of visitors coming to drupa, this represented the perfect opportunity to try it out on a larger scale . . . One of the great things about any social media campaign is that it's so easily measurable.

Xerox was confident that this strategy would work alongside their overall brand message – helping customers to focus on their "real business".

"Helping organizations manage their day-to-day business in such an authentic and open way couldn't be a better fit", Andy added.

The execution

The social media budget for the show was £15,000. But for Xerox the real investment was in sending practitioners to the show, a cost not reflected in the budget. Three team members on the stand tweeted every day about what was going on, while also posting Cirque du Soleil show photos onto the Xerox Facebook page.

Blogging was done by an onsite Xerox blogger. Xerox colleagues around the world were encouraged to show the social media tweet wall in their customer showrooms and join the conversations. Visitors were also able to share their experiences of the stand, including pictures of the Cirque performances.

"The partnership with Cirque played a big part, reminding people when the sessions were on and helping to create a buzz on the floor", said Andy.

The majority of activity, however, focused on the Xerox social media café. It offered people a place to meet contacts at drupa while allowing them to view the trending topics via Twitter from the Xerox visualizer.

Andy commented that the café had a casual, yet purposeful, feel:

> There were plenty of natural opportunities within conversations to lead into individual businesses' digital marketing challenges and how we could help them, and that's where the one-to-ones came in. It was very interactive and educational.

Results

At the show, Xerox was the undisputed leader in drupa's social conversations, according to the visible technologies listening report for Target Social Networks. This put the company ahead of other exhibitors that included HP, Océ, Kodak, Landa and Canon.

The buzz around Xerox@drupa was so significant that it attracted coverage of Xerox's XMPie Facebook Connect application by a local newspaper, *Bild Düsseldorf*.

The social wall in the café was busy throughout the two-week event. Offering compatibility with iOS and Android devices, it generated 4,672 pieces of content, featuring everything from pictures to commentary to videos. Approximately 3,900 of these pieces came from drupa attendees.

Meanwhile, the visualizer, which captured Twitter conversations, showed 2,300 page views. Xerox saw a huge increase in interaction between show attendees and their social media team, revealed by:

- a 482 per cent increase in retweets for @XeroxEvents;
- a 117 per cent increase in mentions for @XeroxEvents; and
- a 78 per cent increase in mentions of @XeroxProduction (the handle that targets companies interested in large production printing technology).

Xerox achieved the social media buzz it had been seeking, but it also directly helped customers with their social media strategy. During the show, 140 social café consultations took place, and 145 print provider guides and 140 field guides were handed out. "To me, this was the most important outcome", said Andy. "In my day-to-day role, I rarely get the opportunity to meet and interact face-to-face with customers beyond the UK, but as drupa is a truly global event, it presented a great opportunity to extend our influence to a much greater range of customers."

Andy added that it was "incredibly rewarding to see that our advice inspired people" and got them thinking about how to use social media marketing to profit their businesses.

Critical success factors

"It would have been easy to keep social media as a back-of-house activity, all done back at the office in the UK", said Minards. He continued:

> Not least because it was quite an investment to have three staff present for 14 days. But by making social media a focus of the stand, we hoped we'd get more followers, more engagement and help customers to realize the benefits of these channels. That's exactly what happened.

From a PR perspective, it helped that this approach was unique. Minards continued: "Nobody at the show was doing anything like this and that alone attracted interest, including from those producing the daily show newspaper."

Among the pleasant surprises for Xerox was the worldwide feedback. "Receiving one-to-one feedback from partners as far away as Australia was great, even though my main focus is Europe", commented Andy. "I was also surprised by how much we learned from the people who came to the stand. It wasn't just them learning from us."

Xerox also noted how much people loved sharing photos and commenting on them. This made it clear to Xerox that incorporating some kind of photo-sharing aspect is a must for all future exhibitions.

Lessons learned

Engaging the Xerox community ahead of the event would have driven further participation during the show. Andy explained:

> We waited to build momentum at the show itself, but really we could have done that earlier . . . For example I'd like to have been able to create video introductions of the Xerox staff on the stand so that they could introduce themselves and explain what they were demonstrating on the stand in more detail.

The team also found there was an opportunity to gain more immediate traction from the one-to-one meetings. For example, by the end of the consultations the team had created a bond with the customer. This presented a great opportunity to take a photo of them that could have been instantly shared via Facebook or Twitter. Andy concluded:

> Following such meetings, the customer is more likely to retweet or tag themselves in these pictures, which would enable us to extend the online conversation further.

Want more? See what has been said about this case or get involved and discuss it with the author and other readers on our LinkedIn group, find it by visiting http://www.socialmedia-mba.com *or search for "The Social Media MBA Alumni".*

Sales

11   ADP – B2B Selling

 ROI is the "risk of being irrelevant" – a risk
that no sales or marketing organization can
ignore. ADP is an example of an organization
shaping the culture of their sales department
around social media to increase demand and
remain relevant to their customers.

Executive summary

Overview

No company, no matter how large, can afford to assume they can grow consistently. ADP has demonstrated that implementing a social selling culture
has enabled the company to grow their social media presence, shape demand
for their solutions and services and provide their sales team with the tools to
reach their quotas.

Key findings

- 79 per cent of sales people who incorporate social media reach their quota,
  compared to an industry average of 43 per cent (Aberdeen Group 2012).
- Younger sales people are likely to need training on how to use social media
  in a professional capacity in the B2B space.
- Shaping demand doesn't always demonstrate the hard measured successes
  sales teams are used to, and requires a different mindset about what

value social selling can add to the traditional sales department distribution model.

Recommendations

1. Get buy-in from senior executives and ensure leaders are comfortable with how and why.
2. Leverage experts and colleagues across the business, they are critical to overall success.
3. A pilot phase is crucial – and expect the unexpected.
4. Use social media channels to educate, inform and add value to conversations rather than jumping straight into "sales talk".

What you need to know

- Studies show that 60 per cent of the sales process is complete before a prospect engages with a sales person, so shaping demand is a critical exercise.
- Find where your audience are meeting virtually.
- Listen before engaging.
- Increase peer-to-peer interaction and participation to build stronger relationships.
- Keep momentum with your sales force, don't forget a culture change is only successful if you keep plugging the message and reinforce with success stories and best practices.

Background

Interviewee

Christine Talcott is currently the VP of ADP's Employer Services Global Sales Operations, a centralized organization supporting the 11 business units that comprise ADP's Employer Services business division. With over 20 years of experience in sales, sales leadership and sales operations, she is responsible for several strategic programmes, including social selling and sales communications, and leads a team

Christine M. Talcott
@cmtalcott

of business relationship executives who are liaisons between the field sales organizations and the centralized sales operations team. Christine held several sales leadership positions within the US-based Small Business Services sales organization prior to her current role. She has achieved numerous sales and sales leadership awards and has been recognized for her ability to lead and contribute to strategic initiatives. Christine holds a BA in Political Science from UMass Amherst. When not at the company headquarters in Roseland, New Jersey, Christine resides in Boston, Massachusetts, with her husband and three children.

Company overview

ADP, Inc., generates around $10 billion in revenues and employs approximately 57,000 people, making them the world's largest provider of business outsourcing solutions. They have more than 60 years of experience and offer a wide range of human resource, payroll, tax and benefits administration solutions to any size of organization across all industries, as well as delivering integrated computing solutions to auto, truck, motorcycle, marine, recreational vehicle and heavy equipment dealers throughout the world.

The case

Background

ADP recognizes that developing innovative and insightful solutions is essential to their clients' success and their own business growth. Therefore, they leverage the internet to deliver solutions to an ever-expanding range of businesses. ADP's innovation in web-based and mobile solutions helps them to better meet the needs of their 600,000 strong client base and those who work for them, as well as attract new clients by providing cost-effective solutions that differentiate them from their competitors.

As an outsource provider, solutions are only half of the delivery. ADP defines service as an ongoing journey toward "service excellence". Service excellence challenges them to consistently reset the high bar of their performance levels to meet or exceed the expectations of an ever-more-competitive marketplace.

Their commitment to service excellence begins with the first impression they make through social media channels, on a sales call, on a client implementation, and ultimately how effectively their solutions deliver value. ADP knows that understanding clients' expectations and identifying their business challenges enables the organization to focus on what matters so they can increasingly develop competitive solutions, build service excellence to heighten client retention and engage with new businesses in order to continue growing profitably.

Having used social media as a thought leadership vehicle for some time, ADP is embarking on a social media journey which will ultimately leverage the expertise and voice of their 57,000 employees across 125 countries. The first leg of their journey began with empowering a 6,000 strong sales force in 14 countries across North and South America, Europe, Australia and China; resulting in understanding how the use of social media within the sales process has the ability to shorten sales cycles and hit their targets faster.

The problem

If you can visualize the sheer scale of an organization that pays 31 million people around the world each and every pay day, is responsible for the security of highly sensitive data and was daubed *The Original Outsourcer* by Gartner, then you can appreciate why protecting their brand reputation is so essential to ADP. Their social media strategy and governance is the responsibility of the marketing group, heavily influenced by their security and legal organizations, who previously exercised caution through a "limit access" ethos. Their policies used to prevent employees from accessing social sites at work in order to mitigate risk to their business and their clients.

The belief that increasing social media activity would be fundamental to future business success was understood across the business, no more so than at the top, where c-level executives acknowledged the power and influence of social networking. The question was: how does a giant organization like ADP handle such a cultural shift, roll out social media to 57,000 employees and control the message? The answer for ADP was simple: you stage your journey and shape the message. In other words, which group of individuals are the biggest advocates for social networking; who's asking for it the most; who could prove most agile in adopting a shift in culture across the world; who would drive a consistent message; and who could benefit most and achieve the quickest wins?

It was recognized very clearly that the sales force was going to be the driver for testing ADP's new social strategy and policy. A major factor influencing the decision to start with the sales team was the shift in the buying process – the buyer had changed faster than the seller. Research studies showed that 60 per cent of the sales process was already being completed even before a buyer connected with a sales person. ADP's own experience verified that their buyers were already accessing a wealth of information on the internet; they were seeking advice, discussing challenges, reading the reviews of peers and forming opinions through social networking circles before they engaged. ADP's sales organization needed to respond and collaborate with "pre-funnel" marketing activities using social media. Rather than just talking about products and solutions, they had to help shape demand and contribute to discussions. What followed was the introduction of their own sales department social media methodology – social selling.

Identifying the obstacles

The fact that ADP's sales organization was supported by a group of sales enablement and operations specialists meant there was already a support framework in place to facilitate the integration of the social media initiative. In 2011, based out of Boston, Massachusetts, Christine Talcott, VP of ADP's Employer Services Global Sales Operations, headed up the introduction of social selling into the sales organization. Christine and her team identified five key challenges to overcome:

- How do they ensure that all sales people have access and the tools to make this work?
- How could they get participation buy-in from 6,000 individuals across the world?
- How could they train those individuals to use social in a business context?
- How could they shape the messages?
- How could they teach their sales people to add value to conversations and not jump straight to the "hard sell" in a social media environment?

"There is only one place you need to start when embarking on a project like this", comments Christine, "and that's the top". Before even tackling the training or any roll-out aspects, the group needed "buy-in" from their top executives in order to drive the project forward. Christine adds, "You have to understand that ADP is a very conservative organization, we have a lot to protect. To ensure we could give the sales team access to social sites we had to work together to satisfy legal, security and IT stakeholders. These stakeholders are stewards of our systems and we worked together to find solutions that both moved the organization forward, yet protected ADP employee, client and stakeholder interests." The team's foresight in identifying potential obstacles to reaching a timely conclusion to the project was imperative. They believed that if they managed any road blocks early on they could clear a path forward and prevent delays or compromising detours.

Preparing to go on the road

The key to project success was collaboration amongst stakeholders. At ADP they are fortunate to have a "One ADP" culture that encourages teamwork, accountability and open discussion. With buy-in from the top to make the project happen, all stakeholders had a clear objective from their senior leadership – take our social media strategy from "command and control" to "guide and enable"!

Drivers

Whilst the sales force were the project leaders, marketing led the way from a company strategy perspective. Other drivers in the project included heads of legal, security, IT and HR, whose role it was to communicate with their peers across the world, remove road blocks, re-write ADP's social media policy and adapt their technical controls.

Vehicles

It was evident to the sales and marketing project leaders that opening access was not enough to encourage their sales teams to adopt a social selling culture. They had to prove the concept added value and gave the sales force the vehicles to continue driving momentum from the outset.

The ADP team could not assume anything; they needed to anticipate every need their sales people would have. How much knowledge existed in their sales organization around using social media? Were their profiles conducive to personal or business? Did they know how to communicate effectively? Did they understand the value of social for business?

Before ADP could establish the training needs and identify essential deliverables, they had to run a pilot.

Driving lessons

ADP felt that establishing a pilot would provide two benefits. First, it would help them to identify training needs and gaps in knowledge. Second, it would provide case study material for an internal selling perspective. "Proof of concept about Social Media is key to adoption", says Christine. "People want to learn from their peers, they don't like being told what to do, they like to make their own minds up and will engage in something that is proven, tested and adds value to their working life."

ADP selected 120 sales people and 20 managers as a pilot to their social selling programme which lasted six months – a little longer than anticipated. There was no training for the pilot; ADP was looking to build training from the questions that were generated by pilot participants. They wanted to learn from their mistakes and capture all the opportunities early on in an effort to roll out an effective social selling programme.

Giving clear direction

In May 2012, ADP's worldwide sales conference held in Washington DC was the stage for rolling out their social selling initiative. Over 500 sales leaders packed a convention centre for what was to be a unique and quite unexpected annual event.

Drive commitment

ADP understood that if they wanted to introduce a new selling methodology and make it stick, they had to demonstrate commitment from the top down. This commitment was evident at their annual sales conference where the theme, the guests and the content all focused on social media. The sales and marketing teams used modern technology to demonstrate the new social face of ADP, including a look at why social media mattered to ADP beyond social selling.

"Introducing the power of social media in general terms proved a solid base to begin with in order to get the audience onboard", commented Christine. "Through third party speakers we wanted to show our sales teams just how their target audience were presently communicating online without them." Christine said that this approach helped build a desire to get involved, but it also stirred trepidation with the announcement that social media access would be opened up. To some sales teams, this meant that stepping out of their comfort zone was imminent.

Lead the way

Learning from the pilot, ADP developed a thorough training programme, which was initiated at the conference. Broken into groups to encourage interaction, sales managers were shown case study videos from the pilot phase, featuring colleagues who had clear results from social selling. They were taught how to set up social media accounts, make best use of their online profiles and separate their social presence into business and personal. All of these things may sound very basic, yet a valuable lesson from ADP's pilot phase was to expect the unexpected. ADP was sure that if they gave too much training and information at the outset, there would be reduced take-up, especially because they asked the sales managers to train their sales teams directly, in a hands-on fashion.

Train the trainers

Back on home soil, ADP's sales managers had the task of initiating social media training with their sales teams. Some were more comfortable than others; some leveraged the experts within the countries' organizations. "We didn't think it was enough to train the managers and expect them to train their staff, we had to give them tools, the training deck and an area which they could learn more from", confirms Christine. The collaboration with marketing enabled ADP's sales organization to build and continually develop an online Social Selling Resource Centre. Accessible through their sales intranet web site, ADP gave their sales people access to best practice guides, learning material, success story videos and "Social Media Content Nuggets" – which provides ready to use "tweets" and conversation openers.

Results

Social selling success to ADP is all about engaging in conversations and adding value in order to shape demand. ADP believes that traditional sales measurements applied to this type of activity are difficult. "We cannot say we are winning deals because our sales people are using social media channels, but we are definitely engaging with prospects who we have not talked with before social selling, expanding our networks and shortening the sales cycle", Christine confirms.

Lessons learned

ADP has multiple sales groups, all selling into different size organizations. As such, the profile of a sales person selling to small businesses is usually different than that of a person selling into the large enterprise space.

Those sales people who are responsible for the small organizations tend to be younger employees who grew up in a digital world and are quick to pick up online trends. ADP found these individuals were eager to engage but needed instruction on how to use social tools professionally. Only around 20 per cent of them truly became comfortable engaging with a prospect in a social network environment. "They're so used to talking about their thoughts, how they feel and what they are doing personally without boundaries", says Christine, "yet they struggled at the onset with how to develop their professional social brand and the guidelines in which they have to operate. Additional training on the how and why proved successful for engaging this important generation."

In comparison, sales people that sell into the large enterprise space were initially more hesitant to adopt the new culture. "I would be confident in saying that 100 per cent of our National Accounts sales team now use social selling in some form or another", Christine said. For this team there is an added benefit to using social selling at ADP. Sales cycles in this arena can take as long as 12 to 18 months to close, so calling these prospects on a regular basis just to see where they are in the project can be uncomfortable for both parties. "There are a lot of ways to engage a company in a sincere way in between calls", she adds. According to ADP, educating, for example sharing relevant information about trends, is more effective than talking about your product or service.

Christine concluded by stating that "ultimately customers expect sales professionals to know as much about them as they do about us. Social media is changing how we sell. It's not a matter of *if* we adopt social selling into our sales process; it's *how well we do* this that will make a difference. Social selling is here to stay."

Want more? See what has been said about this case or get involved and discuss it with the author and other readers on our LinkedIn group, find it by visiting http://www.socialmedia-mba.com *or search for "The Social Media MBA Alumni".*

12 Dell – Building Advocacy

Dell's Social Think Tank programme brings together the most social, vocal industry leaders to discuss trends, challenges and best practices around key trends.

Executive summary

Overview

The programme has held events in five countries over the last four years with online influencers across topics including education, cloud computing and evolving workforce.

An example of the Social Think Tank format was the day of Innovation in Education at Massachusetts Institute of Technology (MIT), Boston, in September 2012. Educators, parents and students came together to discuss the impact of technology on education in an open format that was broadcast to the world through a livestream.

Key findings

- Dell's Social Think Tank programme has grown from two events in 2010 to five events in 2011, with 16 events completed in 2012.

- 18,109,907 Twitter reach; 1,000 livestream views, 98 per cent positive sentiment discussion at Innovation in Education at MIT Think Tank.
- 98 per cent positive conversation rate for the entire event.

Recommendations

1. Identify and build strong relationships with topical influencers on Twitter.
2. Leverage those relationships for in-person thought leadership activities.
3. Create an effective feedback loop so the company can showcase how they are implementing suggestions from influencers.

Bakckground

Interviewee

Richard Margetic is the Director of Global Social Media for Dell, currently responsible for Dell's strategy, governance and presence in social media, cross-segment, around the world. He has been integral to Dell's social media efforts since 2006 when the company began to use social to expand its direct connections with customers. From blogs and wikis to Facebook and Twitter, he has helped shepherd and shape Dell's social media presence across platforms.

Richard Margetic
@Dell

His career has focused on marketing and technology with 18 years' experience on the web. Prior to Dell, he was a senior managing global web consultant for both IBM and PWC Consulting, launched and managed Microsoft's Sidewalk office in Dallas and led his own web marketing consulting firm. His career began in developing marketing and business plans for startups that led to a VP Marketing position at Interactive Media Group in the early 90s.

About Dell

For more than 28 years, Dell has empowered countries, communities, customers and people everywhere to use technology to realize their dreams. Customers trust Dell to deliver technology solutions that help them do and achieve more, whether they're at home, work, school or anywhere in their world.

Customers are at the core of everything Dell does. They listen carefully to customer needs and desires and collaborate to find new ways to make technology work harder for them.

Everything they do is focused on delivering technology solutions to enable smarter decisions and more effective outcomes so customers can overcome obstacles, achieve their ideas and pursue their dreams.

Their social media strategy

Social media offers Dell more opportunities to listen, engage and ultimately understand their customers better than ever before. Going wherever Dell customers are, across the social web, Dell seeks to listen and learn in order to engage in ways to constantly build a better business, ultimately delivering better technology solutions that enable people to do more.

Dell's heritage of direct customer connections and use of the web as a strategic business tool (i.e. an original leader in e-commerce, the first web site enabling customers to custom configure their own PC, as well as using the web for supply chain and inventory management) underpin the company's adoption of the social web as a tool for doing better business.

Dell's strategic approach to the growth of social media is to build a social business. Dell is embedding social media across the fabric of the company (various functions and segments – it is not just about social media marketing or customer support) to be used as a tool in various ways (much like email or a telephone) by employees to achieve better results for customers and the business.

Social business strategy

Social media has proven to be about more than increasing business transactions or top of the marketing funnel awareness. After six years of work in the field Dell has concluded that social media impacts every aspect of the customer experience and lifecycle in positive ways and in some respects impacts the customer lifecycle more than any other medium.

Listening to over 30,000 conversations everyday about Dell is crucial to putting customer centricity at the forefront of all efforts. It is also a significant measurement challenge with more than 300 different search profiles that help Dell organize and prioritize those 26,000+ conversations and make sense of the volume of discussions related to the company. Those 300 search criteria tell the organization about things like location/geography, basic demographics, reach, sentiment, subject matter of the discussions, which sites they are taking place on and more.

Beyond sentiment and this basic information, Dell is also using additional natural language processing software and modelling analytics to further make sense of this tremendous amount of data, making them both measurable and meaningful across our businesses – and as a tool to run the business. That includes faster and automated processing in order to:

- Surface quality issues more quickly and identify customer support needs as they happen (something manually processed now).
- Surface opportunities to share Dell IT solutions with IT customers looking at various technology options.
- Associate and understand the root causes and issues that are generating positive and negative sentiment.
- Identify and connect with people who may be having the most impact on these conversations because of their knowledge and connections.

Dell's current daily listening reports are circulated widely across the company; the company also has specific subject matter reports that are generated at the business unit level or through their central ground control to track matters like commentary around acquisitions, product launches or new service and solution offerings.

This kind of reporting drives deeper understanding of customers, the Dell brand, industry and technology trends, making social media a valuable way to connect with customers as well as a tool to be deployed and used for research, analytics and understanding more deeply their customers' experience.

Dell continues to see "listening" and the related understanding and engagement with people as the very root of their social business strategy and have initiated activities to strengthen listening and the uses and business actions related to it. This includes working on:

- Continued understanding of what content customers engage with and how to further strengthen Dell engagement with customers, improving the data quality analyses (through natural language processing).
- Consolidated and improved set of reports – optimize for insights and leadership vs. volume of reports.

The other key strategic plank that is critical to Dell's journey as a social business is engagement. From the beginning they learned that engagement and follow-up actions are valued by and matter to customers and other stakeholders who use social media. Connecting with Dell makes a difference to those posting about Dell – positively and negatively. In the early years of social media activities, engagement led to an almost immediate 30 per cent decline in negative commentary in just a few short months. Engagement and action also provide Dell with that constant input and feedback to continually build a better business based on customer focus and direct connections.

Social media engagement improves Dell's reach and share of voice online; Radian6 reporting has noted causality between social media activity and demand generation, as well as increased customer revenue. Most importantly, Dell's social media engagement improves customer loyalty through the solid relationships they build and nurture.

Connecting with customers and influencers

Dell has more than 13 million customer connections (August 2012, fans on Facebook, followers on Twitter, Dell Community members and more) across the social web. One of the best examples of how Dell connects across the web is Social Think Tanks.

The case

The problem

Dell's communications department was searching to find a way to have more meaningful engagement with influencers on top areas of interest for the business – education, cloud computing, sustainability, etc. The company wanted to give influencers a socially enabled platform on which to have conversations about how technology impacts each of these topics.

Background

With more than 25,000 online mentions of Dell each day, how do they address some of the real issues brought up in those conversations?

- Dell's Social Think Tanks evolved out of the CAP Days programme. However, rather than a dialogue with customers, it is a conversation with online influencers covering a particular industry or technology. And, rather than a discussion about Dell solutions, the discussion centres on the challenges, opportunities and the future of a particular industry or technology.
- These events are in person for a group of 15–25 influencers and are moderated by a third party.
- Dell has held Social Think Tank events on topics such as healthcare, education, small business, cloud computing, evolving workforce and customer support.
- It provides an opportunity for Dell to listen and understand key priorities and needs of the potential customer base and build relationships with important influencers in the given industry.
- Dell's Social Think Tank programme has grown from two events in 2010 to five events in 2011 and 16 events completed or scheduled in 2012.

The solution

The Dell think tank programme brings together industry leaders who are particularly vocal in social media to discuss trending topics impacted by technology. The goal is to create an open and honest forum that fosters collaboration and reveals unique community needs and opportunities for technology to play a larger role.

For Dell and participating partners, the Social Think Tanks are an opportunity to listen firsthand, discuss business needs and foster relationships with participants and their respective communities. It also gives Dell and co-hosts an opportunity to capture meaningful feedback to better serve their various audiences. Since 2011, Dell have held think tanks on topics including education, healthcare, entrepreneurship and the changing mobile workforce. Events are in-person and extended online for virtual participation on Twitter and via livestream.

What is a Social Think Tank?

- A thought leadership discussion about key industry issues enabled (not controlled) by Dell.
- A relationship with key social media influencers kick-started by in-person dialogue.
- An opportunity for Dell to listen and understand key priorities and needs of their potential customer base.

What does success look like?

- A group of loyal advocates and third party storytellers.
- Captured customer stories, ideas on how Dell can best serve this influential audience and understanding of the priorities of these customers or potential future customers.
- Positive buzz about Dell as an active enabler and a brand that listens to the needs of the industry.
- Increase in positive conversations about Dell in social media – there are different metrics for every social media activity. In this case the goal is to positively impact Dell's thought leadership in education.
- Key learnings and feedback to help drive improvements to Dell's business.
- Ongoing relationships with influencers who can help tell the Dell story and become brand advocates.

Planning and execution process

In September 2012, Dell held an education think tank at MIT, which will be the example.

Identify/select attendees

- Michael Horn of Innosight Institute moderated the think tank dialogue with think tank veterans Ken Royal, Tom Whitby and Adam Bellow, and student representatives Nikihl Goyal, Zak Malamed and Allison Wu, helping to drive conversations with the #DoMoreEDU hashtag. The room was filled with Dell's #DellDozen mom ambassadors, Massachusetts Institute of Technology (MIT) students and Dell customers who continued on with them at the Town Hall later in the day.

- Pre-event communications including save the date, invitation, survey on requested topics for discussion, confirmation note and agenda.
- Distribute event hashtag #DoMoreEdu.
- Develop briefing materials for participating executives.
- Content was shared via:
  - Direct2Dell;
  - Flickr;
  - Storify;
  - Pinterest;
  - One Dell Way – Dell internal communications blog; and
  - Infographic (see the Dell infographic).

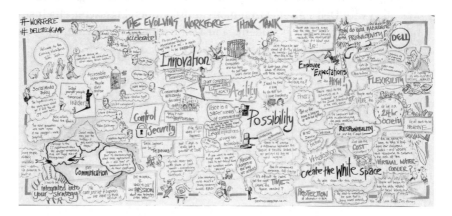

- Conducted research with PSB on how parents, students and educators view technology in education. The key findings were (also see infographic):
  - Although 51 per cent of student respondents said that technology could be a distraction, 63 per cent said its benefits outweigh that possibility;
  - While six in ten US respondents said they do not think students should use social media in class to share what they're learning, most Chinese respondents said they do approve of such use;
  - Forty per cent of respondents from the US and 26 per cent from Germany said their teachers understand technology better than they do;
  - Of student respondents, half said they use technology to interact with school when not there;
  - Students reported using technology at home for school work more than any other activity;
  - Seventy-one per cent of students who responded said that they have access to better technology at home than they do at school; and
  - Most student respondents from the US and Germany reported for two hours or less each day at school.
- Day-of social media posts:
  - John Mullen's Direct2Dell blog post went live on the Friday morning;
  - Tweet Chat day of with #DellDozen (mom brand ambassadors) hosted by @DellHomeUS with participation from @DellEDU, to build awareness and excitement for the think tank;
  - watch the live stream at www.Educationnation.com and www.nbclearn.com;
  - team members live tweeted from @DellEDU and @DellHomeUS;
  - event hashtags included #DoMoreEdu and #EdNatMIT;
  - post-event communications including thank you note, post-event survey requesting feedback; and
  - follow-up plan – keep engaged with attendees via private LinkedIn groups, Twitter lists and a weekly newsletter.

Results

Innovation in education events at MIT
Social media metrics (as of 10 April):

Twitter posts: 14,822
Twitter reach: 18,109,907
Sentiment: **positive**: 97.7 per cent; **neutral**: 1.2 per cent; **negative**: 1.2 per cent
Live stream: 1,000

Additional articles were published by **Chelsea Clinton** in *The Daily Beast*, as well as Dell programme mom ambassador Beth Blecherman, education influencer Ken Royal and Buzz Marketing Group's Tina Wells in *Forbes*.

Twitter reach continued to grow to more than 18 million with a largely positive (97.7 per cent) sentiment to date. Dell hosted a Google+ Hangout with a group of participants to continue the dialogue and discuss where they go from here. One Dell Way internal blog posts generated more than 3,500 views and helped drive internal conversations on Salesforce Chatter service.

Think tank closing thoughts http://www.YouTube.com/watch?v= FXmBNXMl_Lc&feature=plcp

Google+ Hangout

https://plus.Google.com/u/0/106143876839173486558/posts/HzWDbWUZw5r# 106143876839173486558/posts/HzWDbWUZw5r

Top tweets

- @allisonwu Moving to data driven innovation + student driven transparency. Are your schools making data accessible? http://t.co/lm7PhYfn #DoMoreEDU.
- @zakmal @Tech4Moms There are also many ways of interracting using social media that is not so invasive into one's personal life. #DoMoreEdu.
- @sueyoungmedia Social media in higher ed: Interesting Livestream conversation on innovation and risk taking. #Domoreedu.
- @allisonswu We have to bridge the gap b/w what goes on in the classroom and what goes on in the community. #civicengagement #DoMoreEDU.
- @allisonswu We've got to make education a celebration for a student's future. @AnthonySalcito #DoMoreEDU.
- @tech4mom Would you go to an office where all the equipment is old and broken? Public schools are the same, hard to get excited with broken. #DoMoreEDU.
- @jodie_GeorgiaNY: Im rethinking my and my kid's relationship with Technology. #DoMoreEDU.

Dell's social media ground control (SMGC) team was responsible for all reporting. They are the organization responsible for all Radian6 reporting within Dell.

Critical success factors

1. Above all, a commitment to listen and engage customers before, during and after and ongoing management of relationships and feedback are most important to the company's success.

2. For a successful event Dell also needs commitment from the top executives within the company. From the spokespeople, to the product, to the messaging, the team needs support and alignment from the leadership team to make this happen. Roughly $35–50,000 is allocated to each Social Think Tank event.

Lessons learned

- The ideal number of attendees is around 12–15. A more crowded table can make it difficult for everyone to be heard.
- Survey influencers to determine the agenda. Get their input on what they are most passionate about and want to discuss.
- This was the second time Dell had an audience and this event solidified that the audience is a great addition. It increases social media conversations and the amount of content that comes out of the session.
- Ensure names of participants are visible on the livestream so that remote participants can follow along without confusion.

Want more? See what has been said about this case or get involved and discuss it with the author and other readers on our LinkedIn group, find it by visiting http://www.socialmedia-mba.com *or search for "The Social Media MBA Alumni".*

13   Play.com – Monetize Big Data

Rakuten
play.com

This case highlights the retail value of growing and developing a highly engaged social media fan base. With budgets stretched across more channels than ever before, the challenge for many marketers is making social count within the marketing mix and justifying how social spend can contribute directly to a retailer's bottom line.

Executive summary

Overview

Marketing Director at Rakuten Inc.'s Play.com, Adam Stewart, was given 12 months to demonstrate direct returns from social media. The following case considers the data-driven test and learn approach that allowed the retailer to organically grow their fan count by 1,000 per cent, as well as the tools that allowed the retailer to quantify the value of a "like" and attribute over two million pounds of gross merchandise sales to social media.

Key findings

- It's not only the number of fans that matters, but it's their level of engagement that makes a financial difference to your business. Play.com found that an engaged fan was worth 24 per cent more than a non-fan.

- Overemphasis on push messages, such as product launches, will not foster the engagement levels that really stretch the audience reach of your campaign. A blended approach, which includes activity such as social polls, sweepstakes and competitions, is far more likely to increase conversation around your brand. At any one time Play.com has in the region of 18,000 people talking about them, indirectly reaching an audience of over 38 million.
- Investing in social needn't mean paying for fans. Growing fans through organic means can result in higher engagement levels and more direct sales from social. However, there's no such thing as free marketing and significant resource must be invested to make this channel effective.

Recommendations

1. Campaign management and audience analytics tools are essential to social media success. Marketers need to invest in technology that can be used to continually analyse and react to a changing audience dynamic and the ongoing success of activity.
2. Marketing to the self selected is different to other marketing channels. The merit of each post should be considered and used as a benchmark for future posts. Using a test and learn approach marketers learn exactly what gets fans talking and can build on this in future activity.
3. There is no one-size-fits-all approach to engagement and social growth. Benchmarking against competitors is a great way to get ideas, but establishing what works for your community is something that happens over time, so test and learn.

What you need to know

- Rakuten's Play.com started with a Facebook fan base of 35,000 fans, engagement levels were low and up to that point posts had centred on messages pushing products and promotions.
- Rather than mimicking the social activity of other social retailers, the team decided to put audience insights at the heart of their campaigns. By measuring engagement levels at a fan level and also on a post by post basis, the team set about testing content and optimizing personalized communications based on real time audience response.

■ Over an 18-month period Play.com organically grew its social following more than tenfold – from 35,000 to over 380,000 followers. Sales that can be directly attributed to Facebook now account for over £2 million pounds of gross merchandise sales and year-on-year sales through the platform are up 80 per cent.

Background

Interviewee

Adam Stewart's passion for the retail business began at just six years old, when he started growing and selling vegetables on his own street stall. His ambitions grew and by the age of 20 he had set up his own digital marketing agency, Alkemi, in Melbourne. Leaving his brother at the helm of Alkemi, in 2002 he moved to the UK to manage online marketing and digital channel development for RBS. He joined Rakuten's Play.com as Marketing Director in 2011 where he has been spearheading social media, alongside the wider marketing strategy while the brand evolves under the Rakuten Group as they expand globally.

Adam Stewart
@playcom

About Play.com

Founded in 1998 Play.com is the UK's third largest e-commerce marketplace. It has a customer base of over 15 million registered users and employs over 400 people in the UK, in offices across London, Cambridge, Jersey and Bristol. The brand has a strong heritage in entertainment and quickly became known for its wide range of affordable DVDs, music and computer games. Play.com pioneered free delivery on all items, a practice which is now commonplace with many major online retailers.

In 2011, Play.com was acquired by Rakuten Inc., one of the world's leading internet services companies. Rakuten recently launched Rakuten Marketplace, a new proposition that allows sellers to create and promote their own branded shopfronts and design marketing campaigns tailored to their customers to help foster long-lasting relationships.

The case

The problem

As competition in the online retail space becomes increasingly fierce, there has been huge buzz around the potential of social to drive retail growth and improve customer retention. The launch of social shopping tools, such as Facebook stores, fuelled retailer speculation around the possible revenues that could be generated by tapping into the 33 million UK users of Facebook. However, two years on and many prominent brands, such as Gap and JC Penney, have closed their Facebook stores, while the true value of a Facebook fan remains elusive. With marketing budgets stretched across more channels than ever before, the company needed to prove that social growth could deliver real benefit to the business' bottom line. Adam Stewart was given 12 months to demonstrate direct returns from the social media channel.

Background

In January 2011 Play.com had a following of around 35,000 Facebook fans, overall engagement levels on their Facebook page were extremely low and the company's approach to social was focused purely on the short term. The social strategy up until this point had favoured messages pushing products and promotions, rather than seeking to create dialogue with their Facebook fan base. This product-centric approach resulted in low levels of interaction from Play.com's fans. Social messages rarely went beyond the newsfeeds of fans on Facebook, which meant that whilst existing fans were well informed, they were failing to extend the organic reach of the messages to influence and recruit new fans – for example, through the friends of engaged fans.

Adam comments on the true value of the social shopping landscape:

> Shopping has always been both a functional and a recreational pursuit. For any retailer the true power of a social fan lies in that fan's ability to recruit and influence new shoppers. It's not enough to push messages to those that are already invested in your brand; you need to attract the attention of non-fans that could be persuaded to shop with you.

He quickly realized that there was no "one size fits all" method of creating social engagement. Rather than seeking to mimic the Facebook activity of their direct competitors, the company understood that they needed to observe the approach of other brands with high levels of engagement. Adam and his team decided to start by surveying the approach taken by brands beyond the retail sector who were achieving high levels of engagement.

Chris Howard, Head of Online Marketing at Play.com, highlighted some of the trends which emerged from this review of social media best practices:

> It was clear that the brands who used social media most effectively were all seeking first and foremost to add value to their followers. A number of different mechanisms were used, ranging from providing exclusive discounts and unique content, to gauging followers' opinions on future web site developments, to providing real-time customer support.

Every brand's fan base is slightly different, meaning that there is no tried and tested formula for engagement. In order to make best use of their own potential social following, they wanted to put data-driven audience insights at the heart of their social activity moving forward. To do this the organization needed to source a third party social insight tool that could form the backbone of a test and learn approach to engagement. Having looked at various campaign management tools on the market they chose to work with EngageSciences. This tool was preferred because, in addition to being able to create and automate dynamic campaigns on Facebook, it allowed a high level of audience analysis to help understand which segments of their Facebook fan base were most valuable in driving advocacy for the brand.

The solution

The team

First and foremost, the right team needed to be put in place to manage this new approach to social. Marketing resource for social activity was limited. However, it was agreed that to do justice to this data-driven approach the company would need a small team dedicated to social. As it stood, the Play.com Facebook page received two types of interaction: comment on proactive posts and customer queries. As such, one full-time person was recruited to drive proactive posts and tweets and conduct audience analysis on activity, and two people were hired to respond to customer queries on the social page. No budget was allocated to paid-for opportunities apart from an allocation towards a third party technology provider.

Kicking off the test and learn approach

At the heart of their strategy was a test and learn approach to social. It was agreed that the best way to optimize engagement was to analyse audience response to content on a case by case basis. To support this, the social media team was given much greater creative freedom to experiment with the types of post that it used. However, audience reaction to each post was to be analysed daily to inform the ongoing campaign. The team was not seeking fan growth for its own sake, but it was agreed that in order for social to drive tangible business returns they needed to grow both audience size *and* levels of audience engagement.

Adam elaborates:

> When it comes to social retail, we're in relatively unchartered territory. Yes, many forward thinking brands have become more sophisticated in their approach to the social channel, but true social strategy is in its infancy. There are so few experts and each brand audience is so different that we needed treat our own social strategy like a good scientific experiment. So, using our audience analytics tool we created a truly measurable social environment, and then altered the variables of interaction on our page to see which campaigns yielded the greatest levels of interaction and fan growth.

Engaging the self-selected

"Social media represents a unique environment and opportunity to market to self-selected individuals", explained Chris Howard.

> The group is already bought into the brand and its products, but is seeking to develop a more personal and privileged relationship with the retailer. So naturally the types of conversation you encourage should reflect this dynamic.

In order to get the new social approach off the ground quickly, they took advantage of the campaign automation functions within their social media marketing tool. This allowed them to quickly design more dynamic campaigns. The team stepped away from their heritage in pure product and sales posts and began creating campaigns that focused more on driving fan engagement. These campaigns took many different forms, from social polls on their fans' favourite super heroes, to sweep stakes where fans could win "money can't buy" prizes and experiences. Using a variety of styles of post was an essential part of the strategy, as the team wanted to see which performed best in terms of generating the biggest social buzz.

The evolving audience

It's important to note that there was no watershed moment or stand out post that increased the value of the social channel for them. The social programme centred on constant incremental improvements to communication content and its delivery. Improvements were made based on insights around audience interaction, gathered over time direct from the company's fan base.

Play.com created a sophisticated database of fan interactions. This database allowed the team to see at a glance how the social following was segmented and which types of content elicited the greatest response from core audiences. The team was also able to identify brand champions within its fan base on an individual basis. By pinpointing those individuals that had the greatest circles of influence, or were the most vocal brand advocates, the team was able to better tailor campaigns to inspire and reward these groups.

Most importantly, they started to track the shopping cycle of engaged fans so that they could determine whether or not an engaged fan was worth more than shoppers attracted through other channels.

Adam expanded on the point:

> Social would be so much simpler if there was a simple template for success. The reality is that for social activity to make a long term difference to a business's bottom line, teams must constantly question the quality of their posts and seek to learn from their efforts. Marketers that succeed in creating brand personality add huge value to a business, just look at Innocent smoothies or Red Bull. If used effectively social is one of the most powerful and measurable tools for the job, but underpinning every post and every campaign should be a solid measurement model which informs ongoing activity.

Results

Without any paid-for media promotion Play.com were able to attract more than 1,000 per cent organic growth, taking their community from 35,000 to more than 380,000. At any given time, over 18,000 fans are actively engaged and talking about the brand, reaching a potential audience of over 38 million. Most importantly, growth and engagement have resulted in tangible business results. Year-on-year sales achieved through social are up 80 per cent and the company has been able to quantify the value of a "like", finding that the average value of an engaged customer is 24 per cent higher than a non-fan. More than £2 million of gross merchandise sales (GMS) are the direct result of Facebook.

Critical success factors

1. The success of this campaign, and others, is centred around Play.com's ability to understand their audience. By tailoring social conversations according to insights gleaned from their database on audience interests, they were able to provide fans with a reason to engage regularly with the brand.
2. Social even proved its worth beyond sales. Having a 300,000 strong audience of engaged social followers proved to be a huge asset in negotiations with publishers and large vendors, all of whom were keen to tap into this audience to promote upcoming launches. As a result, the company received more exclusive products and special prizes from publishers to be used on Facebook, which naturally reinforced the appeal of the fan group to shoppers.

Lessons learned

Adam concludes:

> Don't assume that because everyone is talking about social media, that it's simple to succeed in this channel.
>
> While it would be foolish to ignore social altogether, its effectiveness as a communications channel must be considered on a case-by-case basis. Marketers should invest in audience analytics tools from the outset and use these to constantly re-evaluate and optimize their campaigns, and push the business to utilize and capture the rich customer data that can be obtained to personalize future customer experiences.
>
> Ultimately there is little value in chasing fan growth for its own sake. It's far better to make sure that every fan counts, by creating

content that keeps your fans engaged and makes your brand a talking point rather than a nuisance in the news feed.

Want more? See what has been said about this case or get involved and discuss it with the author and other readers on our LinkedIn group, find it by visiting http://www.socialmedia-mba.com *or search for "The Social Media MBA Alumni".*

14   Hobart – B2B Community Building

UNITING A COMMUNITY OF BAKERS FROM SCRATCH

This case will discuss "Get Back to Scratch", Hobart's aggressive venture to unite a professional community through social media. The Get Back to Scratch movement harnessed the passion of professional bakers and chefs by creating an online outlet for peer-to-peer sharing and education, while ultimately positioning Hobart as the brand of choice.

Executive summary

Overview

The Get Back to Scratch movement tapped into the growing passion for, and presence of, scratch-made goods in restaurants, bakeries, schools and grocery stores. To grow the movement organically, Hobart turned to social media.

Key findings

- Approximately 600 establishments registered in the directory, primarily driven via social media. These establishments are all potential leads for Hobart. At the time of writing, the site had received more than 110,000 visitors.

- Supporters ran their own advertisements promoting the movement, their love of Hobart mixers and their passion for their craft. The ultimate engagement goal was to create ambassadors for the brand without being overtly promotional in the process, and Hobart have succeeded.
- The initiative received social media support, engagement and promotion via key influencers, customers, potential customers and fans. The @Back2Scratch Twitter handle has sent over 2,200 tweets (as of the time of writing), received hundreds of twitter mentions, retweets, "favorite" tweets and gained over 600 twitter followers specific to the precise target audience. It has been "listed" by 13 other influential Twitter accounts, and @Back2Scratch regularly engages with key influencers of the baking community.

Recommendations

1. Integration from all marketing avenues to support efforts is a necessity.
2. Need to tap into the audience's passion and give them a forum to rally.
3. Help them – provide them with benefit (being able to increase business success, promote themselves, gain knowledge, connect with peers, etc.).

What you need to know

Hobart needed to solidify awareness of its status as the preferred food equipment brand among professional bakers and chefs despite its higher price point in a sales landscape crowded with lower-price, lower-quality competitors.

To do this, Hobart harnessed the passion food professionals and consumers have for scratch baking and cooking into a nationwide movement that celebrates, elevates and empowers those who literally build their businesses from scratch. From this, the Get Back to Scratch movement was born.

The results of the Get Back to Scratch movement were unprecedented for Hobart. Awareness of Hobart as the premier supporter of businesses that are at the forefront of the new real-food movement was huge. This was evidenced by hundreds of thousands of page views on the web site, with tens of thousands of unique visitors per month during the initial contest period. In addition it has helped drive leads and tradeshow attendance at Hobart events and provides an ongoing platform for selling Hobart products.

Background

Interviewee

Jenni Bair has worked in foodservice for Hobart for nearly 15 years. She began her career at Hobart as an application specialist/technical writer and served in a variety of roles including marketing analyst (weigh wrap), territory sales representative and manager of administration (supplies). She later served as business unit manager (supplies) until being promoted to her current position as brand marketing manager.

Jenni Bair
@hobartcorp

About Hobart

Hobart manufactures commercial kitchen equipment for the foodservice and grocery industries. Its primary product lines include equipment for cooking, food preparation, dishwashers and waste handling, weigh wrap, Baxter baking and Traulsen refrigeration. Hobart equipment is supported by a national network of factory-trained service representatives in hundreds of locations across the USA.

An international company, Hobart has facilities around the world with manufacturing plants in the USA, Brazil, Canada, China, France, Germany, Italy and the UK. In the USA Hobart have approximately 3,295 employees.

Their social media strategy

The strategy for this particular campaign was to tap into the growing passion for, and presence of, scratch-made goods in restaurants, bakeries, schools and grocery stores. To start and grow the movement organically, the company monitored social media channels, taking a closer look at this passionate segment – where they were talking, what they were talking about and how they were engaging with one another. Ultimately, the company identified this segment's need for an online outlet to share their passion with one another, celebrate and promote their craft and engage their peers – a place where they could exchange tips, recipes and best practices, among other things.

With this research, Jenni and her team were also able to identify the influential bakeries, restaurants, chefs and foodservice industry professionals that have a strong and growing social media presence to target for the launch and growth of the movement. Through social media engagement efforts, Hobart enlisted the support of the TLC network's "Cake Boss", Buddy Valastro, to drive additional attention around the launch of the social media-driven movement and ignite the Get Back to Scratch movement for scratch-made goods among bakers, foodservice providers, grocers, restaurateurs and consumers.

The movement uses social media to build a community and drive traffic to GetBacktoScratch.com, which was designed to serve as an easy-to-use and entertaining resource for baking and culinary professionals to access resources, connect with the Get Back to Scratch community, participate in contests, promote their businesses and engage with peers and customers. The three primary means of engagement arose through Twitter, Facebook and the Scratch-Baking Blog that is housed within the GetBacktoScratch.com web site.

They established the @Back2Scratch Twitter handle, created a profile and identified key influencers to follow and monitor upon launch. The research conducted was used to create and share content relevant to the target audience, participate in popular twitter chats (#FNIchat, #Cupcakechat), frequently and consistently engage with target audience and employ the use of hashtags and handles when relevant to the content. The team also used Twitter to drive traffic to Facebook, the Get Back to Scratch site, the directory and the interactive Scratch Knowledge blog.

The blog enables further engagement with consumers and is housed within the GetBacktoScratch.com web site in order to profile scratch bakers, chefs and establishments, as well as to share tips, tricks, best practices and other content of interest to the target audience. The blog was also used as a forum to share Get Back to Scratch campaign updates, contest updates and news regarding industry events.

With Facebook, the team created a Get Back to Scratch Facebook fan page and used it to engage with key bloggers and bakeries, chefs and establishments that joined the Scratch directory on GetBacktoScratch.com by "liking" their pages, sharing images of signature scratch items, sharing useful links, and movement updates. Hobart also created tabs to promote registering in the directory and to promote the Signature Scratch Item contest. Engagement on Facebook served as an opportunity for users to share with each other, celebrate their craft and the movement and learn from their peers, as well as provide further insight on the company's target audience.

In addition the company launched a mobile application for Get Back to Scratch foodservice professionals and their consumers; where they can search and find scratch bakers and chefs in their area, as well as share scratch baking and cooking tips from professional bakers and chefs.

The strategic responsibility for Get Back to Scratch rests within the brand marketing group at Hobart. Since its inception, the budget to support the launch of the Get Back to Scratch community web site, social engagement, 2011 National Restaurant Association (NRA) trade show unveil, contest and media relations totalled less than $500,000.

The case

The problem

Jenni found, through social media listening, that many people in the food-service business have a strong passion for their craft, and in some instances, even their foodservice equipment (i.e. bakers and chefs love their Hobart mixers). She also found that, despite this unified devotion, these foodservice professionals had no outlet to share their passion and celebrate their craft of baking and cooking from scratch.

With this vital insight in hand, she saw the opportunity to help these establishments and professionals. And, because this audience is such an important part of Hobart's business, she wanted to find a way to engage them, build relationships, increase brand awareness and drive leads while doing so. However, this audience is not always an easy target. Foodservice equipment is a large investment and often results in a long purchase decision cycle. So, any marketing strategy needed to be bold and needed to focus on the buyer at numerous touch points.

Jenni worked together with an agency called gyro and determined that the best way to reach this audience was to create an outlet for this segment – a community for foodservice professionals. So, they set out to create Get Back to Scratch, an integrated marketing movement that utilized a variety of avenues but placed specific emphasis on digital marketing and social media. The movement was designed to give foodservice professionals a place to convene, communicate, share challenges and solutions, celebrate their craft and passion and gain visibility for their businesses, achievements and the common desire to encourage baking and cooking from scratch.

Background

Hobart, Traulsen and Baxter, all members of the Illinois Tool Works Food Equipment Group, are leading providers of mixers, ovens, dishwashers and other equipment to the foodservice industry. Their business is committed to, and dependent on, the success of restaurants, commercial and educational foodservice facilities, bakeries and other establishments that create menu items with fresh ingredients. To support and promote scratch cooking, the companies needed to find and reach foodservice decision makers through media outlets that are appealing and relevant to them.

Through research, they found independent bakeries, restaurants, chefs and foodservice industry professionals were growing a strong social presence online. The target audience was increasingly using social media channels including Twitter, Facebook and LinkedIn to exchange tips, recipes, best practices and, most importantly, share their mutual passion for creating food made from scratch. Using Twitter lists, Jenni and her team identified key influencers in the space and tracked topics popular among the target audience. A third party contacted current Hobart, Traulsen and Baxter customers to gather feedback and insight on their views of scratch baking and cooking to help in crafting the movement. Ultimately, the research confirmed there was no single online outlet solely dedicated to celebrating and promoting the craft of cooking and baking from scratch, and that the target audience was highly passionate about all things "scratch". Furthermore, competitors were not targeting these audiences or taking advantage of the opportunity to engage with them. Hobart saw this as an immense opportunity to position themselves as an engaged provider to their target audience.

When Hobart was first presented with this opportunity, a variety of avenues were discussed including celebrity spokespeople, an online television series, more promotional methods, etc. Ultimately, Hobart chose the route of helping their customers celebrate their shared passion and achievements, enhancing their business successes and engaging with a community of their peers. The approach was focused on engagement and support as opposed to direct promotion. The unique aspect about this movement is just that – it is a movement, not a campaign. Get Back to Scratch created a marketing phenomenon allowing Hobart to gain brand awareness and build brand excitement without ever having to directly promote its brand. The movement's supporters are so excited about the initiative that they have promoted the brand without even being prompted (establishments ran their own ads promoting their involvement in the Get Back to Scratch movement and discussing their desire to one day have a Hobart mixer – their passion for the product and their craft was communicated clearly by the members of the movement, not by Hobart).

Ultimately, the movement utilized a unique approach to position Hobart, Traulsen and Baxter as the leading supporter of scratch cooking and as the source for everything required to cook and bake from scratch.

Results

The Get Back to Scratch programme quickly built a community of small businesses and institutions, earning praise from bakers and culinary professionals. The initiative has received social media support, engagement and promotion via key influencers, customers, potential customers and fans. The @Back2Scratch Twitter handle has sent over 2,200 tweets (at the time of writing), received hundreds of twitter mentions, retweets, "favorite" tweets and gained in excess of 600 twitter followers specific to the precise target audience. It has been "listed" by 13 other influential Twitter accounts, @Back2Scratch regularly engages with such key influencers as @CakeBoss-Buddy, @THEtoughcookie, @CookingwCaitlin, @CakeSpy, @bakingaddiction, @poojasway, @cupcakestakethecake, @nella22 and others, with a total reach of well over 300,000 individuals. Likewise, the Facebook page receives an average of 30,000 monthly post views and has garnered over 850 "likes".

The engaging dialogue has resulted in multiple guest blog posts, blog coverage, media coverage, new and important introductions, the creation of Get Back to Scratch net promoters and successful peer-to-peer connections. For example, Get Back to Scratch shared a question that CakeSpy, a celebrity food blogger, posted on her Facebook wall. Get Back to Scratch ended up with more responses than CakeSpy received, and Cakespy asked permission to use Get Back to Scratch's responses instead of those on her wall. Similarly, natural foods chef and popular online personality Pooja Mottl found Get Back to Scratch on Twitter and reached out to ask if she could participate in the movement by submitting a guest blog post. Other industry professionals have been connected through Get Back to Scratch's social media efforts. Get Back to Scratch has become *the* go-to resource for all things "scratch". In addition, the initiative has already seen approximately 600 establishments registered in the directory, most of who were driven there via social media. These establishments are all potential leads for Hobart. The site has received more than 110,000 visitors and user engagement is significant with hundreds of comments in support of scratch profiles and blog posts!

Also, during the movement's launch at the 2011 NRA trade show, more than 30 registered media outlets and over 500 individual NRA show-goers attended the unveiling of the giant Hobart mixer replica cake and press conference. One hundred and two establishments added themselves to the Scratch directory, and coverage of Get Back to Scratch at NRA included mentions by more than 150 media outlets and blogs.

Ultimately, the supporters took over and promoted the movement and the Hobart brand themselves. Hobart did not have to do any direct promotion, which built trust and excitement from the beginning. Supporters ran their own advertisements promoting the movement, their love of Hobart mixers and their passion for their craft. This was the ultimate engagement goal, and Hobart succeeded.

Critical success factors

Success factors for Hobart included:

1. Real engagement with the target audience. This was at the core of Hobart's efforts.
2. Creating brand ambassadors for Hobart. The company built a strategy that would allow supporters and loyal consumers to promote the movement and the Hobart brand (without Hobart having to directly promote their own brand).
3. Research, identifying trends, a need and an opportunity/solution.
4. Utilizing a high profile event or component to jump start the programme and create buzz (i.e. the contest and Buddy Valastro appearance).
5. Full marketing integration.

Lessons learned

The Get Back to Scratch campaign was a success for Hobart, and as with any strategy and in this case, "movement", there were valuable lessons learned, including:

- Integration from all marketing avenues to support efforts is a necessity.
- Listening is more important than talking.
- Need to tap into the audience's passion and give them a forum to rally.
- Help them – provide them with benefit (being able to increase business success, promote themselves, gain knowledge, connect with peers, etc.).

Want more? See what has been said about this case or get involved and discuss it with the author and other readers on our LinkedIn group, find it by visiting http://www.socialmedia-mba.com *or search for "The Social Media MBA Alumni".*

15 Allianz – B2C Selling

HOW ALLIANZ YOUR COVER UTILIZED SOCIAL MEDIA TO BOOST BRAND REACH AND ACHIEVE SIGNIFICANT SALES GROWTH

 Allianz Your Cover saw huge opportunity in the prolific nature of social media in helping to achieve brand reach to support sales growth. The company also used social media to extend the life of PR campaigns and enhance customer relationship management (CRM) activity.

Executive summary

Overview

Part of Allianz Insurance plc, one of the UK's largest insurers, with more than 100 years of heritage, Allianz Your Cover was a relatively unknown direct to consumer brand. In order to communicate the company's unique proposition, build consumer trust and nurture customers and prospects, they invested substantial portion of their marketing budget in social media.

Key findings

- Achieved reach of over 40 million people in eight months.
- Despite insurance being seen as a relatively "dry" subject, and without the use of characters or gimmicks, grew their Facebook and Twitter fan base to 25,000 fans and followers within 11 months.
- Social media activity drives the same level of traffic as search engines – but much more cost effectively.

Recommendations

1. Understand from the outset what you want to achieve from social media, how it aligns to consumer needs and, finally, how it aligns to your business goals. As part of this, make sure you understand your customer and create content specifically for them. Moving into social media with no clear strategy or understanding of how your customer interacts with that channel will lead to disappointing and potentially pointless results.

    Finally, understand the halo effect of social media and how it can be aligned with search engine optimization (SEO), public relations (PR) and, more interestingly, CRM. Social media is an unparalleled prospect-nurturing and customer-engagement tool, which can bring a whole new dimension to CRM campaigns. Allianz Your Cover has enjoyed success at both the acquisition and retention phase of the customer lifestyle by aligning social and CRM activity.

2. Focus on the quality of your fan base and the subsequent web site traffic you receive from social channels. Growing a massive fan base is great to report in the short term but when your hear questions such as "Do these fans align to our core demographics?" and "How many quotes, sales and advocates do our social channels generate?" ensure that what you report back directly aligns to your business goals.

3. Make sure the entire business is on board with what you are doing. Identify and engage your key stakeholders before launch – don't just think about how customers and the marketing department will react to social media. Allianz Your Cover identified operations (contact centre staff, complaints, claims and information security teams), PR and legal to name a few. Information and feedback sessions were held with all departments and a training guide, including information on anything from how to respond to complaints to where to escalate a number of issues. (Another tip – keep this document streamlined and practical so that stakeholders can refer to it. A monster, overly complicated document will be ignored.)

What you need to know

The Your Cover case study outlines how a relatively unknown financial services brand managed to engage their target customer demographic in social media, growing their fan base month on month with only a small marketing investment. Topics covered include:

- How the company achieved long-term engagement amongst their target audience to bolster brand awareness and long-term sales growth.
- How social media was built into the business by identifying and engaging key stakeholders to achieve a joined-up approach to social media management across the business.

Background

Interviewee

With ten years' experience in digital marketing, Natalie Woods is part of a team that launched Allianz Your Cover's direct to consumer car and home insurance products almost three years ago, managing the digital marketing and CRM functions of the business, focusing on sales acquisition and brand and customer relationship marketing. Natalie instigated the launch of Allianz Your Cover into social media in February 2012.

Natalie Woods
@YourCoverUK

Social media activity is key to the Your Cover business, helping to build the brand and relationships with customers throughout their lifecycle from prospect through to year-on-year retention.

Despite being a lesser known insurance brand in the UK direct marketplace, Your Cover achieves success via a multi-niche, highly segmented marketing programme of digital, CRM and aggregator activity.

About Allianz

Allianz Your Cover is a new breed of insurance product, offering car and home cover that customers can build themselves to suit their own lifestyle and circumstances. Using an easy to use "Quote and Buy" web site, Your Cover makes it simple for customers to design, obtain a quote and manage their insurance online.

Prior to the launch of Allianz Your Cover, consumers were only offered "off-the-shelf" insurance policies that didn't necessarily meet their needs, leaving many customers underprotected or overpaying for benefits they didn't need.

Allianz Your Cover is a product from Allianz Insurance plc, one of the largest general insurers in the UK and part of the Allianz SE Group, the largest property and casualty insurer worldwide.

Allianz UK employs 4,500 members of staff and generates an annual gross written premium of £1.8 billion. Allianz Your Cover are entering into the third year of trading.

Their social media strategy

From the outset, Allianz Your Cover needed to boost brand awareness in order to achieve sales growth. Above all else, the following were necessary for the company to achieve their growth targets:

- Expansive brand reach and awareness.
- Communicating their unique proposition clearly.
- Connecting with customers on a more personal basis, in order to make the brand offering less "faceless".
- Retaining customers beyond year 1 – building long-term "relationships" was key to keeping the brand "front of mind" at renewal.

Due to budget restrictions, wide reaching marketing opportunities such as television advertising were not an option for building the brand. Instead, Allianz Your Cover had to find other cost-efficient ways to engage the target audience to purchase.

Allianz Your Cover saw huge opportunity in the prolific nature of social media in helping to deliver these objectives. With a budget of £200,000, the company enlisted a digital agency called STEAK to help with the following strategies:

- Customer prospecting – gaining prospects and nurturing them into customers via our social channel.
- Customer service – an alternative channel for customers to contact Allianz Your Cover.
- Customer engagement – a means to build a relationship with customers, keeping them informed, engaged and the brand "front of mind" throughout the year.

Customer service strategy

Opening a new communications channel meant that Allianz Your Cover had to plan customer service carefully. The company felt that social media could provide customers with an alternative support channel as well as enhanced service and value. It was decided that social media should be integral to the business, ensuring that customers were always dealt with efficiently and treated empathetically. Being seen to do this would ensure that the brand's reputation was well thought of by customers, who it was hoped would, in turn recommend the company and their products.

The social CRM strategies of market leading insurance brands, as well as organizations demonstrating best practice polices in alternative verticals, was researched. This helped Allianz develop a "social media training guide" detailing how and when to respond to customers, where to escalate different issues and highlighting the importance of excellent service and empathy at all times.

Allianz Your Cover then embarked on a company-wide, multi-divisional social media training and customer service programme that spanned the contact centre, PR, marketing, claims division, complaints division, HR and market management. All staff from contact centre associates to company directors received training.

Audience engagement strategy

Prior to setting-up their social media channel, Allianz Your Cover profiled their customer base to better understand what appeals to and motivates their audience. The outcomes of this research helped to develop the content strategy to ensure maximum engagement and interest from prospects and customers.

Research confirmed that Allianz Your Cover customers trust word-of-mouth recommendations above advertising messages and are more active in the social arena than any other group.

Engaging high profile bloggers whose content appeals to their target audience became a key part of Allianz Your Cover's strategy. Using key bloggers to share and promote the company's content and messaging within their personal networks drove even higher levels of qualified traffic to Allianz Your Cover's social channels.

Allianz Your Cover manages that strategy and direction of the social media function, which is implemented by an agency that also manage the day-to-day BAU (business as usual) for the channels.

Channel development and evolution

Allianz Your Cover's first year in social media has largely focussed on growing fans and followers and optimizing the level of content engagement.

To maximize their social media investment, Allianz Your Cover integrated social campaigns with PR (extending the value of PR content that typically has a very short media value shelf life), CRM (to enhance customer advocacy, loyalty and engagement), mobile and SEO (content is king in SEO and social generates a lot of content) to derive maximum value from the investment whilst providing a joined-up experience for customers.

Finally, Allianz Your Cover made social media an integral part of their customer experience in the following ways:

- It's an alternative support channel for customers, providing enhanced service and value.
- It is plugged into CRM activity to deliver added value, enhancing advocacy, loyalty and engagement.
- PR campaigns are stretched into social media to extend the value, rendering activity more cost efficient.
- Social activity supports their SEO programme where "content is king".
- Allianz Your Cover can be relevant, topical and conversational with consumers.
- It enables the company to live its brand values – "reliability, trust and transparency".

It encourages new business acquisition via word-of-mouth recommendations. Allianz Your Cover built social media into their business model in the following ways:

- They invested in a training programme (considered world leading across Allianz worldwide with other OEs (Operating Enterprise) using the same programme) – all contact centre staff are trained to respond to social queries and complaints.
- Senior managers were also trained to respond.
- Key stakeholders such as operations, PR, marketing and technical were involved.
- Complaint and query escalation charts touching several areas of the business were created.
- To drive cost efficiency, they aligned social campaigns with PR, CRM mobile and SEO content to derive maximum value from the investment whilst providing a joined-up experience for customers.

The case

The problem

Tasked with launching a new (and largely unknown) "fast-growth" brand into the already overcrowded UK car and home insurance market where big-name brands spend hundreds of millions on advertising in comparison, Allianz Your Cover needed to find a way to cut through the "noise" and communicate their unique proposition of "build your own insurance". A further challenge is that consumers naturally prefer and trust established well-known brands. With a comparatively small marketing budget, Allianz Your Cover needed to: Reach their target audience.

- Build brand awareness recognition and sentiment.
- Generate online traffic and quotes.
- Encourage word-of-mouth advocacy and recommendations amongst potential and existing customers.

By year 2 of trading, Allianz Your Cover was faced with a new challenge – retaining customers. The company utilized social media to actively engage their target audience throughout their lifecycle, helping to build the brand and ensure that it stays front-of-mind at renewal.

Their target audience trust word-of-mouth recommendations above advertising messages and are more active in the social arena than any other group.

As an online-only insurer, every piece of activity they do is tied to key metrics and social activity is no exception. They use Social Analytics (a Google tool) to understand the customer journey from their social pages to their web site and use Hitwise to benchmark the social downstream traffic they received against competitors writing a similar profile of business.

Allianz Your Cover's next challenge in the social arena is to monetize the channel by better engaging a profile of social user more aligned to their pricing profile, namely Mosaic profiles B, F and G.

Background

Mass marketing a standard insurance product is not a financially sustainable business model because of the large investment required to compete with price comparison web sites who dominate the market.

Allianz Your Cover's largest competitors employ high-cost above-the-line advertising to communicate their brand and product proposition, but do comparatively less in the social media space.

Because Allianz Your Cover's target market is segmented into niche, profitable groups, television and outdoor advertising were not an option. These were too expensive and could not deliver the targeting necessary to cost effectively reach the desired audience.

The decision was taken to market Allianz Your Cover as an online-only proposition, taking advantage of the highly targeted prospecting and retargeting opportunities available to create highly relevant customer journeys (Allianz Your Cover's marketing mantra is: Reach the right customer, at the right time with the right message and offer) leading to higher, more cost-effective conversions.

Social media played a key part in this strategy, as the company's approach would enable them to reach desired prospects via lower cost Facebook advertising and word-of-mouth promotions generated by a highly engaged blogger network.

Before launching into the social space, it was important that Allianz Your Cover engaged all departments in supporting the channel.

Before embarking on any social activity, Allianz Your Cover commissioned an audit of the external social environment; a market-wide assessment using a combination of social listening tools and detailed granular analysis. Allianz Your Cover wanted to know if negative sentiment already existed and whether customers were already commenting about the brand on the web. Outcomes from this enabled the company to build up a dossier of customer compliant and query examples which helped shape their social media training programme. The audit also allowed them to see what other brands in the vertical were doing. They took key learnings from the good and the bad, which ultimately fed into a strategy that was underpinned by data.

A social media training guide was created, detailing how and when to respond to customers in a number of circumstances and where to escalate a myriad of different issues across the business. Social media training took part across the entire business including the following departments: PR, claims, complaints, marketing, brand, legal, compliance and the call centre. Staff from call centre agents to directors all took part in the training.

Once all internal processes had been set up to ensure that customers were dealt with efficiently and appropriately in the social space, the focus turned to launching into the channel.

Having requested Cameo and Mosaic information from their pricing and technical teams, Allianz Your Cover had a very clear idea of exactly who their target audience was.

Audience profiles were created to ensure that Allianz Your Cover understood the audience, what they liked, how they liked to engage socially and what content was likely to appeal to them enough to share it within their networks.

Launch content was created to appeal directly to this audience and seeded out to bloggers with a similar audience profile leading to greater reach.

Allianz Your Cover launched into the social space with a smartphone app named "Chores Worth", designed to appeal directly to the audience. Household members input their housework duties and time spent on them and the app calculates the monetary value of the duties and tallies who does the most. A four week themed campaign designed to build brand awareness and spark positive engagement was built out.

The launch campaign encouraged households to share who did the most and "acts of kindness" were awarded to those who did a lot of work, whilst rubber gloves and low-cost domestic appliances were sent to lazier household members. Content was themed around household tips, which sparked an impressive amount of conversation around the Facebook and Twitter pages.

Previous apps have launched on iTunes and Marketplace with no promotion. However, Chores Worth was Allianz Your Cover's best performing app in terms of downloads, as the word spread across Facebook, Twitter and parent bloggers, extending both the life and value of the campaign.

The solution

The primary goal of Allianz Your Cover's social media activity is to improve customer satisfaction and increase brand awareness and advocacy. Ultimately, improvements in these areas translate into increased sales, loyalty and life-time value to generate long-term, sustainable profit for the organization.

£200,000 was allocated to social activity and the agency was retained to manage content creation, community management and paid advertising. Six campaigns were rolled out spread throughout the year. These were mainly used for prospect on-boarding. During non-campaign months, they had themed content campaigns and built out "business as usual" social updates based on themes that resonated with the Allianz target audience. This approach helped them maintain social growth and an engaged audience outside of campaign periods.

Results

Social activity distinguishes Allianz Your Cover from competitors by adding value and highlighting through continuous conversation what the brand stands for – namely transparency, sustainability, reliability and trust.

It drives more cost-efficient brand communication than traditional advertising, reducing their overall expense base.

In just 11 months, Allianz Your Cover's social media campaign has achieved the following:

- Brand awareness, recognition and sentiment (achieved 21,000 fans at 98 per cent positive sentiment). They picked this as a measure of brand awareness.
- Online traffic, quotes and sales (social media activity now drives the same level of traffic as search engines – but much more cost effectively). This was critical to their success – Facebook driving prospects to take action off the back of social activity.
- Word-of-mouth advocacy and recommendations amongst potential and existing customers (131 Facebook recommendations).
- Reach – over 40 million people – a measure of simply "getting the word out" about Allianz Your Cover.
- In 2012 six social campaigns for Allianz Your Cover:
  - 20,000+ pieces of engagement,
  - 10,000+ competition entrants,
  - 3,300+ Twitter followers,
  - Over 83 per cent Facebook followers sit within the target demographic,
  - 8,768 views of the blog.
- Established a best practice model that has been used as a benchmark for other brands within the Allianz Group.

Lessons learned

- Attribution modelling.
- Tone of voice.
- Quality, not quantity!

Want more? See what has been said about this case or get involved and discuss it with the author and other readers on our LinkedIn group, find it by visiting http://www.socialmedia-mba.com *or search for "The Social Media MBA Alumni".*

Customer Services

16   giffgaff – Customer Support by Customers

 The case will explain how we set up the community, why it is important to the business, how we approach the community and some of the benefits the business and the customers get out of it.

Executive summary

Overview

giffgaff are constantly pushing the boundaries of what can be achieved with a community, all the way from highest in industry Net Promoter Scores, to tremendous cost savings in customer service, and they claim they haven't reached the limit yet. Creating a truly involved community for your business creates tremendous results, especially if the business is open to it, willing to spend time and resources, open to change the way it's working and really involves the community in its business decisions.

Key findings

They have been able to:

- Create a consistent Net Promoter Score of 75.
- Sustain a Customer Satisfaction Index of 80.
- Reduce customer service costs by a minimum of 50 per cent.

Recommendations

1. Ensure you have the buy-in and support from the entire business. The more support the community gets from the wider business, the better your community will flourish by being able to address any and all questions that come from the community.
2. Create processes that ensure you can make decisions fast, and have the ability to change your roadmap depending on the feedback of the community.
3. Make sure you have the resources in time and money to support a great team of community managers as they are essential to your community. The money you invest in a well-run community will be well worth the benefits you get out of it.

What you need to know

giffgaff is a mobile virtual network operator (MVNO) run in the UK, who have put an online community at the core of their business. The organization involves their community in business decisions that need to be made, listens to and implements ideas from the community and involves the community in sales, marketing and customers service with tremendous results.

We will look at how and why the company was set up. What they do to keep running on a day-to-day basis and the results they get.

Background

Interviewee

Prior to giffgaff, Vincent Boon's career had focused on the computer games industry. After graduating from Utrecht School of the Arts with an MA in gaming, he worked as an animator at NOB Virtual Productions and then Eidos where he gained his first taste of community management. This led to a community coordinator and community team leader role at Sony Computer Entertainment Europe where he spent four years before being poached to join giffgaff.

Vincent Boon
@VincentBoon

About giffgaff

giffgaff is an MVNO with roughly 75 employees, which is an incredibly small team for the industry the organization operates in. giffgaff breaks the mould as far as a regular business model goes for a mobile telephone operator. Run with the help of their members, who get rewarded for answering questions in the community, recruiting new members or helping to market and promote the business, all the way through to coming up with new products and services and helping set the direction for the company, giffgaff has seen this approach rapidly gaining traction in the mobile market.

Although they can't share their annual turnover, it would be fair to say that giffgaff easily beats its targets of revenue, profit, customer acquisition, OIBDA, Customer Service Index, Net Promoter Score and others year after year.

Their social media strategy

To set the scene, the reader needs to be aware that giffgaff makes a distinction between social media and community management, and so here we will be looking at online forum community management, rather than social media, as a strategy. The reason for this is that they feel there are more lasting benefits to creating an online forum community because it is a platform that they have control over but which also allows them much deeper engagement than would be possible on platforms such as Twitter or Facebook.

Budget: community team (20), 1 million+ on customer acquisition through their community, 400,000 on customer payback for help in running their customer service.

The strategy for the giffgaff community is one of deep engagement with members on an online forum and putting customers at the core of their business to ensure that some of the benefits that will be touched upon later start happening. This means that every member of their network has a voice. They can let giffgaff know how they are doing as a company, if they are heading in the right direction and what things might possibly need to be added or removed from how they work or what they offer.

From a decision-making point of view, this means giffgaff have an ideas section within their online forum, in which members have added thousands of their ideas and the organization's aim is to implement as many of these as possible. On average they have been implementing one community idea every three days since they started this journey.

giffgaff also regularly engage their members in discussions on decisions they need to make. From price rises to changing the product portfolio, they ask for their users' input in the decision-making process. The company lay out their problems or challenges with as much detail as they can and run the discussion from there, adding in their opinion and reasoning for the direction they feel is best. The team then look at the suggestions put forward by the community and adjust their direction or policies accordingly.

Through all of this they aim to create and give the members a sense of ownership in the company, while at the same time being very clear that they are a profit-making organization. This allows people to help give direction to what they do, while at the same time staying realistic to giffgaff's needs to survive as a company.

This sense of ownership translates into a variety of other benefits for the company, which they actively encourage through many different processes of community management. The benefits include, but are not limited to, increased SEO, brand defence and advocacy, product development, and of course a fantastic customer service, provided by the customers themselves through the online forum community. There giffgaff encourage members to ask any questions they might have and at the same time urge yet other members to answer these. What this means for the organization and the customer is an answer within 90 seconds (on average over a 24-hour period) and at least 50 per cent reduction in customer service cost (part of which they pass back to the customer through lower pricing), while at the same time having one of the highest CSI scores in the industry, which consistently sits around 80.

The company also encourages their members to get involved with all kinds of projects and marketing for the company, which has seen members creating over 30 different mobile applications for them with countless downloads. As well as that, their members account for well over 25 per cent of all their customer acquisition. This in turn translates to a Net Promoter Score that consistently sits around the 75 mark.

The case

The problem

In 2009, within the UK telecoms industry the costs were mounting in terms of customer service, while at the same time the industry as a whole didn't have a great reputation in terms of customer care. On top of this, a leading telecoms provider (O2 UK) looked at their base and found their brand was underrepresented with a certain group of people, in this case the free thinkers and early adopters, and needed to come up with a solution to both these problems. How could they get these people on board and provide a new form of customer service that would reduce the cost but keep or improve the service to the customer?

Background

The main challenge was:

How do you get people to start delivering the customer service for you and
  get them to start answering questions on an online forum, about a product
  they don't know anything about?
How do you get them involved?
And how do you keep them there?

giffgaff looked at different solutions, such as getting the customer service agents involved in the forum, setting the example showing customers how they could help answer questions from fellow customers. Technical solutions, such as auto-escalations to ensure people were warned when questions weren't being answered. An all hands on deck approach of everyone in the company being involved in the community, answering questions where they could, as well as scouring the internet for forums on mobiles and finding people there who were willing and able to train and asking them to get involved, by offering them rewards for their participation.

And once people were there and helping, they needed to come up with solutions to keep them motivated and engaged. So a content strategy, on top of the customer service questions that would come in, was needed.

Should this all take off, with having many people involved in answering their customer service queries, do they simply take that for granted, thank you very much, and pocket the difference, or do they look at somehow showing their appreciation for this help? And who should get it? The whole base? Or just the people that help out?

None of giffgaff's competitors were doing anything of the sort, and pretty much the only industry with any kind of real experience in online community management was the computer games industry where Vincent came from.

So although from a community management perspective they had the experience, to really leverage the community to do customer service for them was a different problem all together. Previously having worked with communities in terms of creative collaboration projects and getting people involved and working together on many different games, leagues and ladders, that would have to be the starting point.

The solution

There were a few things that needed to be done right from the start. The online forum community needed to be set up intuitively and work as effectively as possible. The messaging throughout the site and all other communications needed to be clear to ensure people would understand how the proposition worked: i.e. if you're looking for customer service, please go to our community first. The customer service team (who deal with any type of query that needs access to the back-end, think account related queries) needed to be brought up to speed with how they wanted this to work. Then they needed to start making people aware of who they were, what they stand for, how the idea works and what's in it for them. And last but not least, they needed a few people ready to start answering questions for the company, should they come in.

Setting up the community

At the very beginning, before the founders even had a product to launch, before people could buy the service, and before the team had fully worked out what to offer, they created a blog on which people could comment. The founders set out their ideas, introduced the team and talked about what they envisioned. This slowly started to gain a little bit of traction up to the point where they felt it would be right to start the community itself. giffgaff needed to create a forum that was as clear and concise as it could be. They needed to keep the boards on which to interact to a minimum to ensure that the people would virtually bump into each other as much as possible, to create as much conversation as they could. Their biggest fear was that people would ask their questions, but no one would actually be answering them. So ensuring people would not only ask but also answer questions, they needed to make sure the questions being asked could be seen while at the same time involving people in other discussions that they set up. The idea being that once you're there, talking away anyway, you might as well answer a question or two.

Messaging

The messaging throughout the site as well as the messaging throughout the on-boarding process all the way through to when people would leave, should they choose to do so, consistently referred to the community as the primary way to contact giffgaff or to get problems resolved. This was very important to the organization as no one had set up a company yet whereby a forum community was the only way in which you could get any type of customer service. They understood that not everyone would like or even understand this approach, but they did need to ensure that people were aware of how it works without upsetting anyone if they could.

Customer service agents

The customer service agents employed needed to be brought up to speed with how the company wanted this to work. So no longer would it be a traditional model where people could phone in; no, they could only be contacted through a ticketing system. However, should any queries come in that were not account related, i.e. something they deemed the community itself should be able to resolve, the agents needed to respond in the best way possible in order to push back on answering any of these types of queries and redirect the people towards the community. Again they felt a lot of work needed to go into making this as smooth a process as possible, ensuring people would not feel too miffed about contacting customer support only to be pushed back to the community.

Making it work

As previously mentioned, the team started it off with a very simple blog, on which they posted articles introducing the concept of the company. The trade press picked up on this as well and so the first few interested people started coming in and asking their questions. Depending on who wrote the original article giffgaff made sure any questions that came in were responded to. As there was no product yet, this was more of a philosophical debate rather than any type of customer service related questions.

From there they started the full online forum and seeded some of the very first discussions. As the product was not live yet they asked things like what people would find a fair price, how they would like their service delivered and how they would like to get involved.

And shortly before they actually launched the product they got in contact with a few very involved users on other mobile related communities to ask them if they would like to get involved with the company and possibly keep an eye out for any questions that came in from the very first users to sign up. They talked to them extensively and made sure they understood the product and how the service worked, so that, when the questions started coming in, they would understand how to help these people.

The team was now ready for launch, and the rest, as they say, is history.

The starting team

The starting team and budget for the entire operation was relatively small. The first year and a half they ran the company with just 20 people and the community itself was run by just one person. With no existing starting base it takes a while to get a good running community off the ground and to reach that tipping point where you really need to increase the team. Once it takes off, however, you need to be ready to scale up relatively quickly and have budget allocated to increase that headcount. The total headcount for the company is now roughly 75 people, with the community team making up 20 of those.

Results

Vincent looks at the volume of content that is reported to them, which in itself is a measure (the more content that is reported the better for them as it helps manage the community), on top of that they look at the volume of "abusive content" and try to keep that volume below 2 per cent. The actual number is 0.3 per cent of all content created.

The other measure they looked at is how well the service is provided in terms of community members giving the correct answers to questions and how happy people are with the service in general. And there they look at the Customer Satisfaction Index, which they get out of monthly surveys. The scores they see are consistently around 80.

And the last measure they also look at is their Net Promoter Score, as this is very important to them in terms of customer acquisition. The scores we see are consistently around 75.

All of these results are derived from internal tools and surveys.

Critical success factors

1. Critical to the success of the community is getting the buy-in from the business. They need to be ready to answer the questions of the community, when it comes to business decisions or practices they have, should they be questioned.
2. On top of which the business needs to have the flexibility in the roadmap to swap and change what they do depending on member feedback, ideas or suggestions.
3. Most important is to have a dedicated resource running the community on a day-to-day basis. This is not something that can be done by someone part

time and with no experience. It is equally important for the person or team that runs the community to have the freedom to hold discussions and talk to their customers without needing sign-off for the things they say.

Lessons learned

For Vincent the most important lesson learned is to really listen to your customers and treat them with respect. As a collective they often surprise him with their in-depth knowledge of the industry and how it works. They are fantastic at coming up with credible solutions and solid ideas.

The few times they did not listen or ask for feedback they got burned. Vincent found that if they did not explain themselves properly there was the risk of a massive backlash in the community. This is something that is hard to do halfway. There needs to be a commitment to always include people in the important decisions the company makes, whether this is giving in-depth information on the decisions made, including people in the decision-making process or giving them multi pre-set options to choose from; it always comes down to putting people at the centre of the business.

In conclusion Vincent adds:

> We learned that the more information we could give our members the better the discussion was that we could have. The more information provided, the more readily they understood our situation and the more realistic their suggestions for change or the quicker the acceptance of the things that are inevitable.
>
> Information and inclusion are key.

Want more? See what has been said about this case or get involved and discuss it with the author and other readers on our LinkedIn group, find it by visiting http://www.socialmedia-mba.com *or search for "The Social Media MBA Alumni".*

17   Go-Ahead – Customer Service

Go-Ahead Go-Ahead organized an internal social media summit, which brought together representatives from across its businesses who were keen advocates of the use of social media, together they redefined how the business provide customer service.

Executive summary

Overview

UK bus and rail operator Go-Ahead has embraced new and developing social media platforms, which are adding to the established methods of communicating with passengers and stakeholders.

Key findings

- Go-Ahead's bus and rail companies have pioneered the application of social media in the passenger transport sector, using Twitter and Facebook to keep passengers updated with service-running information.
- Go-Ahead achieved 250,000 social followers in one year.
- Go-Ahead rail company London Midland improved its passenger satisfaction scores around communicating with passengers by 17 per cent after the company started using Twitter to update people about delays.

- Go-Ahead bus company Oxford Bus doubled the number of Facebook "likes" overnight while providing service updates during bad weather in early 2012.

Recommendations

1. Start small, build confidence and get your back office in order.
2. Get the right team of people for the job and provide training if required.
3. Keep the messages simple and professional.

What you need to know

Go-Ahead responded to the changing passenger communication landscape by starting to embrace tools and technologies used by its passengers in their daily lives. Go-Ahead organized a "social media summit", which brought together representatives from across its businesses who were keen advocates of the use of social media and were in most cases using it in their personal lives.

Background

Interviewee

Samantha Hodder has worked as an in-house communications professional for over 20 years, in both the public and private sectors.

About Go-Ahead Group

Samantha Hodder
@GoAheadGroup

The Go-Ahead Group is one of the leading providers of bus and rail services in the UK. A FTSE 250 business, the company focuses on delivering high-quality, innovative, customer-focused transport, which meets the local needs of passengers and communities.

The company is the largest bus operator in London, working in the regulated environment on behalf of Transport for London. It also runs commercial bus services largely across the south of England. It operates three rail franchises for the Department for Transport, carrying more passengers than any other rail operator in the UK. Go-Ahead manages its businesses in a devolved manner, with local management teams in each business responsible for day-to-day decision making.

The company has four strategic principles:

- to run its companies in a safe, socially and environmentally responsible manner;
- to provide high-quality, local-focused passenger transport services;
- to focus its operations on high-density urban markets; and
- to run its business with strong financial discipline to deliver shareholder value.

Go-Ahead employs around 23,000 people and invests in staff to further their development and ensure high standards of services are maintained for their passengers.

Their social media strategy

Go-Ahead's bus and rail services are used by more than 1.7 million passengers a day.

Passengers today want access to quick and accurate information about their services, delivered in a way that's relevant to them. The challenge for transport operators is to improve that flow of information to passengers, especially when services are disrupted. In the last couple of years a number of Go-Ahead companies have set up Twitter and Facebook accounts in an effort to improve the flow of service information. Those initial trials were tested in earnest during the bad weather of 2010 and proved popular with passengers.

Samantha Hodder, Go-Ahead's Corporate Affairs Director, said:

> Twitter and Facebook have delivered a new way of communicating with our passengers and means we can exchange information about our services quickly. We are committed to becoming a social business and to embracing new and developing communication platforms which add to our established communication tools such as our award-winning web sites.

Since 2010 social media has been introduced across the majority of Go-Ahead's business. Most operating companies have incorporated it in their customer service centres, training existing staff or recruiting a small number of additional people. The cost of implementing the strategy has been small.

The case

The problem

Looking at the rail industry in particular, customers in the past have relied on paper timetables and service update boards at stations. There was little or no on-train communications and public address systems were scarce. Passengers used the telephone to contact call centres for information about their service.

Since those times, the information landscape has altered dramatically. Passengers can access real-time online journey planners and stations have digital screens with live updates. National Rail Enquiries (NRES) can be contacted via telephone and the web, and hand-held devices give passengers instant access to live departure boards. Stations and trains now provide automatic announcements to keep people informed. Operators have also focused on giving staff the right tools to do the job – equipping them with smartphones, for example, through which they can also access information to pass on to passengers.

So what is the best way to adapt to this change?

Background

These developments provide a solid base for operators and make it easier to communicate when things are going well. But the statistics speak for themselves – while overall customer satisfaction has steadily risen over the past ten years from 73 per cent to 84 per cent, dealing with delays remains a challenge: passengers score rail operators in London and the South East fairly low on that count – the Spring 2012 National Passenger Survey revealed a satisfaction score of only 35 per cent.

In addition, these improvements to communicating with passengers have taken place while social media has grown in popularity and more and more people want to be able to access information – and expect to be able to find out about their train and bus services in the same way.

The solution

Go-Ahead responded to the changing passenger communication landscape by starting to embrace the tools and technologies used by its passengers in their daily lives. Go-Ahead brought together representatives from across its businesses, who were keen advocates of the use of social media and were in most cases using it in their personal lives, for a social media summit. Go-Ahead also sought insight from external businesses who were already experienced social media users. This combination of enthusiasm and external advice and guidance assisted Go-Ahead in the early days and enabled the business to start its social media journey.

Social media has proved invaluable. All three rail franchises now use Twitter to communicate with passengers – London Midland has 28,000 followers and has sent nearly 140,000 tweets. The company uses Twitter to provide service information in a brief but engaging way. The company receives regular feedback from followers impressed by the company's proactive approach to keeping them informed. This improved advocacy has been translated into better passenger satisfaction scores, with London Midland's score rising in just one year from 32 per cent to 49 per cent – 12 points ahead of the national average.

On the bus side, Go-Ahead's businesses across England now user Twitter and Facebook to communicate with passengers about their bus services and also use both to promote news about latest products. One company, Go North East, worked with a local PR agency to launch a new smartcard ticket, with the campaign using social media platforms to push out flash mob videos and launch updates. Earlier this year, Oxford Bus Company doubled the number of Facebook "likes" overnight while providing services updates during a period of heavy snowfall. Metrobus provides updates to its 13,000 Facebook fans 24 hours a day.

Samantha commented:

> Twitter has really transformed the way London Midland, for example, interacts with passengers during delays. Information is targeted to the passenger and people aren't bombarded with reams of detail that simply isn't relevant to them.

London Midland has been recognized by the rail industry for its pioneering work, winning the Putting Passengers First ward at the last two National Rail Awards.

Critical success factors

1. Go-Ahead has been successful due to the gradual roll-out of social media at the pace most suited to each operating company.
2. Go-Ahead's businesses have learnt from each other on the social media journey, sharing best practice, understanding what's worked well and adapting those lessons to suit their own local audience. For example, early

in 2013 the Group corporate communications team set up a Twitter and Facebook account for Go-Ahead plc, recognizing how successful both had been when set up by their operating companies. The team used the knowledge and experience of colleagues already familiar with using social media for business purposes to get started and adapted the existing styles to suit the Go-Ahead requirement for a more corporate approach, which is geared towards providing information about corporate news rather than service information aimed at passengers.

Lessons learned

Go-Ahead's social media journey has suited the nature of its devolved approach to running its business. It was, however, somewhat driven by individuals' understanding of the growing move towards the use of social media. Not every business appreciated the pace of change in this area or that social media is here to stay and must be seen as a complementary means of interacting with passengers rather than a replacement of traditional channels of communication.

Social media continues to evolve and Go-Ahead intends to provide refresher training for their practitioners.

Samantha said:

> My advice would be to start small, build confidence and identify a handful of people in your business who are keen and enthusiastic and either have – or can be trained to use – the right kind of tone of voice on Facebook or Twitter.

She continues:

> Get your back office in order and the right people lined up, then make sure you keep the messages simple and professional, avoid technical language and abbreviations and be prepared to provide two-way communication in specific circumstances.

Want more? See what has been said about this case or get involved and discuss it with the author and other readers on our LinkedIn group, find it by visiting http://www.socialmedia-mba.com *or search for "The Social Media MBA Alumni".*

18   NHL Minnesota Wild – The True Value of a Fan

TURNING SOCIAL MEDIA CONTENT INTO VALUABLE, ACTIONABLE INFORMATION

MINNESOTA SPORTS & ENTERTAINMENT

Originally, Minnesota Sports & Entertainment (MSE), owners of the NHL's Minnesota Wild Hockey Club and the Saint Paul Arena, had looked at the world of social media from the outside in. On monitoring social media channels, the organization were concerned they lacked the online presence that businesses strive for today. This case study examines the evolutionary process that MSE went through to transform their social media strategy from something that initially centred around push promotions, to a mechanism for encompassing, and driving, sales, marketing and customer service.

Executive summary

Overview

For MSE, maintaining their fan base and keeping valuable customers while attracting new ones, even during losing seasons, is critical to the overall success of their business. Yet the effects of the recession caused MSE's season ticket holder base drop to around 10,000 fans. The challenge was to look at how MSE could use social media to develop new relationships with potential customers while keeping existing fans happy and winning old ones back.

Key findings

- MSE recognized that while fans were still using traditional methods of communication such as email, phone and mobile text for sales purposes, they were increasingly turning to social media to express more emotional reactions to events, such as frustrations with customer service, and excitement about promotions. MSE understood that in order to achieve all of their aims the company had to complement their current methods of communication with newer social media channels.
- To ingrain their social media activities into existing business processes, MSE chose a flexible IT solution that would enable the integration of their CRM system, their customer service function and their customer loyalty programme with social media channels.
- By integrating their social media activities with their CRM solution, MSE was able to use all of the information to which they already had access to gain greater insight into customers' behaviour, and make strategic decisions based on that knowledge.

Recommendations

- Social media is all about being social. It's about engaging people, developing a dialogue with them, and building relationships with customers. Give social media accounts personality; using the first person in conversations, for example, shows you are engaged, and asking questions shows you are interested. Only then will people see that you are listening and will start telling you things about themselves.
- Interact with, and respond to, people via social media exactly as you would in person. If you are going to have a presence on social media, be prepared to answer people's queries and address their frustrations immediately as they will expect as quick a response as if they were talking to you on the phone or face-to-face.
- When you are integrating a new IT solution for social media, take the time to involve your social media team in the discussions and not just those from the IT department. It is hugely important for the people who will be using the technology on a daily basis to develop an understanding of how it works.

What you need to know

MSE started out by experimenting with social media but solidified their strategy by selecting an IT solution that would aggregate and combine the power of their CRM solution, customer service function and customer loyalty programme. This would enable the organization to:

- Complement traditional methods of communication such as phone, email and web site with social media communications, driving traffic to the site and raising awareness of events and promotions.
- Use social media as a method for two-way communications to keep customers engaged with the brand.
- Recover from service issues, celebrate service successes and respond as quickly as possible to potential service opportunities.
- Look at collective groups expressing excitement or frustrations about the same topic and respond appropriately.
- Make communications relevant to the customer by data mining the company's CRM system.
- Monitor for tweets that mention specific topics, determine the relevance and sentiment or emotion, and use this as the basis for strategic marketing decisions and to prioritize areas of focus for customer service.
- Understand how happy or frustrated a customer is and take suggested responses from the new integrated solution. This will take the topic and customer history into account and assess whether the action is to retweet, clarify the comment or question or send a direct message to the customer.

Background

Interviewee

Jim Ibister is responsible for the overall operations of the Saint Paul Arena Company, which runs The Legendary Roy Wilkins Auditorium. Jim's role involves overseeing campus-wide IT efforts, getting to grips with technology to understand how different solutions can best be applied to different parts of the business in order to drive sales and improve customer service.

Jim Ibister
@mnwild

About MSE

Minnesota Sports & Entertainment (MSE) is a premier sports and entertainment provider with gross annual sales of approximately $92 million. The company was formed in 1997 when it was awarded the rights to an expansion of the National Hockey League (NHL) franchise for the City of Saint Paul, Minnesota, USA.

MSE owns the NHL's Minnesota Wild Hockey Club along with the Saint Paul Arena Company, who operate venues including the state-of-the-art Xcel Energy Center where the Minnesota Wild team plays. As well as showcasing the world's greatest hockey players, this venue has hosted concerts for stars such as Pavarotti, Neil Diamond and Eric Clapton, and college and high school athletic tournaments.

MSE currently has 200 full-time members of staff supported by approximately 750 part-time employees. Around 100 of the full-time employees are part of the Saint Paul Arena Company and 100 work for the Hockey Club.

Their social media strategy

MSE currently uses social media to support three key communications objectives that feed into their overall key business objective to drive ticket sales.

Firstly, they use social media channels such as Twitter and Facebook to complement traditional methods of communication, such as phone, email, SMS and the company web site, which are used to push information out to customers about upcoming games and concerts taking place at the Xcel Energy Center.

Secondly, social media is used as a way of engaging those customers to give them reasons to stay connected to the information push. Trivia, contests and play-by-play activities are employed across Twitter and Facebook as well as traditional channels.

Finally, MSE are using social media as a means to recover from service issues, celebrate service successes and respond as quickly as possible to potential service opportunities.

MSE's social media strategy was not one that was clearly defined from the beginning, however. Rather it was a process of discovery and as such its approach to social media has evolved over time. Originally, MSE looked at the world of social media from the outside in. On monitoring social media channels, the company was concerned that they were underrepresented and lacked the online presence that businesses increasingly strive for today.

MSE slowly started to look internally at first – at how they could build their presence. The company created accounts on the major social media sites such as Twitter and Facebook and began pushing information out about upcoming matches and promotions. Yet, as they did this, it quite quickly became apparent that MSE could not build the strong social media presence they desired by dictating information to friends and followers.

> People started to respond and feed back to us on what we were telling them. They started asking questions. It was then that we realized it had to become a dialogue. If we were going to push information out to our customers via these very social channels, then it's only natural that they expect a response.

This was quite a revelation for the company and, as a result, what had started out as an experiment shifted quite dramatically to form a social media strategy centred around two-way communications and customer service. It was from this moment on that MSE understood that social media was about engaging people, developing a dialogue with them and building relationships with customers. The company, therefore, started trying to develop personalities for their social media accounts. They began using the first person in conversations to show they were engaged and asking questions of their friends and followers to show they were interested. That changed everything for us. It was suddenly as if people knew we were listening and that's when they started telling us things about themselves.

With an annual budget in the range of $100,000–200,000 for social media activities, MSE now employs a full creative team, including one full-time social media manager, a web editor, a director of marketing intelligence and two database support personnel. The purpose of this team is to work together to build a comprehensive data footprint of the company's customers – including Minnesota Wild fans and concert guests – in order to gain greater insights into who they are and what they want. Ultimately this helps the company to make smarter marketing decisions and more impactful marketing and sales choices.

Integrated into the team is the MSE IT staff, who are critical in delivering the solutions that allow for the collection and management of these data. They work together with the director of marketing intelligence to plan collection software and hardware implementations.

The case

The problem

Minnesota Wild (National Hockey League franchise) based in the city of Saint Paul, Minnesota, USA, has a strong season ticket base of approximately 12,000 ticket holders and aims to fill 18,000 seats at 44 hockey games a year.

From the late 1960s to the early 1990s, Minnesota enjoyed strong support for the local professional hockey team. When a new, younger team was introduced in 2000, the support from the old hockey community continued despite the fact that the new team was less experienced and saw fewer wins. It was during this period that MSE started focusing on delivering a real customer experience to fans. With a brand new arena, for almost ten years the overall experience helped to compensate for the fact that the team wasn't winning games. But, by 2008, the honeymoon period with the fans began to wane and the club took a natural hit on ticket sales. This was also the year that the recession kicked in and the added stress of a difficult economic climate meant that by 2010 the number of regular supporters had dropped by roughly 10,000.

Maintaining the fan base and keeping valuable customers while attracting new ones, even during losing seasons, was and still is critical to the overall success of the business. The question Jim was asking himself was: "How can we develop new relationships with potential customers while keeping existing fans happy and winning old ones back?" It was at this low point in the company's history that the marketing department at MSE started to look into solutions that could help them to address this challenge.

Background

As the demand for the shrinking entertainment dollar increased, MSE realized that it was the one-on-one relationship with the fans that had sustained a strong base through the early years of the franchise. The company knew that rekindling and reinforcing these relationships was the key to retaining the remaining base and enticing new customers.

MSE looked back to their research to see where they could reignite the fading relationships. For some time the company had recognized that their fans were avid users of technology and, as such, the company had invested in building a technology-rich culture over the years. It seemed that the time was right to amplify that connection.

Traditionally MSE has used email, fixed line phone and mobile text via the contact centre to communicate with customers and to develop one-to-one relationships. For example, if a customer says "Call me if the team makes the playoffs" the system would automatically notify the customer service team to contact the customer the day the playoff news is announced.

However, while email and mobile remain good channels for communication, it was becoming increasingly difficult for the customer service team to reach the 12,000 season ticket holders by phone due to "do not call" lists and the growing use of mobile phones in lieu of land lines. With this channel of communication closing in on them, they knew they had to look at other options.

Meanwhile, MSE had realized that fans were already starting to use new social media channels such as Twitter as a way of communicating their frustrations with the customer service at games. On one occasion, the game had attracted a greater number of supporters than the facilities team had anticipated. As a result, the company had underestimated the number of food and drinks vendors they would need to have open to serve fans. As queues started to form and customers started to vent their frustrations at having to wait in line, Jim checked the company Twitter feed and saw the negative comments come flooding in. At that moment he realized that he had no way of getting an immediate response to customers to pacify them and to offer them compensation. Instead, he had to notify the customer service team and ask them to get responses out to each customer who had made a complaint. This was a wake-up call for the organization to investigate how technology could help them to automate these processes for more efficient and effective customer service.

Before they had seriously considered a social media strategy, MSE had already begun aggregating their CRM system and existing phone set-up. Jim knew he needed to move to an internet protocol (IP) phone set-up, and he recognized that he needed access to richer data and to foster better integration with this IP system and ultimately the customer service agents. This would primarily assist the hockey sales group and the sales teams in selling more tickets. Jim commented:

> We were starting to understand that the future was about taking the information we have access to and using technology to pull it all together in order to get a better insight into customer behaviours.

As part of this conversation, Jim began to explore whether it would be possible to integrate social media communications with this upgraded CRM system. Previously, he had started looking for reference points as to how other companies had approached similar opportunities. He quickly realized, however, that it would be difficult to gauge what MSE's competitors were doing in this field: while they could see outwardly what was being done via social media, they didn't have a window into how the back-end processes worked internally with their marketing and sales teams. What he did do, however, was spend time looking at what other hockey teams were doing in terms of social media. He explained:

> We recognized that successful teams had been working a lot on database management. They were becoming sophisticated in the art of data mining and in collecting information about their fans.

This insight gave MSE an even greater impetus to use the CRM system to help the company gather valuable information about their customers. Yet Jim was still concerned about how best to leverage the system to its full potential, especially if the implementation would lock him into a solution that couldn't then be customized as the business' needs evolved:

I was very aware that I didn't want my decision to limit our flexibility in the long run and I didn't want it to hinder us as we progressed along the learning curve. From an IT perspective, the event world changes every day. Regardless of the type of event you're hosting, you can pretty much guarantee that they'll all have different requirements in terms of technology.

The solution

Having considered all the options, MSE decided that the best approach was to go for a flexible solution that would enable the integration of their upgraded CRM system, customer service function and customer loyalty programme. Jim explained:

> When selecting an IT partner, you can end up going down certain decision paths that you're not actually comfortable with. We agreed as a company that we wouldn't put all of our eggs in one basket. It was important to us that the new technology worked with the solutions we already had in place, even if they had come from competitors. We wanted to maintain our freedom to select best-of-breed technology so we made the decision to transition to an Avaya Contact Centre Suite as it was simple and allowed us flexibility to work with the assets we had already built up.

As Jim started working through the implementation process, he made a conscientious decision to involve his social media team in the discussions and not just those from the IT department. He felt it was important for the people who would be using the technology on a daily basis to develop an understanding of how it worked. However, what happened next, Jim explained, was not what he had anticipated:

> Looking back, the reaction from the social media team was really quite interesting. Despite their expertise in the field of social media, they just couldn't get their heads around the product and the process; all the information goes into the system at one end, and then something quite different comes out the other end. But what happens in between, and what do we do with the information we're left with? The product was brand new and perfect for what we wanted, but what we were suffering from was a learning curve deficiency.

Up until that point, the social media team had been using social media channels as a vehicle for push marketing, fielding information out to customers but not responding. They hadn't been using social media as a way of engaging in a dialogue with them and as such they didn't understand why they should be excited about it.

The deployment got off to a slow start as a result. As Jim worked through the perception challenges with the implementation team he realized that on paper the solution seemed very complex. His social media team were finding it difficult to grasp the concept because they hadn't experienced it or seen the output. Fully sold on the solution, however, Jim knew that if they were taken through how it works step by step, they would believe in where it could take the company. He, therefore, decided that he would take the reins and show them manually how it would work in practice and how valuable it would be for the business. Jim explained:

> To start with, I think the team were concerned that they were going to be bombarded with every single piece of information on every social media channel that related to MSE. But I explained that this is exactly what the system helps to avoid. In fact, the two important factors the solution monitors closely are immediacy and sentiment and these are exactly the two things that we need to be aware of.

Jim jumped in head first and started applying rules manually to the system. For example, asking the system to only monitor tweets that mention tickets or sales. He knew therefore, from sifting through the relevant tweets, that people were really excited about season tickets going on sale that year. This he took from the positive sentiment. He also knew, from the immediacy, that sales were going up as a result of announcements around new signings by the team. Where there was negative sentiment around the signings, he was able to tell from the geography connected to people's Twitter handles that they weren't from the area and in fact came from a completely different fan base. He was then able to show the team how the system worked and the benefits it would bring in terms of prioritizing areas of focus for customer service.

To start with MSE was getting around 10,000 tweets a week that it had to analyse and respond to. With the system sifting through those tweets and prioritizing them based on immediacy and sentiment, that number dropped by more than half to just over 4,000 tweets.

Now that the team are fully on board, the next step is for the new system to be integrated with MSE's complete contact centre solution. So the actionable information that was previously being sent by email to a series of inboxes that the social media and customer service teams constantly monitor will be routed directly to the most appropriate customer service agent, allowing them to respond immediately as tweets come through. This means that the customer service team will be able to easily and systematically monitor "relevance" and "emotion" and respond in a strategic way.

One of the benefits of the new system, Jim explained, is that it gives suggested responses to tweets. It takes the topic and customer history into account and assesses whether the action is to retweet, clarify the comment or question, or send a direct message to the customer.

> Overall it helps our customer service team to understand and judge how happy or frustrated the customer is, and based on that assessment, we can make the call on how best to respond. For example, if a season ticket holder complains on Facebook about the beer served in the arena, our customer service agents will be notified immediately. By assigning it to the right agent, the contact who has perhaps dealt with that customer in the past and built a relationship with them can respond before the complaint escalates into a social media crisis.

Results

While it's too soon to do an in-depth evaluation of the return on investment, Jim is content to base his assessment so far on pure intuition:

> What we have taken away this far is an understanding of the incredible volume of people who are talking about us via social media channels. For me, that's enough to justify the steps we've taken to engage with our customers who are using these channels.

MSE is currently focusing on fine-tuning the solution in advance of the upcoming season, after which they expect to gain great insight into their customers' behaviour. Having put in place a market intelligence team, they now have the ability to collate and take value from the information they have gathered from fans and customers. Moving into the future, MSE will be looking to benchmark the extent to which customers are spending as a result of loyalty to the brand.

In the meantime, additional insights are being developed daily by review-ing how relevant Twitter and Facebook interactions build or repeat on each other. This will be an important metric to use in the long-term analysis of the project's success. As the organization begins to interact more often and more quickly, MSE will be keen to see whether there is a drop-off in negative com-munication and a multiplication of positive comments.

Critical success factors

1. Immediacy became one of the most critical success factors for MSE as the company looked at how to get the right information to the right person as quickly as possible to enable them to respond while relevancy still exists. According to Jim, taking the time to get that part right is where 80 per cent of the effort is directed:

> This type of social interaction slowly loses its importance as time passes. Therefore, collection of data, while critical, could drive the initia-tive into the ground if the weight of the collection process either slows or confuses the real intent, which is communication.

2. Another important part of MSE's success so far is down to its technology-savvy workforce. Although the social media team were sceptical at first at the capacity for the technology to improve the process of managing a com-pany's online presence and activity, Jim believes his team has been instrumental in ensuring the company communicates with fans in the right way, and he adds:

> Having a sales team that's confident using technology has made a huge difference. Knowing this has made us smarter about who we recruit.

Lessons learned

Jim concludes:

> Some companies look at social media as a way of collecting data and this is something we were guilty of at first. Once you dip your toe in the water, it's difficult not to get sucked in by the sheer volume of content referencing your company. But eventually this has to give way to the immediacy of the medium and the opportunity to start two-way com-

munication to build customer relationships. What works really well is if you have a process that can combine the two, allowing you to collect interactions that cover the same issues and then use them in a positive way to recover from a service issue or celebrate a service success.

Want more? See what has been said about this case or get involved and discuss it with the author and other readers on our LinkedIn group, find it by visiting http://www.socialmedia-mba.com *or search for "The Social Media MBA Alumni".*

Product Development

19 Barclaycard US – Customer Collaboration

A member of the **BARCLAYS** Group

What happens when you put customers in charge of your product development?

Executive summary

Overview

Barclaycard US recognized a fast-changing environment and moved to take advantage of how social media can bring together consumers with a shared interest – and self select into a programme that offers good value in exchange for disciplined financial management. Barclacyard Ring is the first crowd-sourced credit card in which members decide critical elements of programme management.

Key findings

- When consumers have a hand in developing the product, they use it more – and responsibly.
- The community even works together to make decisions, such as to share some of the card "giveback" bonus with a national charity.

Recommendations

1. Businesses can trust their customers to make good decisions that benefit all.
2. By maintaining an ongoing dialogue with customers via social media, the provider can frequently take the pulse of its customer community.
3. Digital influencers can help businesses connect providers with potential customers.

What you need to know

In response to changes in the regulatory environment, consumer attitudes and the emergence of social media channels, Barclacyard US created Barclay-card Ring the first crowdsourced credit card in which members decide critical elements of programme management. Key decisions about the programme – such as how much to share in programme "giveback" – are made by community members. With this interest in the programme, the business sees better than average behaviours in usage, balance build, credit losses and usage of economical service channels such as online.

Background

Interviewee

Jared Young creates and implements plans to manage this ground-breaking new payment product that lever-ages social media and crowdsourcing. Jared joined Barclaycard US in 2003 and has held a variety of roles in marketing and marketing analytics since that time. Previously, he worked at Bank One's First USA unit – conducting marketing analysis for its credit card business as well as at Walker Digital and Next Card. Jared holds a master's degree from the University of Pennsylvania's Wharton School.

Jared Young
@JaredEYoung

About Barclacycard US

Headquartered in Wilmington, Delaware, Barclaycard US creates customized, co-branded credit card programmes for some of the country's most successful travel, entertainment, retail, affinity and financial institutions. The company employs 1,200 associates and was named a Top Workplace in Delaware in 2012. Barclaycard, part of Barclays Global Retail Banking division, is a leading global payment business that helps consumers, retailers and businesses to make and accept payments flexibly, and to access short-term credit when needed.

Their social media strategy

Barclaycard US leverages multiple properties to have a conversation with its customers. The programme, managed overall by David Goodman, senior director of digital marketing, utilizes a segmented approach to match consumers with the Barclaycard product that holds the greatest interest for the consumer. Barclaycard US announces corporate news and updates via its Barclaycard global Facebook page and Twitter feed. The business also operates an active and fun Facebook site to support its NFL Extra Points Reward Card. At that site, consumers discuss card spending promotions, talk football and learn about new programme options. With Barclaycard Ring, in a programme managed by Jared Young, the business takes social media to the next step by allowing members of the first crowdsourced credit card to get to know each other and co-manage the card programme.

The case

The problem

Can crowdsourcing work in credit cards? In November 2011, a small team within Barclaycard US decided to find out if it could – and create a better credit card in the process. Consumer trust in big banks was at an all-time low, the credit card industry faced unprecedented regulatory pressure to be simpler and more transparent and the proliferation of social media and community-based reviews had redefined how products were made and priced, changing companies' abilities to interact with and serve their customers. Barclaycard's answer to these trends was a virtual cardmember community and a new business concept called Barclaycard Ring – the first community crowdsourced credit card.

The 300-year-old bank knew how to do credit cards very well from a technical standpoint, but combining that with a transparent online, community platform and single sign-on servicing site was a big change to implement.

Beta testing with an invite-only cardmember base went live just months after the idea was first conceived and the product was launched for the broader public by April of 2012.

The Barclaycard Ring® MasterCard® offers simple, easy-to-understand terms and benefits, including:

- One, low 8 per cent interest rate for all balances (not 7.99 per cent).
- No annual fees.
- No balance transfer fees, enabling revolving credit card holders to transfer balances from higher interest-rate reward cards and still earn points.
- Giveback™, allowing community members an opportunity to share in the profit generated from their collective decisions.
- A simplified summary of the standard cardmember agreement.

Throughout the evolution of the product, Barclaycard US has utilized the power of social media to gather feedback and enable its cardholders to be involved in decisions and have a say about what they want the product to be. New cardmember acquisition is driven largely by word of mouth and referrals from within the community, with no large-scale paid advertising support. Barclaycard Ring has been hailed as a disruptor to the current credit card marketplace and its success relies on Barclaycard's ability to create a strong bond and high level of trust with its community.

Background

Card competitors recognize it's time for change – but have not pursued such dramatic solutions. Most, in the recessionary environment, moved to halt late fees, make terms more clear and ramp up service.

The Barclaycard Ring community represents step change by providing a forum where cardmembers can exchange ideas, share knowledge and provide direct feedback to Barclaycard US to help determine future product features. Through weekly online polls, the current community has already provided input on topics ranging from product feature preferences to marketing programmes.

The financial goal of the programme was to create a community of responsible customers who care about their credit rating and picture – and drive better than average spending, payment performance and e-statement usage – as well as a more profitable programme.

The solution

The Barclaycard Ring® MasterCard® is the first social media credit card designed and built through the power of community crowdsourcing. For the first time, cardmembers have a say in how their credit card works for them. An online framework provides cardholders with the ability to influence decisions that impact how the card is managed and serviced. A rarity, cardmembers also have visibility into the card's financial profit and loss (P&L) statements and are part of a unique Giveback™ program that enables them to share in the profit generated from the community's collective decisions. This helps Barclaycard US show cardmembers how good behaviour can drive good financial results, making for a more successful and profitable credit card product and greater level of trust between the bank and its cardmembers.

- The simplicity of Barclaycard Ring has helped the bank respond to new regulations and maintain compliance. For instance, it has adapted the standard six-page cardmember agreement to provide a two-page summary of the important terms and conditions that are contained in it.
- While regulation has made it difficult for banks to change someone's financial product, Barclaycard has put the power in the hands of its cardmembers and offers them the ability to opt out of decisions the community makes. Barclaycard may ask the community if it wants their late fees to be $10 or $25 with the offset that APR may change from 8 per cent to 8.25 per cent. Since the bank makes the same financial return, it comes down to what is important to the community.
- To collect feedback, Barclaycard developed a unique polling system that works seamlessly with its credit card servicing platform. Cardmembers only need to sign on once and can continuously jump back and forth between the community and their account servicing site.
- The bank is also breaking new ground in how it communicates with its cardmembers, using mechanisms such as Twitter and working closely with the legal team to ensure responses are approved ahead of time but still timely, easy to read and helpful.
- Sharing the credit card's P&L with cardmembers is something no other credit card issuer has been willing or able to do in the past. It is so unique to the marketplace that Barclaycard has filed 14 patent applications around the business process.
- PR around the launch was extensive with the new product being covered in the *New York Times, Fast Company*, the *Washington Post* and *Wall Street Journal*.

- Digital influencers, bloggers who write and tweet about personal finance, picked up on the concept and millions of Twitter followers learned about the new product.

Results

Already, the bank is seeing stark differences with its Ring cardmembers compared with other cards in its portfolio: 75 per cent of Ring cardholders are active online, versus just 48 per cent for other Barclaycard branded products. They log in more (66 per cent compared to 41 per cent), pay their bills online more (51 per cent versus 44 per cent) and have decided to go paperless (55 per cent compared to 25 per cent).

Critical success factors

Barclaycard Ring was quick to launch arguably the most disruptive credit card product on the market and is leading the industry in what many say could be the future of credit cards. Even still, the community has already voted to change the late fee policy on the credit card. And they had a great turnout, as 46 per cent of the community logged in to vote. That's incredible engagement and shows that customers truly value having a voice.

Lessons learned

Barclaycard US has learned that a community – connected by social media – is really a group with shared interests. In this case, Ring brings together a community that understands and wants a good deal in a credit card. They are engaged in the product – they use it and revolve on it to drive revenue to the programme. They care about it and make timely payments – and use cost-effective online servicing and e-statements. By aligning the interests of the issuer and the customers, both are satisfied with the product.

Want more? See what has been said about this case or get involved and discuss it with the author and other readers on our LinkedIn group, find it by visiting http://www.socialmedia-mba.com *or search for "The Social Media MBA Alumni".*

20 Sony Mobile – Managing Quality Control

SONY

make.believe

Use social media to detect consumer issues as they break to improve products and services, manage potential brand damage and avoid costs.

Listening to consumer discussions in social media to identify the key issues expressed about your products and services is the fastest, most cost-effective, statistically relevant and efficient way for you to harness the value of these globally networked conversations.

Executive summary

Overview

A large and statistically significant number of global consumers, many of them your current customers, express detailed comments and preferences, likes and dislikes, about your products and services in online communities. They don't just express their opinions about your products and services, they express their opinions about your competitors' products and services, and they often compare.

Consumers often do not mention corporate brands, like Sony, but rather express their opinion at a product level like the "Xperia", and frequently at product feature level: the camera; the WiFi connection; the battery; the screen; the user interface; the application; and the "look and feel".

Implementing a social media *listening* programme that harvests this information, and accurately categorizes and identifies issues consumers express in the early lifecycle of a hardware or software release programme, supports the implementation of remediation activities to avert larger scale issues causing, in the worst event, widespread consumer dissatisfaction with a product or service and brand or reputation damage.

Key findings

- The value of mining and analyzing social media data for valuable consumer insights into your products and services is significant, but it is in its infancy, and is only slowly gaining commercial recognition in the corporate landscape.
- Correlating consumer data from social media with internal channel data from CRM systems is greatly assisting in improving the reliability of forecasts around product sales, repairs and issues.
- Acting on issues detected early in the life cycle can avoid significant costs and brand reputational damage, and significantly enhances the probability of improving customer service satisfaction ratings.
- Understanding customers preferences through the analysis of how they discuss smartphones in social media is a valuable input to product design and quality to better develop products.

Recommendations

1. Map the social media landscape to understand the topics of conversation in your sector or category. What are consumers talking about, where do they talk about it and who are they? Correlate this data to internal channel data for resonance.
2. Analyse how consumers discuss products and services to identify the root cause issues driving tonality and sentiment. What do they like and what do they dislike and why? Who is winning, who is losing?
3. Assess the value of this information to your business, area by area: design, development, manufacturing, marketing and sales, service, corporate communications, etc. Who are the data of the biggest value to in helping to improve the products and services you deliver to consumers?
4. Establish small pilots to action the key findings and measure the impact of the actions on the customer and the organization. Are customers better

satisfied? Is the organization responding better to issues? Move successful pilots into measurable business line programmes that execute, measure and continuously improve.

What you need to know

Social media is increasingly seen as a media for marketer's to seed content and ultimately drive product sales. The increasing focus on social media ROI, and the market buzz around Facebook advertising is all well and good and will play out for all to see in a relatively short period of time.

What is often overlooked is that social media is the "world's largest focus group" and it is free. It is just that it is uncontrolled and unstructured. Organizations that have the knowledge, skills and tools to structure these data, analyse them to identify key consumer preferences, and act upon them, are better positioned to deliver improved products and services.

The volume of social media discussions about your products and services is statistically relevant. Consumers in social media express meaningful feedback about your products and services, articulately and often in great depth.

A disciplined programme of harvesting and analyzing social data to identify the top positive and negative drivers of sentiment for your products and services is essential. Acting on this data in a planned, timely and organized fashion can avoid significant costs, potential brand and reputational damage, and help to improve your future products and services.

Find the best partners to help you on your journey, but don't be afraid to get your hands dirty digging in the data, it is the epoch of big data so you better get good at it.

Background

Interviewee

Olle Hagelin started in the mobile phone business in 1993 as a production engineer. He has held many roles as a Project and Quality Manager for the Industrialization and Development department, responsible for the Ericsson Mobile Development process and quality at a company level. He is currently the Quality

Olle Hagelin
@OHagelin

Manager in Field Data Management as part of Quality and Customer Service at Sony Mobile Communications (SoMC) and is responsible for consumer feedback from the field about products and support performance across internal and external channels.

About SoMC

SoMC, formerly Sony Ericsson, employs 7,000 people, and is a subsidiary of Tokyo-based Sony Corporation, a leading global innovator of audio, video, game, communications, key device and information technology products for both the consumer and professional markets.

With its music, pictures, computer entertainment and online businesses, and unique sub-brands like Sony PlayStation™, Bravia™, Vaio™, Walkman™, CyberShot™ and now Xperia™, Sony is uniquely positioned to be the leading electronics and entertainment company in the world.

Through its Xperia™ smartphone portfolio, SoMC delivers the best of Sony technology, premium content and services, and easy connectivity to Sony's world of networked entertainment experiences.

Their social media strategy

Olle explained:

> With the strategy that customer service "should be *where* the consumers are" it is easy to understand why SoMC is present in social media, but our journey started long before this was a part of the strategy.

In 2005 the company began to look at what was happening "on the web" regarding the brand. Together with a social media partner, a listening programme was put in place to better understand consumer behaviour online and how the perception of the brand was impacted in online conversations. The programme also helped to guide on better customer communications in these emerging online communities in marketing. Olle commented:

> The listening programme allowed us to tap into a completely unfiltered and unbiased source of consumer opinion, not just about our brand and products, but as importantly, about our competitors' brand and products.

At the heart of the customer service strategy, and the focus area for this case study, is the use of social media as an intelligence source together with information collected internally from contact and service centers to understand how to improve products, services and support to Sony customers and target consumers.

In 2010, the global support forum http://talk.sonymobile.com was launched, which enables real-time communication to support consumers with the usage of Sony phones. Consumers can also engage with SoMC through Developer World (http://developer.sonymobile.com/) and the Sony Mobile Blog Portal (http://blogs.sonymobile.com/).

Social media, contact centers, and the support forum are the first places consumers go to find solutions to problems and communicate issues. The normal behaviour today for many consumers who have a problem is "to Google it", which increasingly drives consumers to these channels.

Currently, the strategy is being *extended* to analyse "new" and emerging social media channels and CRM data and combine them with "historical" data, such as sales and repair channel data, to be able to forecast, as early as possible with degrees of certainty, the impact an issue may have on a product, service and support quality, costs and sales.

The case

The problem

Detecting consumer issues in 54 markets and more than 20 different languages for up to ten major product launches every year is a forensic task, a sort of "CSI social media"! To be best positioned to successfully solve consumer problems, the very first instance of an issue should be detected when it arises in social media in order to assess its impact and track its trajectory.

It is impossible to manually collect and analyse tens of thousands of daily social media mentions accurately and identify and rank those that are specific product issues. In fact, despite the vast number of purported technology solutions claiming to be able to easily do this, there are few.

It can also be difficult to identify new issues in contact centres. CRM systems deploying pre-defined codification hierarchies often use restrictive product and service mnemonics and make the assumption that the system "knows" all of the potential issue categories. This can be restrictive and prone to errors, and users often rely on "other" categories or "free text" as a means of describing a customer problem.

With thousands of daily entries from contact centres around the world, rapid and accurate analysis of these data in helping to identify new customer issues can be problematic.

And then there is the question of how to assess the threat of an issue. For example, how important is one consumer issue about your product in social media in China at 08:00 CET? How important is it if there are ten similar issues by 15:00 GMT from France, Italy, the UK and the USA? At what point do you take action on this insight, and what action do you take?

Background

It all started with the Sony Ericsson K800 handset in June 2006. Two weeks after the product was released, a comment in social media appeared: "the coating on the keypad was peeling off", and after having contacted the customer service centre, the customer was told that "this was not a product issue but was a customer issue". Over the coming days, 15 users from six different countries reported the problem. Olle explained:

> 15 users from six different countries might not sound like many customers . . . but at SoMC, we use the 1 per cent rule.

The 1 per cent rule states that the number of people who create content in an internet community, like a social network or a forum, represents approximately 1 per cent (or less) of the people actually viewing that content. For example, for every person who posts on a forum, generally about 99 other people are viewing that forum but not posting.

The product launch support and maintenance team acted quickly to equip customer service centres with the information to deal with the problem. Customers were offered new replacement products in the shops. An internal investigation revealed there were problems in the manufacturing production run, which was corrected within days. The resulting quick actions saved the company tens of thousands of dollars in costs and potential damage to the brand by avoiding a much larger crisis.

Fast forward six years later to 2012, and the issue tracking programme has moved from initial pilots into mature business processes that are integrated into the operations in customer services quality feedback (CSQF). Daily global issue tracking covers:

- All major social media networks.
- Over 150 specialist mobile/handset/gadget forums, discussion boards and blogs.
- More than 12 major languages.

The KEY process "listens to consumers" to detect and identify issues early in the product lifecycle, in order to implement an appropriate remediation strategy. In 2012 alone, the programme had:

- identified over 15,000 unique issue reports in social media;
- across 400 issue categories; and
- spanning 35 products.

The process of continuously monitoring social media to detect issues early, and the subsequent analysis and prioritization of issues through a "triage" system, led to the identification of three big issue categories in a period of 24 months. The remediation strategies for these issues have saved the company tens of thousands of dollars, and visibly improved customer satisfaction, most notably as measured in social media.

Wi-Fi issues compete with battery life issues for the number one spot with consumers in social media for smartphones across ALL manufacturers. By analyzing in detail the root cause issues as communicated by users of the different handsets, for example router, handset and location related causes, SoMC identified the most significant problems related to their own products, and issued a major upgrade to solve these issues. In addition, a completely new section on the support forum was created to help consumers improve their Wi-Fi connection.

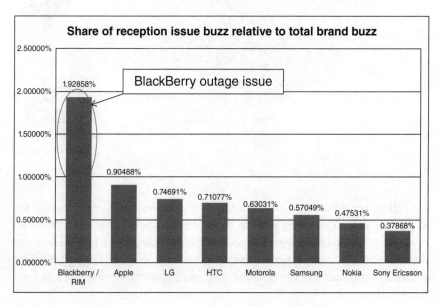

Competitive smartphone benchmark, June–November 2011, reception issues

Battery life issues are a major area of complaints by consumers in social media for ALL smartphone manufacturers, and the Android platform in particular. By analyzing feedback in detail, and understanding the extent of consumer negative sentiment associated with the issues, SoMC developed ESM: "Extended stamina mode" (official name), also known as "Extended standby mode". This function was introduced in 2012 following the Android OS Ice Cream Sandwich update, and is designed to increase the battery life of the handset when it is in standby mode.

Top 5 root causes for overheating

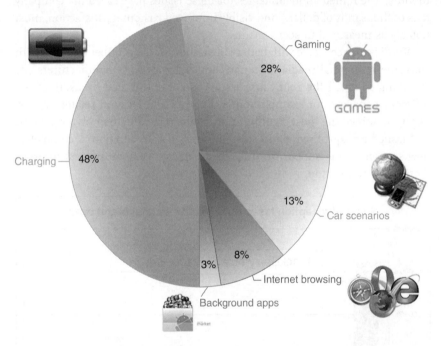

Root cause analysis, overheating issues

Yellow screen issues were identified by consumers in social media for Xperia S handsets, where a portion of the display appeared to be "yellowish" in contrast. These issues were immediately remediated in the hardware of the handset model, and the issues were announced on the Support Forum, encouraging customers to exchange their old handsets for new ones at local Sony outlets.

Olle explained:

> We would not have been able to do the issue tracking programme without Integrasco's Analytical Services and Technology . . . they are an integrated part of the global monitoring team and have provided all of the technology we use for social and CRM mining.

In addition, the SoMC analysts have been trained through "Integrasco University" to further develop skills in social search, Boolean taxonomy, trend analysis and root-cause analysis.

The solution

Sony Mobile started to receive structured information from social media about consumer issues with products in 2005, from its services and technology supplier. The information is the result of a daily social crawling and filtering process, of tens of thousands of social media networks, forums, discussion boards and blogs using large Boolean search expressions.

The search expressions, collectively referred to as taxonomies, are continuously updated and evolve as new products and software updates are released. The search taxonomies enable the quality filtering of social media conversations on a product or software level.

```
(((("sony ericsson" OR "sony ericson" OR "sony erikson" OR "sony-ericsson" OR
"sony-ericson" OR "sony-erikson" OR Сони OR эриксон OR ериксон OR "Сони
ериксон" OR "Сони-ериксон" OR" Сони эриксон" OR "Сони-эриксон" OR ericsson
OR 索爱* OR 索尼* OR 爱立信* OR xperia) OR subject:("sony ericsson" OR "sony
ericson" OR "sony erikson" OR "sony-ericsson" OR "sony-ericson" OR "sony-erikson"
OR Сони OR эриксон OR ериксон OR "Сони ериксон" OR "Сони-ериксон" OR
"Сони эриксон" OR "Сони-эриксон" OR ericsson OR索爱* OR索尼* OR爱立信* OR
xperia)) AND (arc OR x12 OR subject:(arc OR x12)))OR(lt15i OR lt18 OR so01c OR "arc
s" OR anzu OR subject:(lt15 OR lt18 OR so01c OR anzu)))
```

Sample product taxonomy

Furthermore, advanced search expressions enable the decomposition of conversations to a product feature and issue category level (build quality, Wi-Fi, reception, camera, display, application, etc.).

((akkuproblem OR (("Akku hält"~3 OR Akkulaufzeit OR Gesprächszeit OR "Standby-Zeit"
OR "akku laufzeit"~3 OR akkuladen OR "akku laden"~3 OR akkukapazit* OR akkuverb*)
AND (kurz OR gering OR wenig OR klein OR schlecht OR schlimm)))OR (("battery life"~ 3
OR "battery duration"~3 OR "battery charge"~3 OR "battery capacity"~3 OR
((subject:battery OR battery) AND (day* OR hour* OR hrs OR minut*)) AND (low OR small
OR short OR "not long" OR "not enough" OR less OR weak OR poor))OR ((batteria OR
"Tiempo de conversación" OR "Tiempo en espera") AND (corto OR breve OR poco OR
pequeño OR bajo OR escaso OR rápido OR pequeño OR menor OR pobre* OR malo)) OR
((bateria OR "tempo di conversazione" OR "tempo di standby") AND (povero OR scarso
OR scadente OR cattivo OR breve OR corto OR poco OR piccolo OR basso OR
insufficiente OR basso)) OR((待机* AND (很短* OR 太短* OR 短了* OR 不足* OR 不够)) OR
待机短* OR 待机很短* OR 待机太短* OR 待机时间短* OR 待机时间太短* OR 待机时间不足* OR
待机时间不够* OR 待机弱* OR 待机太弱* OR 待机很弱* OR 放电し過ぎOR 充電ならない))

Issue category taxonomy

The net result of this initial crawling and filtering process is a "clean" set of data that is quantitatively structured. The data are then qualitatively analysed by experienced analysts to identify key customer issues.

Each product and category taxonomy has its own variations for key markets and languages, which allows for the investigation of volume trends (peaks and troughs) to guide the qualitative analysis.

The programme tracks all SoMC products in social media on a daily basis, and flags and reports an emerging issue as soon as it is identified, subject to a threshold and priority level.

When an issue is identified and monitored in social media or a contact centre, a rapid assessment is undertaken:

- All findings are collected, analysed and cross-referenced;
- The issue is checked to establish if it is known, or if there are similar or related issues reported; and
- The issue is assessed to understand its commercial impact by reviewing the issue volume, momentum and sentiment.

Depending on the result of this rapid analysis, new information may need to be created for consumers and pushed to the support forum, social channels, customer contact and service centres. A severity rating is associated with each issue.

Weekly issue reports summarizing key issues and trends for each of the products and product families are produced and distributed across the Sony Mobile FDM team. Consumer verbatims and links to social media conversations support all findings and key issues observed in non-English markets are translated into English. The links are used by the consumer engagement team to engage with users in social media and the support forum to take preemptive measures or ask the customers for further details on their issues when needed.

By tracking and reporting issues at both a product and product family level, the FDM team can identify issues specific to certain devices and issues affecting entire product families or specific software versions.

The social media data are correlated and combined with data from contact centres, service centres and relevant external market data, and a holistic consolidated issue report is prepared and distributed to all product projects, customer services heads and the engineering community responsible for improving products and support.

The programme also allows SoMC to measure the positive impact of software updates as they are released by analyzing reductions in issues reported, returned and service centre inquiries.

Weekly and bi-weekly call-outs are conducted with key stakeholders, depending on product lifecycles and launch update cycles. The weekly call-outs enable the gathering of further input, requests for further analysis on specific issues and the sharing of information across customer service and quality channels.

Olle commented:

> Regardless of the perceived severity of the issue, consumers see Sony Mobile are acting on the information they provide, and actively listening to their concerns generates positive sentiment towards the Sony brand. In some cases, evidence has indicated that this has turned the loss of a customer to a retention, or a new sale, because Sony Mobile are acting quickly and effectively.

Results

The results of the issue tracking programme have been impressive. The benefits from proactively putting in place actions to fix detected problems with products or preventing further widespread customer dissatisfaction have led to a range of both tangible and intangible benefits:

- Identification and prioritization of the KEY issues for SoMC.
- Benchmarking issues across competitive products to understand relative performance and issue severity.
- Avoidance of costs.

- Avoidance of brand and reputational damage.
- Improved consumer satisfaction.

As important, the issue tracking programme has demonstrated the value of "listening to the consumer" to the SoMC team, and has helped better align the awareness of customer issues and the importance of proactive actions to help to solve issues.

Critical success factors

There are a large number of success factors in effectively developing and executing a programme the size and scale of the SoMC issue tracking programme. Boiling down the main experiences at SoMC clearly highlights three major success factors:

1. Select a partner with quality solutions that adds value to your team – the data, technology, and analytical infrastructure, knowledge and skills required to harvest and analyse SoMC requirements is sophisticated. Make sure your partner solutions can deliver "industrial mining" and not just "pan handling".
2. Put the processes in place to be able to execute quickly – it is not helpful to invest in a sophisticated issue detection system if, once issues are identified, they cannot be actioned across the organization's channels rapidly and effectively, and the outcomes can't be measured.
3. Excellent communications and perseverance is required to get your team onboard – social and CRM data mining are relatively new areas for the business (even though SoMc has been at it for seven years), but they have a significant commercial value that is not recognized in most businesses. Work hard at aligning your entire team to the benefits of these new tools and processes, including the sceptics, and do not give up.

Lessons learned

Olle explains:

> The volume and content of global social media data from discussions about smartphones can be overwhelming . . . having the skills, processes, tools and partners to "mine the nuggets" from social media for the key issues, and correlate those quickly with information mined

from your own internal channel systems is one of the most powerful, reliable and real-time key performance indicators we have come across.

Listening across global social media channels to harvest a statistically significantly set of consumer data that can be analysed requires investment in a tool set, methodology and partners to deliver accuracy and rigor, but is still more cost effective, faster and arguably more accurate than traditional methods of regularly soliciting consumer opinion.

Detecting and analyzing issues early in the product lifecycle can promote remedial actions to avoid the issue becoming larger in the community; averting potential brand damage and avoiding costly damage control activities. An issue detected early may involve only a handful of consumer complaints globally, but the experience of analysis better enables the reliability of identifying those issues that have a probability of going viral.

Benchmarking issues about your product's features compared to those of your competitor's can help to better identify outliers related to your product versus generic problems common to all manufacturers' products. For example, "overheating" was a problem for all mobile manufactures in 2010 and 2012, and understanding the issue with your product relative to your competitor is key to an accurate evaluation of the problem.

Remediating big issues that have been identified early in the lifecycle through direct communications with consumers in social and on the support forum including: preparing contact and service centres in advance for the resolution of new in-coming issues, and substituting products that have problems, contributes to significant cost avoidance and potential negative brand and reputation damage.

Correlating social data with internal data from customer services, sales and customer surveys can identify highly correlated trends. For example, the pre-launch social media buzz for a product is often highly correlated to sales data, which can be correlated to repair, unit return and service data. This provides a more accurate business forecasting process and assists with the deployment of human and capital resources.

Want more? See what has been said about this case or get involved and discuss it with the author and other readers on our LinkedIn group, find it by visiting http://www.socialmedia-mba.com *or search for "The Social Media MBA Alumni".*

21 Getty Images – Socialize your Products

gettyimages® As social media becomes a more established way to communicate with present and prospective customers, businesses can be more innovative than ever on emerging platforms. By socializing products, as Getty Images has done, businesses can gain customers, increase brand engagement and show themselves as leaders in their field.

Executive summary

Overview

Through innovative new technology, Getty Images has been able to showcase its award-winning editorial imagery across the social sphere. The company now has the ability to listen to social conversations and automatically return relevant trending images almost instantaneously, giving consumers timely, engaging content.

Key findings

- High quality editorial images can now appear on Getty Images' social media platforms just minutes after creation.

- Social conversations can be listened and reacted to, with images of trending topics returned in real time.
- Getty Images can now be at the centre of conversations – predicting and tweeting trends almost instantaneously.

Recommendations

1. Be innovative: don't be scared of trying something new.
2. Pick your team wisely. Use the most knowledgeable and passionate people, and if possible try to limit the number of people involved to keep communication tight.
3. Think about whether or not you are able to socialize your products. It's not right for everyone, but if it works it is a great tool to engage customers.

What you need to know

- Getty Images has a wealth of award-winning editorial content to showcase across social media platforms. The new technology harnesses the power of social and emerging platforms, giving customers engaging and timely content through Facebook timelines, a Twitter account and a trending app.
- Photos can now be uploaded to social media sites within minutes.
- Images can be scheduled to appear as soon as a topic trends on social networks.
- As social channels evolve, so too will The Feed by Getty Images.
- Analytics have been key so far in informing Getty Images' online strategy, as well as pointing to important developments and changes to be made to The Feed.

Background

Interviewee

Since joining as vice president of marketing in 2010, Yvonne Chien has overseen the customer segmentation and digital marketing strategies across the organization, including the implementation of The Feed by Getty Images.

Prior to Getty Images, Yvonne held senior marketing positions for various internet companies, including

Yvonne Chien
@GettyImages

Google and social network Bebo. She holds an MBA from Harvard Business School and a BA from the University of California Berkeley.

About Getty

Getty Images is one of the world's leading creators and distributors of still imagery, video and multimedia products, as well as a recognized provider of other forms of premium digital content, including music. Getty Images serves business customers in more than 100 countries and is the first place creative and media professionals turn to discover, purchase and manage images and other digital content. Its award-winning photographers and imagery help customers produce inspiring work, which appears every day in the world's most influential newspapers, magazines, advertising campaigns, films, television programmes, books and web sites.

In 2012, the company was acquired by private equity firm Carlyle Group for $3.3 billion.

Social media strategy

Social media has been an important part of Getty Images' marketing strategy for a number of years and the company now has over 800 thousand fans on social media platforms. With around 200,000 fans on Facebook, this has been a key way to communicate with current and potential customers across a number of areas, from advertising and creative industries to media owners. Equally, Getty Images communicates via a number of Twitter feeds, with its two main handles @GettyImages and @GettyImagesNews attracting in excess of 65,000 and 24,000 followers respectively. Other Twitter feeds include video and music handles, as well as individual Twitter profiles for a number of markets worldwide. Getty Images also communicates through a Tumblr site with over 150,000 followers, increasing at almost 1,000 per day.

In order to make sure the Twitter feeds and Facebook accounts are managed successfully and the content is both engaging and informative, they are run by marketing managers and product specialists. These are the people in the business that know the different areas in depth and are passionate about them: for example, Getty Images' Reportage (photo journalism) profiles are run by editors. These experts also know how to connect with influencers in their specific areas, through what channels and using what content. Another good example is the fashion and entertainment-related feeds that contain references, tags and links to fashion houses and labels to further engage with clients in the fashion industry.

While social management is decentralized, there is an overarching global team that makes sure everything is on-brand and all messages are consistent. Over an 18-month period, Getty Images achieved this consistency by putting in place a common set of social management tools, analytics and processes to drive a more global approach. Social media managers are able to track brand mentions and measure the impact of their activity, using data and shared learnings to further increase the company's engagement and reach across social media.

The case

The problem

Getty Images delivers thousands of photos and videos daily that end up in newspapers, magazines, advertisements and on web sites around the world. Getty Images is known for distributing content quickly to news and picture desks worldwide, from breaking news to key events like the Olympics or Oscars. Speed to market is paramount to the media industry. The marketing team at Getty Images wanted to reflect that same speed and timely relevance in their social channels not only to showcase the speed of Getty Images' platform but also because social media itself has become an outlet for what is trending around the world.

The challenge, of course, was that curating and posting on social media is labour intensive and would require 24/7 human coverage. There had always been a disconnect between the fast pace of distribution happening on Getty Images' web site and the much slower posting of new content onto its social media profiles. Historically, every Facebook and Twitter post was populated manually. The social media manager had to physically choose the images and upload them; to trawl through Twitter, see what people are talking about and then tweet relevant images. By the time the post happened, the images were often no longer current or timely.

It was this very business problem that spawned The Feed by Getty Images.

Background

As part of its overall brand strategy, Getty Images tasked their agency to find an innovative and creative way to bring its wealth of premium visual content to the fore: a ground-breaking project that could show the company as an innovator, who was at the forefront of new technologies.

Social media was a ripe area for innovation. Recent insight from two of Getty Images' partners, communications agency M Booth and analytics and reporting agency Simply Measured, had shown that photo and video content on brand pages drove the highest levels of engagement. On average, photos are "liked" twice as much as text updates, and videos over 12 times that of links or text. This was the insight Getty Images felt supported the investment of the time and resources to create what was to become The Feed. The company and agency felt it would set them apart in the industry and help to increase the engagement with prospective and current customers through social media.

A number of initial concepts, all based on social media, were developed by leading digital agency R/GA London in May 2012. Once the concept had been finalized, development began in August, with soft launch commencing in November 2012 and final launch in January 2013.

The solution

The brand new concept, The Feed by Getty Images, is an innovative new technology that links Getty Images' Connect API to social and emerging media platforms. This powerful new software showcases the company's award-winning editorial content based on top trending topics, conversations and thought leadership that produces up-to-the-minute news, sport and entertainment imagery.

The Feed by Getty Images has been implemented through three separate stages: Facebook timelines (News, Sports and Entertainment), a Twitter account @FeedMeGetty and a trending responsive web application (thefeed. gettyimages.com).

Facebook timelines

The Feed leverages the Facebook platform to showcase the trending capabilities by creating up-to-the-minute themed timelines for Getty Images' coverage of current sport, news and entertainment events. These images are based on matching search terms as well as spikes of relevant chatter on Twitter. Getty Images' audience is diverse, but by dividing the feeds into these three global subjects, they add both flexibility and speed, giving the user the opportunity to focus on what they want, and only what they want.

The process behind this part of The Feed can be controlled through a number of different techniques, making it as automatic or manual as needed.

Push: this allows for images to be manually searched and selected using a custom admin interface and publishes it directly into Facebook albums and onto timelines, without even leaving the admin interface. For example, one of Getty Images' social media managers could, at the touch of a button, choose the images they wanted from that night's film premiere and it would automatically upload them to the "Entertainment" timeline.

Scheduled: the automatic search, selection and publishing of images from events directly into albums and onto timelines. These searches, as the name suggests, are scheduled beforehand and run at the desired time. The Feed will automatically select the best images based on certain defined parameters as well as a special search algorithm. This is especially useful for events, for example a football match, when consumers are likely to want to see high profile moments as and when they happen. A social media manager does not have to trawl through hundreds of images highlighting them and uploading them, instead images with select keywords or meta data will upload automatically.

Trending: this tool takes into account what people are talking about on Twitter and publishes relevant images at a desired time. As with scheduled posts, trending searches are configured in advance of the event and run automatically when programmed to do so, listening to Twitter conversations to inform what to post.

Twitter feed: @FeedMeGetty

Further enriching Getty Images' social media presence is the creation of @FeedMeGetty. This integration with Twitter uses The Feed's capability and features a dual functionality, firstly tweeting the top trending images and secondly responding to content queries in real time. Followers can Tweet @FeedMeGetty a request for an image that will then be returned to them.

The Feed Trending application

Finally, The Feed Trending app is a browser experience that links from gettyimages.com. It allows users to explore editorial imagery related to a trending topic on Twitter by geo-location. Images associated with what is globally and regionally trending are automatically posted to the The Feed Trending app microsite.

The Feed currently has a patent pending, so the technology and ideas around the smart search will be uncopyable and solely owned by Getty Images.

How the roll-out worked

The creation and launch of The Feed by Getty Images was a collaboration between R/GA and the team at Getty Images. While it started as a marketing-led project, it became a cross-functional effort across the business. With six stakeholders at R/GA involved and double that number at Getty Images – some in the UK and others in USA – the process was intensive and iterative. Four months from conception, the project was live. There was a lot of toing and froing when it came to design, plans and final sign-off on the roll-out, and almost hourly calls were needed to make sure everything was in place and would be ready to meet the launch deadlines.

When The Feed's Facebook timelines soft launched at the end of November 2012, photographs were appearing on the social network within two minutes of creation. This enabled sports fans, for example, to see images of their favourite football players scoring, almost in real time.

The Feed by Getty Images Trending app and @FeedMeGetty Twitter account officially launched on 14 January 2013 and so it is too early to see just how successful these have been. However, Getty Images' monitoring suggests that engagement levels are high and growing by the day.

What's next for The Feed?

The Feed was built to open up ways for Getty Images' content to be showcased to its customers through today's top social media networks, enable real-time engagement and create new experiences. Because of this, it is highly customisable and extendable, and Getty Images has big plans for it. There will be a healthy list of enhancements to the existing offering to take the innovations even further, as well as application to other platforms. The specific platforms that will be integrated are still being determined, so watch this space!

Another key development will be making sure the three aspects of The Feed interact well with each other. While they naturally fit together, they do not necessarily talk to each other as much as the marketing team would like. In the future it is hoped that @FeedMeGetty will be key in driving users to the Facebook page, and vice versa, with immediate interactions between the tools.

Furthermore, as social media becomes more entwined in Getty Images' overall business strategy, it will enable The Feed to grow and evolve at a faster pace. The business was built long before social media arose, and therefore

Getty Images' business proposition will naturally progress to suit the environment.

Results

Although still in the early stages, the results so far have been positive. The smart search used in all three techniques, by far the most complex part of the project, launched in mid-November and has been a great success. This has fed timely, relevant images to the Getty Images Facebook page and so far fans seem to be engaging well with the tool. Images are now being uploaded onto Facebook timelines within two minutes of creation: far quicker than anybody ever imagined.

A great example of The Feed in action was a "scheduled" Facebook album for the final Formula 1 Grand Prix of the 2012 season in Brazil. As it was Michael Schumacher's last ever F1 race, it was clear that there would be a big focus on him. Before the race, Getty Images created a scheduled Facebook album for Schumacher to populate his imagery as it was captured. This meant that at exactly the same time as Twitter announced Schumacher was the number one trending topic in the world, the images were on Getty Images' sports timeline. At the same time, @FeedMeGetty populated a photograph of Schumacher walking onto the grid moments before the race started that mirrored the content in the Facebook album. With planned activity such as this, the content feed is instantaneous, showcasing Getty Images' speed and coverage when the conversations are happening.

Because this project is the first of its kind, it has been impossible to set targets: there is no precedent or benchmarks to use. Measurement, through both Simply Measured for the Facebook and Twitter accounts and the Omniture codes tied to the Trending app, at this point aim to help Getty Images adapt, rather than proving The Feed's worth.

One of the biggest results, which is certain to impact the whole of the Getty Images business, has come from the Omniture codes. The subsequent analytics have enabled the company to discover a number of things that will help with the overall online and search strategy. These include key search terms that have never been targeted before, as well as new ways of looking at traffic referral to the Getty Images web site. In time, these analytics will be fundamental to the online marketing strategy of the business.

Getty Images is pleased to have succeeded in creating the world's first automated social posting engine for imagery, tapping into social media's capabilities in a way that has never been done before. Additionally, the Facebook timeline API has only been around since April 2012 and no other company has ever tapped into it in this way: The Feed has proved that it can be done and is sure to set a precedent for all other social-savvy businesses.

Critical success factors

To bring The Feed to life so quickly required the following:

1. A clear brief: identifying and clearly laying out the business problem and objectives at the outset.
2. Creative and technological vision: understanding of the possibilities in social media, ability to navigate the world of APIs and what is doable.
3. Focus and urgency: a clear timeline, minimal scope creep.
4. Dedicated resource: buy-in from senior executives at the start; dedicated project managers from both agency and client.

Lessons learned

As with any project of this scale there must be learnings and failings along the way. Any challenges related to the current limits of the Twitter API are being addressed as they arise. Additionally, the image matching for @FeedMeGetty and The Feed Trending app needs to be tuned slightly in order to provide the most relevant images possible.

Working with so many different people, all of whom want slightly different things from the project, can be difficult, but obviously vital if you are to get the best results. Working together from the start is key, and having key people at the fore who can challenge each others' ideas helps to make the project a success. Also, making sure that senior stakeholders are involved, and keeping this to as limited a number as possible, can help to make things run more smoothly.

Some of the key figures in implementing and progressing the campaign came in part-way through the process. In particular, it would have made sense to involve the Getty Images product team and business development team to evaluate productizing The Feed for customer use. By doing so, The Feed could have had a greater impact to help clients with their own social strategy as opposed to boosting Getty Images' own social presence.

Yvonne Chien concludes:

> The Feed by Getty Images was a great learning curve for all at Getty Images and R/GA. My advice to all social media practitioners is to aim high and don't be scared of new ideas or being innovative. We had a challenge: we wanted to socialize our products in a relevant and timely way to show off our range of editorial content, and we came up with a successful and innovative solution to that. That's all we can really ask of our staff and agencies.

Want more? See what has been said about this case or get involved and discuss it with the author and other readers on our LinkedIn group, find it by visiting http://www.socialmedia-mba.com *or search for "The Social Media MBA Alumni".*

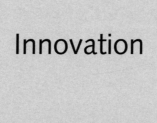

Innovation

22   PricewaterhouseCoopers – Crowdsourcing

This case study explains how PricewaterhouseCoopers (PwC) has amplified "one firm" working to create a client-focused team of thousands in order to deliver value for clients in a way never done before.

Executive summary

Overview

Social networking platforms have provided the opportunity for PwC to capture the power of their people and deliver exponential value for their clients. It has enabled 16,000 minds that don't think alike to collaborate and focus their experience and specialist expertise on a client's business issue.

Key findings

- It is critical to understand your client's business issue and then communicate this to the crowd in a clear and concise question.
- Gamification of ideas management does drive engagement – in a first client campaign, close to 70 per cent of PwC's people participated.

- You must identify a clear process for implementing ideas and communicate this to the crowd if they are to know that their efforts will make a real difference.
- A well-engaged team creates exceptional value for clients.

Recommendations

1. Crowdsourced innovation is not an abstract exercise to generate isolated, unstructured ideas.
2. Explain the rules of the game from the outset so that the crowd understand what is expected of them to win and how they will be recognized and rewarded.
3. Clear creative communications are required to fuel engagement and encourage favourable behaviours.

Background

Interviewee

Norman Lewis is a director at the UK firm of PwC and has been with the organization since July 2011 specializing in innovation and crowdsourcing.

Dan Schwarzmann is a partner with PwC and is responsible for One.

Norman Lewis
@Norm_Lewis

About PwC

PwC was created by the merger of Price Waterhouse and Coopers and Lybrand in 1998. For 160 years they have provided a vast range of clients with accounting, advisory and tax services. PwC's UK revenues in FY2012 were £2,621 million, and they have a headcount of more than 16,000, making them the leading professional services firm by revenues in the UK.

Their social media strategy

PwC's social media strategy is part of their digital strategy. This is focused on creating an environment

Dan Schwarzmann

that enables PwC's people to use their networks to build relationships through content, ideas and experience.

In the UK their approach has been very much based upon client expectations, which are to provide a modern experience rooted in their traditional strengths. This includes enabling:

- Clients to set rules of engagement – how, when and whom.
- Access to the firm's people, content and thinking – anywhere in the network and at anytime.
- Content that respects clients' time and finds them, rather than making them work to find it.
- The easy sharing of ideas among colleagues, networks and followers.
- Digital interaction to augment face-to-face relationships.
- An organization open to dialogue and collaboration.

Meeting this challenge has required a shift in culture and mindset. It has demanded the introduction of new content production processes, and the implementation of new approaches to communicating the company's ideas, thoughts and perspectives with their clients. It has also meant making the content fit for the digital age ensuring it is easy to consume, share and is produced in multiple formats, i.e. text, video, audio, links. It also has to be available wherever and whenever the clients want it. One such example is the PwC mobile application, which has already been downloaded 25,000 times from the Apple iTunes store and was cited by the *Sunday Times* as a top business web site.

The 2012 tax Budget is another good example of the strategy in practice. The company moved from a print and event based approach to digital engagement with their tax clients. The instant reaction of the partners watching the budget speech was pushed out on Twitter (to over 15,000 followers), so clients and journalists could be kept updated with their views in near real time. A few hours later on the same day they ran a live webcast with an in-depth discussion around the issues raised, during which clients could ask questions to panellists. The coverage was very well received and all centred on the day of the Budget and moved beyond their traditional approach of waiting for the overnight written analysis.

PwC's digital strategy is relentlessly focused on the needs and requirements of their target audiences – particularly the C-suite. It does not simply provide a showcase of PwC expertise. They now enable their people to use their networks to build relationships through content, curating the expertise clients need and offering this content how and when they choose. This has maximized the investment in their intellectual property, deepened relationships with clients and has brought their brand promise to life.

The case

The problem

As a professional services firm, PwC prides itself on providing creative solutions to client issues. In order to provide excellent client solutions, PwC have recognized the need to work as "one firm" – drawing on professionals across the firm's different specialisms to provide a seamless cohesive service for their clients. Until now working as one firm has taken the form of distinct teams across the organization working together.

The growing movement of social networking platforms into the enterprise, particularly those focused upon collaboration and idea management, provided an opportunity to take the one firm approach to a new level. These platforms could facilitate the creation of a truly one firm team, whereby all PwC employees could work together to generate ideas to solve a client's business issue.

Background

Like many things in life, a chance encounter was the catalyst for an innovative idea. Dan Schwarzmann and Norman Lewis met as a result of being on the same panel at the Battle of Ideas in 2011. During an exchange of views shared over a follow-up meeting, an insight emerged that brought together Norman's expertise in crowdsourced innovation and Dan's experience and passion for innovation in PwC: crowdsourcing, or the wisdom of crowds, now enabled through enterprise-grade social network platforms, could provide an opportunity for PwC to capture the creativity of their people in a fundamentally new way. The source of new solutions would not be just any crowd; it would be a "smart" crowd – all of PwC's people regardless of grade, location or line of service. And the focus of PwC's crowdsourcing activity would not be PwC itself, but rather its clients' business issues. The emerging crowdsourcing paradigm was to be "smartened" and inverted.

The concept works because it amplifies PwC's client-focussed culture. Instead of offering clients a small team of dedicated resources, PwC now had the possibility of offering its clients a team of thousands. By focussing on client issues in this way, PwC could bring a unique perspective and approach to clients in a manner that has never been done before.

The solution

PwC decided to create "One", a new "smart sourcing" innovation service, which invites all employees to generate ideas to solve a client's business issue. Whilst generating ideas using their 16,000 people, they wanted to move away from the traditional suggestions box and instead have an open and transparent process for idea generation, which relied on people to identify and filter the best ideas. In order for the process to be a success and truly promote collaboration across the company, there needed to be a level playing field where grade, location and business unit were irrelevant. The use of an idea management platform would be instrumental in facilitating the engagement and recognition of 16,000 people's involvement in the process.

Web site selection

The IT team undertook due diligence on a selection of idea management platforms. The chosen platform met their requirements in terms of filtering functionality, transparency and providing a level playing field for all participants. It also "gamified" the ideas generation process in order to enhance competition and promote collaboration in a way that drives engagement and structured outcomes. For example, individuals earn virtual currency for participating in the ideas generation process, including posting ideas, commenting and voting on their favourite ideas. They can then use this virtual currency to purchase items from a virtual store. Leader boards make visible the top ideas, top contributors, reputation scores and thus promote competition and recognize participation.

First pilot with a white goods manufacturer

In order to prove the One concept, PwC ran a pilot with one business unit of approximately 1,000 people focusing on a global white goods manufacturer's business issue. The pilot gave them the opportunity to gauge people's appetite for One, which exceeded their expectation with a high level of engagement across the business unit. Some excellent ideas were generated and the client's sales and marketing director commented:

You have come up with some really clever ideas and if that's three weeks' input then I am really impressed with what we can get out of this long term.

Second pilot with the partners and directors

As One was very different from any other PwC offering, it was necessary to obtain the buy-in of key stakeholders within the organization, including explaining the concept and the value that it would generate for their clients. The team responsible, therefore, decided to run a second pilot with the senior people across the firm. All partners and directors were invited to participate in a campaign that asked them for suggestions as to who should be the client for the first PwC-wide campaign. In addition to the partners it was necessary to obtain the support of other groups including the innovation team, the communications team and key members of the human capital team.

The second pilot highlighted the importance of managing a One campaign. When designing a campaign question you cannot be too prescriptive as this can stifle creativity. However, when you create an open forum for people to give their opinions or perspectives, there is the possibility that people will take the opportunity to raise issues that have not been dealt with elsewhere. They realized that careful community management is the best way to ensure that the campaign moves in the right direction. For example, sending out emails that highlight those ideas and behaviours that best meet the campaign requirements.

First company-wide campaign

The second pilot identified a FTSE100 company as the client for the first company-wide campaign. Through the engagement contract they aligned themselves with the success of the campaign so that they were remunerated according to the value that the employees created for the client.

Pre-launch teaser campaign

PwC launched a firm-wide teaser campaign in advance of revealing the details of the campaign to the staff. People were asked to provide a short response to the question "What does One mean to you?" and visual aids were placed in the entrance of their London office to promote anticipation of the upcoming campaign.

Campaign question

The team worked with the client to understand the complex business issue they faced and to identify a clear and concise question to ask the PwC employees. They created a short entertaining animated video to explain the client's complex business issue to their people.

Campaign launch

To launch the campaign, PwC's Chairman, Ian Powell, sent an email to the whole organization announcing the campaign question and encouraging employees to get involved. His email provided a link to the One site, where there was more information regarding the question, a video of an interview between Ian and the client explaining the challenge and a copy of the animated video. Within the first hour they had over 3,000 people visit the One site.

Communication strategy

Throughout the campaign they used a rigorous communications strategy to educate the people about the One process and to drive people to the site. This communication took the form of notifications via the firm's intranet news site PwC News, company-wide emails and plasma display screens. As they were communicating with the whole organization it was necessary to involve their internal communications team. These communications were subtly flexed to drive messages to the right areas and encourage favourable behaviour.

Expert reviews

The top ideas were subject to a review by both the PwC experts and the client's experts. Each idea was rated according to criteria previously agreed with the client. This review process helped to refine the ideas with the best potential to add value for the client.

Winning ideas

The "winning" ideas as selected by the "crowd" and the experts were presented to the client. The client selected 11 of these ideas and three with significant revenue potential are in development.

The idea owners were publicly recognized by the chairman and each person and their friends and family were invited to attend a special event hosted by their executive board.

The CEO of the global division of one FTSE100 client commented:

> I spend a lot of time working with big multinational companies all around the world and I have to say that this One idea is really unique. I've not seen anything else like it and I take my hat off to the individuals who put this together . . . it's a very innovative and forward looking initiative.

Results

The measures they use are based upon verifiable data. The most critical relate to outcomes for the client and levels of engagement of PwC staff:

Outcomes: 50 ideas were presented to the client of which 11 were selected and three with large revenue potential are currently in development.

Levels of participation: over 10,500 PwC employees participated across all regions, lines of service and grades, generating over 500 ideas, nearly 34,000 page views, 1,805 comments and 4,206 votes.

Critical success factors

Crowd or smart sourced innovation flourishes in environments where problem solving is ingrained in the culture of the organization. This is the case for a number of reasons:

1. Understanding the client and their issues is ingrained in the culture. This is crucial to framing the correct question that facilitates participation and generates ideas that deliver new value.
2. Partners and employees thrive in solving client problems and adding value. One also enables and values employee participation; making it easy for people to get involved, as well as recognizing and rewarding participation.

Lessons learned

Crowdsourced innovation is not an abstract exercise to generate isolated, unstructured ideas. As mentioned already, it is necessary to understand fully the client's issue. The next step is to work with the client to pose the question in a clear and concise way so that everyone can understand and engage with the problem.

It is important that the "crowd" understands the rules of the game from the outset, i.e. how the process works, what is expected of them to win and how they will be recognized or rewarded. Reward and recognition must be transparent, as well as aligned to the community's values. Diverse workforces need a range of rewards and recognition, which could include charitable donations, financial incentives or a simple thank you from senior stakeholders.

Communications throughout the campaign are essential in driving participation and engagement. The frequency and mediums need consideration;

using a combination of different media worked well, including emails, videos and posters.

Finally, a clear process of implementation must be identified and agreed upfront and updates on implementation are required long after the campaign has ended to ensure the "crowd" know they are making a real difference and, therefore, are incentivized to engage in the next project.

Norman concludes:

> It is critical to understand your client's business issue and then communicate this to the crowd in a clear and concise question – if you are not solving the right problem, you are creating new ones and no value for your client or yourself.

Want more? See what has been said about this case or get involved and discuss it with the author and other readers on our LinkedIn group, find it by visiting http://www.socialmedia-mba.com *or search for "The Social Media MBA Alumni".*

23   Electrolux – Internal Crowdsourcing

 Household appliance group Electrolux engaged 40 per cent of their white-collar employees in a global, 72-hour ideation event. The result was a step forward on their journey towards becoming a world-class, market-driven consumer innovation company.

Executive summary

Overview

The Electrolux Group's innovation ambition is to create new products consumers prefer and to do it faster than the competition. One way for a large, global company to make size a virtue instead of an obstacle to increasing speed is to create cross-regional, cross-functional connections between employees and engage them in the ideation challenge.

Key findings

- Employee passion and creativity can be effectively unleashed in the crowdsourcing environment. The benefits include accelerating the innovation pipeline of the company and creating a lasting impact on corporate culture by making it more highly engaging, inspiring, collaborative and entrepreneurial.

These changes to the culture could potentially lead to innovations in all functions, not just product development.

- When an online ideation session is properly constructed, it is possible to get a high level of engagement. Electrolux inspired more than 7,200 employees (out of a target audience of 18,000) to contribute more than 3,500 ideas, 14,000 comments and 20,000 votes in its first global innovation jam.
- Visible backing by senior management is the single biggest success factor in overcoming scepticism. A single email from the Electrolux president and CEO led to a three-fold increase in participation within a day.
- Creating a playful competition helps generate enthusiasm and underlines that the initiative was out of the ordinary for this relatively conservative corporate culture.
- A single successful internal social media exercise can overcome very strong scepticism and create momentum for more engagement via social media. The Electrolux Group's first innovation jam was so successful that they continue to plan and run more global innovation jams. Several of its business areas are also planning their own crowdsourcing projects: in total, Electrolux will run seven crowdsourcing initiatives in any one-year period, all based on the platform for the original innovation jam.

Recommendations

1. Make sure your event is well enough designed that you can get top management to personally engage in the event and support it visibly, putting their credibility on the line.
2. Do not underestimate scepticism, lack of understanding, time conflicts or lack of interest. Plan communications months ahead and be a warrior.
3. Anticipate that once scepticism is overcome, employees will want to contribute and participate as long as the purpose is clear – and especially if they will be recognized or there is something to win. To be seen within the organization, to make a difference and to connect with colleagues are highly motivating. So are prizes.
4. Use every trick you know of that you would use in a product launch. Succeed once and every similar initiative will be much easier to promote.

What you need to know

Electrolux is striving to be a market-driven consumer-oriented innovation company that creates new products, accessories, consumables and services that consumers prefer faster than its competitors do. One way it is doing that is by engaging its employees in global, cross-regional, cross-business area, cross-functional idea creation. Last year, Electrolux ran its first online innovation jam ideation session focused on a key innovation area: culinary enjoyment.

As a project, the innovation jam faced a certain amount of scepticism. Overcoming that required the services of a PR agency and a great deal of support to heads of communications in various parts of the Group. Top management backing and high-quality supporting materials such as videos and posters were instrumental in getting buy-in from communications heads within the Group's business areas. Communications emphasized the business relevance, which was reinforced by the participation of a cross-functional project team. Communications also emphasized the fun of it all, the chance to be heard and the chance to connect with others. The CEO asked employees to bring their passion and creativity.

Thorough, detailed planning for driving engagement for each stage is important. These plans should be shared at a very early stage with the people responsible for communication.

Background

Interviewees

The project is owned by the heads of the Electrolux Innovation Triangle Council – marketing, design and R&D – who are members of the Electrolux Group's senior management team,

MaryKay Kopf has a BS in finance and an MBA in group management. Previously she has held senior management positions at DuPont North America, Europe, Middle East and Africa, and globally, 1991– 2003. MaryKay joined Electrolux in 2003 as vice president of Brand Marketing, Electrolux Major Appliances North America, 2003. She has held the CMO and senior vice president positions since 2011.

MaryKay Kopf

With a PhD in architecture, Stefano Marzano has been chief design officer since 2012. He was previously senior designer for Philips Ireland, major domestic appliances division, 1973–1978; design group leader for

Stefano Marzano

Philips Data Systems and Telecommunications division, 1978–1982; director of Philips Ireland Design Center (major domestic appliances) 1982–1989; vice president and head of corporate industrial design at Whirlpool International (a Whirlpool and Philips joint venture) 1989–1991; and executive vice president and chief design officer at Philips 1991–2011.

Jan Brockmann joined Electrolux as head of R&D, major appliances in 2010 and is currently chief technology officer, since 2011. With an MS in mechanical engineering and an MBA, Jan has held management positions in Valeo Group, 1994–1999; was project manager in Roland Berger Strategy Consultants GmbH, 2000–2001; and held senior management positions in Volkswagen Group, 2001–2010.

Jan Brockmann

About Electrolux

Electrolux is a global leader in home appliances and appliances for professional use, selling more than 40 million products to customers in 150 countries every year. The company focuses on innovations that are thoughtfully designed, based on extensive insights to ensure they meet the real needs of consumers and professionals.

Electrolux products include refrigerators, dishwashers, washing machines, vacuum cleaners, cookers and air-conditioners sold under brands such as Electrolux, AEG, Eureka and Frigidaire. In 2011 Electrolux had sales of SEK 102 billion and 58,000 employees.

Their social media strategy

Electrolux have an integrated approach to social media and PR.

The Electrolux innovation jam and the communications surrounding it were largely based on the Electrolux global consumer engagement strategy. The project team verified its communications plan with Mattias Rådström, vice president of social media and PR, who is responsible for the strategy.

As in the consumer strategy, engagement is important and the first step was to determine the right engagement strategy towards employees. With consumers, social media also integrates with and amplifies traditional PR, as well as impacting shopping and 360 consumer experience. This thinking was adapted to an internal audience, as the team set priorities and objectives for interactions and engagement within different areas such as participating, voting on ideas, commenting on ideas, interactions per registered user, etc.

Whether it is an internal or external social media exercise, one task is to define which platforms to use and what role they will play. This means evaluating each platform in the engagement ecosystem on its own merits, since people have different uses and expectations on each and one common metric will not fairly judge different platforms. Sharing may prove most important to you on Twitter, while commenting might be the primary goal for Facebook and simply driving views the goal for YouTube. In this case, there was one platform, the "innovation jam" platform, and the metrics were straightforward: employee participation rate per division, ideas and comments submitted, favourable and unfavourable votes recorded and, finally, expert judgement on the quality of the ideas.

The Electrolux social media strategy is global and local and Electrolux uses the word glocal. The reason for this is that brand is global and the global presence should reflect the efforts that best embody the position and vision of the brand. Social and traditional PR must be tied together. All content should be consumer based and reflect the best of the brand. But social is local and country communications (e.g. a local country Facebook page) should be in the local language providing relevant and relatable messages that engage the audience in a conversation around programming as well as supporting product news. The Electrolux innovation jam followed this pattern to a large extent, with centralized messaging and centrally produced communications assets (videos, posters, T-shirts, stickers, intranet articles, etc.) that regions and countries could translate and adapt. Regional, divisional and country organizations also adapted the communications to the channels that had proven most effective in reaching their employees. In North America, town meetings were effective. Elsewhere, phone calls and word of mouth were decisive.

The Electrolux vision is to have millions of conversations conducted on Electrolux channels – on key social networks in all major geographic markets. This will build brands and deliver sales opportunities. The consumer experience is enhanced through publisher-quality storytelling that delivers the right information at the right time in the right place. Another important aspect is the "always-on" approach. The old method of having few large campaigns has now been replaced with an always-on approach. The Group strives to have an ongoing conversation with their audience every day of the year and believe they cannot afford to be silent during long periods. Their philosophy is that by being responsive to customer needs and expectations, trust and loyalty will naturally follow.

While there will not be millions of conversations, innovation is an always-on theme at Electrolux. Moreover, for the real benefits of the innovation jam to be fully realized, significant follow-up communication is planned. This will cover what is happening to the ideas, how they are being developed and how the database is being used. Related future innovation initiatives are also being tied into the original 2012 innovation jam.

The case

The problem

A passion for innovation has long been a core pillar of Electrolux. Today, the company is striving to be a market-driven, consumer-oriented innovation company that creates new products, features, consumables and services that 70 per cent of consumers prefer and to do it faster than their competitors. In line with that ambition, the company has formed an innovation triangle council, made up of the heads of marketing, R&D and design, and undertaken a number of initiatives within the organization. One of these initiatives was a global, 72-hour, online ideation session called the Electrolux innovation jam, which took place in the autumn of 2012.

Before the innovation jam, the most accessible way to share an idea was an email drop box to the CEO. In this scenario, the burden of evaluation, implementation and tracking starts with one person and then is delegated outward. There was no universally accessible tool that:

- Took advantage of and encouraged crowdsourcing.
- Collected and categorized ideas.
- Self-evaluated ideas.

"When we started this, we did not have a way to formally harness the knowledge of our employees beyond emails, suggestion boxes, surveys and meetings", recalls Heather Hanson, head of marketing effectiveness, global marketing. "We knew there had to be a better way", she continued.

"We asked ourselves do we gain access to all of that knowledge and experience that our people have? How do we engage them, motivate and inspire them, and leverage their natural collaborative inclinations?"

The proposed solution? A crowdsourced innovation jam that was self-regulating and fully trackable and reportable.

If successful, the event would not only result in a database of new ideas, it would:

- leverage untapped creativity in their employees worldwide, allowing everyone in the company to be an innovator;
- forge new connections between employees across regions and functions;
- promote cross-functional, cross-regional collaboration;

- demonstrate to employees how much senior management values creativity;
- lead to innovations in all functions, not just product development;
- improve the strength of the company innovation pipeline with more rich ideas that cut across multiple offer types and solutions;
- cultivate an entrepreneurial mindset across the Group;
- be a step towards creating a culture of market-driven innovation throughout the company; and
- bring employee engagement to the innovation strategy.

"We wanted to channel all our employees' brainpower towards a defined strategic challenge, send a clear message about where we should focus our attention and resources, create a transparent way to track and report progress on innovation throughout the company", comments Li Zhen, innovation marketing manager.

Background

The notion of getting every employee to bring creativity to his or her work and become an innovator is not new. Electrolux has taken several initiatives to accomplish that in order to deliver on their innovation ambition, which is to deliver new products that are preferred by consumers and do it faster than competitors do. It is a tall order and requires making the whole organization more agile and more innovation-oriented from top to bottom.

Yet, like any other large, global organization, Electrolux faces challenges in getting people to break habits, change silo thinking and work across regions and functions. With a sustainable, solid, financial track record, the organization does not face a crisis or existential threat that would drive people to change longstanding habits.

Against this background, Electrolux decided to launch their first ever global innovation jam session. The idea was to activate employees, "the crowd", with a combination of game mechanics (leaderboards, scores and ranking) and enterprise-wide recognition (earning points and badges along the way). The initiative would integrate social collaboration with enterprise workflow, use the crowd to create new innovations to meet business opportunities, channel participation towards areas of mutual interest and create a formal way of managing the "idea funnel".

In January 2012, Electrolux paid a visit to Volvo Technology to exchange good case practice between the two companies on innovation. "We were inspired by the innovation jam they conducted in 2011", recalls Li Zhen, "We shared the Volvo case back to the innovation team and started the sell-in process."

Meanwhile, CMO MaryKay Kopf learned how Citibank approached innovation. They had also done a successful innovation jam but in a different way. By then, organization engagement had also been identified as one of the three innovation building blocks for Electrolux. With the inspirational external benchmark and identified internal needs, the ground was prepared to run the innovation jam on a global scale.

"I considered our first innovation jam a 'global pilot'", Kopf recalls. "I never considered doing it regionally or on a smaller scale."

> There were several reasons for that. First, our focus is to drive global innovation versus regional innovation so we can leverage our strengths and scale. Second, regionally we have different areas of excellence in innovation but we needed a better mechanism for sharing and collaborating. And I believed that the innovation jam could unleash that.
>
> Finally, it was an opportunity to put innovation in the hands of our people. It was very much about improving the social dynamics and grass-roots idea sharing, idea building and listening to the voice of our employees through voting. In a way, that was what we were really piloting – changing the spirit and culture of how we work.

Nothing like this had ever been attempted before at Electrolux, the concept of crowdsourcing was unfamiliar to most employees and there was no obvious benefit to individual employees nor any obvious bottom-line benefit to their work groups.

It was therefore necessary to overcome this lack of understanding (and even, in some cases, outright scepticism, as if the innovation jam were an "ivory tower" initiative of no practical importance) and find ways of not just informing them about the initiative but engaging their active participation.

The solution

The innovation triangle council chose "culinary enjoyment" to be the theme of the first global Electrolux innovation jam. Culinary enjoyment is one of the company's innovation focus areas. It was chosen because it is one of the most important areas and because it is the most applicable to all Electrolux employees, whether they work on major, small or professional appliances. Innovation jam participants would be asked to submit ideas on a product, feature, accessory, consumable or service related to culinary enjoyment – the process from shopping for food to storing, cooking, eating and cleaning up.

iJam
Innovation iJam

Electrolux

TOP 10 SELECTED: ON TO THE DRAGONS' DEN!

The Top 10 have been selected. Now the idea owners will be working on their pitches to the Dragons' Den starting at 13:00 CET on December 7. So mark your calendar and plan to tune in with some friends and colleagues as we take one more step towards becoming a world-class consumer innovation company!

The challenge: By 2017, Electrolux will be known for its world-class **Culinary Enjoyment** by consumers and professionals around the world. **Culinary Enjoyment** is the **pleasure** you can take in the **moments** of planning, cooking, eating, socialising and cleaning during your working week and weekends, whether you are in your home, on the move or at a restaurant. Look for inspiration in your own life and share your ideas with us.

THE QUESTION:

How can we bring *culinary enjoyment* to consumers and professionals around the world?

VIEW ALL IDEAS

SEE HOW IT WORKS

BE INSPIRED

"The brief to employees was based on the importance of innovation focus areas in the portfolio globally", says Anton Lundberg, vice president of market driven innovation, global marketing. "The ambition was to improve our existing innovation portfolio to be populated based on crowdsourcing input."

After a competitive bidding process, Electrolux selected a vendor specialized in these types of initiatives. The Electrolux project team, together with the vendor, tailored the functions, chose the graphics, wrote the instructions and determined the flow of the event.

The innovation jam event took place over a 72-hour period. Participants first registered on the site and then submitted their idea(s) and commented on other people's ideas. For each idea, the idea owner had to fill in answers to questions in text boxes about who the idea would be for, what problem it would solve, how it would work, etc.

Participants added comments, made suggestions and clicked on a "thumbs up" or "thumbs down" button for each idea, gaining points for their participation. Innovation coaches from the marketing, R&D and design departments were trained for each regional time zone. These coaches looked closely at the ideas that attracted the most attention, made comments and moved some of the ideas into a second stage of the top ideas. Because of the overwhelming response, that second stage grew to several hundred ideas.

After the 72 hours were up, innovation coaches took a week to look into the ideas that received the top ratings by participants and created a short list of 20 ideas. These ideas were then entered into a game in which participants invested the points they had gained during 72 hours into the ideas they liked best. At the end of a week, the list was reduced to the top ten ideas backed by participants and innovation coaches.

Two weeks later, these ten ideas were submitted to a panel of the Electrolux president and CEO, the heads of the six divisions and the heads of the innovation triangle council. The panel met in the boardroom in Electrolux headquarters in Stockholm and by video conference. As insurance against technical problems, the idea owners and teams were required to submit a video presenting their ideas. There were also two dress rehearsals to test communications and iron out any technical kinks. The ten videos were each followed by a live presentation and Q&A from the panellists. The panellists selected three winners.

High-stakes communication

Overall, the central communications plan was designed to create awareness that this was a game-changing initiative, not just another roll-out. The project

Welcome Message (Post Idea)

How can we bring *culinary enjoyment* to consumers and professionals around the world?

Title *

Description* [?]

| B | I | U | ≡ |

Who is your idea for?* [?]

| B | I | U | ≡ |

What are the needs and problems that your idea is targeting? * [?]

| B | I | U | ≡ |

Please indicate if this is a team submission* [?]

Please supply the names of the Team Members [?]

Innovation Feedback (Review For Use Only in Stage 2) [?]

| B | I | U | ≡ |

Category *

--Select One--

Review Submitted Ideas
Make sure you have taken an opportunity to read through other submissions. If your idea has already been posted by someone else, add your comments and recommendations to the existing post. You can also show you like an idea by clicking on the "thumbs up" icon.

Give your Idea a Descriptive Title
The title should clearly articulate your idea. This is what people will see first as they scan the ideas. Try to keep your idea title specific and simple.

Describe Your Idea
Write a clear and succinct Description of your idea. What is the solution it provides?

For whom is your idea?
Include some information regarding the person, consumer group or corporate who would benefit most from your idea. Try to be specific.

Needs and Problems?
Describe any problems your idea is targeting. What issues will your idea resolve for your target. Consider motivation, wishes, physical and emotional difficulties.

Provide Enough Detail
Make sure that your post has enough detail so that a reader understands the topic. This will help generate discussion on your post and will make it easier to evaluate.

Team Submission
Is your idea the result of a team effort? If yes, please complete this question in the Idea Form.

Team Member Names
Provide the names of each of your Team Members. Be sure you include everyone now!

Champion Your Idea!
You can promote your idea by using the Tell a Friend option. Monitoring the status of your idea by reviewing and responding to comments made by other participants will encourage on-going collaboration. As the champion of your idea, feel free to make adjustments to your idea submission as needed.

team knew that if the initiative failed, it would be a while before a similar project would be approved again. If it succeeded, however, it would not only make a positive impact, it would lead to the demand for more innovation jams in the future, each of which would be easier to promote based on the success of the first one. The project team therefore used a variety of tools including stickers, posters, PowerPoints, intranet articles – even a jazz band "jamming" at Electrolux Group headquarters in Stockholm – to launch the three-day event.

Core messages were also developed. In a video, the Electrolux president and CEO asked all employees to "Bring your passion, bring your creativity"; a message that appeared prominently in an animated banner on the intranet. In another video, CMO MaryKay Kopf made the connection between strategy and fun, saying that the innovation jam would be "part of our journey to becoming a world-class innovation company. It's also going to be a lot of fun and a chance to share ideas with other employees throughout the company."

The CEO, the innovation triangle heads and the heads of all of the business areas also set an example by announcing the times and days they would be participating, further reinforcing the idea that everyone should take part. Other themes included empowerment and the chance to make one's voice heard, as well as the chance to be recognized by peers and managers.

Central support for local plans
Electrolux is divided into six different business areas, each with its own head of communications. It was therefore important to task the business areas'

communications heads with creating and implementing communications plans that were appropriate for their resources and organizations. The central role was to provide communications assets and whatever support was requested. This approach, which was based on the Electrolux glocal social media strategy outlined already, allowed the use of communications channels that were most effective at each division or location (discussed further).

It also proved to be useful to set up competition between the business areas. For this, Electrolux chose as a KPI the percentage of each business area's employees who had registered for the event. These figures were updated daily and published on the Electrolux Group's intranet. They were also presented to the CEO and the business area heads in a senior management team meeting. When the head of one business area, who was an innovation champion in the group, saw how far behind his organization was in the percentage of employees registering, he called in his senior management team and told them how important this initiative was – he wanted high participation. Within a day, that division became one of the leaders.

The project team commissioned an external PR agency to produce high-quality video interviews with the CEO, the CMO, the chief R&D officer and the chief design officer. These demonstrated senior management backing. To convey the idea that it was a fun and interesting challenge, the agency also produced a video of employee ambassadors urging their colleagues to register and participate. These videos were filmed in the Electrolux Group's new innovation lab in Stockholm to help tie the innovation jam into the Group's overall innovation strategy. The videos were uploaded to the intranet in the final two weeks before registration officially opened.

The intranet was also re-skinned with innovation jam-themed graphics and animated banners. This was the first time that the intranet look and feel had ever been changed to promote any initiative or that animated banners had been used. This not only drew attention to the event, it also served to underline that something extraordinary was about to take place. The PR agency created a consistent, fun-looking graphic profile for all communications – PowerPoints, posters videos, the intranet skin, the innovation jam platform, etc.

Building interest via guerrilla and word-of-mouth
Like a major product launch, a gradual build-up of interest leading to a big reveal was a key success factor. The vendor had recommended a registration period of between two and six weeks before the 72-hour event. The project team discussed the benefits of each time frame. This was one of the most important decision points.

A long registration period would be the more cautious approach. It would allow more time to get sign-ups, diagnose problems and make adjustments. The downside would be a possible drop in interest over a several-week period. So the team decided to gamble, compressing the window between the official opening of registration and the start of the event to just eight working days. This would maximize the intensity of the communications spotlight on the event.

With such a short window between the start of registration and the event, it was important to build buzz ahead of time. Therefore, in the weeks and days leading up to the official announcement on the Electrolux Group's global intranet, posters and stickers were also prepared and distributed to local offices. These included cryptic posters that did not refer to the event directly but were used as guerrilla marketing in the days leading up to the launch of registration.

It was clear from the beginning that informing people and raising awareness was only part of the challenge. They also had to be motivated to act. That is why the communications plan relied heavily on person-to-person communication, not just traditional media tools.

A top-down word-of-mouth campaign was also created. This operated on several levels. Communications heads distributed a PowerPoint presentation explaining the event for managers to cascade through the organization during presentations to their teams. Communications heads and innovation coaches also appointed ambassadors to advocate for the event and answer questions. An innovation activation community previously created, with its own intranet site, was also brought into the loop.

Personal email appeals

And everyone involved in the project sent personal emails to some of their close colleagues advocating the event and asking the recipients to pass the message along to their close colleagues. To prevent people from feeling spammed by multiple emails about the event, the advocates were asked to personalize each email, not just cc a lot of people from their address books. These pre-launch activities resulted in nearly 1,000 registrations before the official launch of registration.

Constant support throughout

A dedicated communications manager also worked full time to respond to miscellaneous requests for information and such additional help as pre-written texts for managers to email, additional PowerPoint slides, taking points, etc.

Buy-in by the business areas' communication heads was a decisive factor and they came up with some creative ways to communicate. Registration activities included:

- In São Paulo, actors playing the role of chefs (in line with the event's "culinary enjoyment" theme) walked desk to desk helping people register.

- In Singapore, jars of specially labelled "i-Jam" were given to the first 100 people to register, temporary murals were created and displayed on office walls and adhesive placemats were stuck to cafeteria tables.

- In Charlotte, North Carolina, a member of the communications team set up a registration table in the company cafeteria and asked people to register.

Activities to kick off the 72-hour event included:

- In Sydney, tea and scones were served.
- In Singapore, a "war room" was set up, where trained staff helped people with the language differences.
- In Stockholm, a jazz band was hired to "jam" in the lobby of the headquarters building and fortune cookies with customized fortunes were handed out to people as they arrived at work.
- Globally, the Electrolux president and CEO called for everyone to participate for at least one hour.
- Globally, the Electrolux president and CEO, the division heads and the heads of the innovation triangle council all added ideas and comments and publicized their own participation in the 72-hour event.

Results

The results were easy to quantify and automatically tracked by the site's software. A total of 41 per cent of the target audience of 18,000 white-collar employees signed up to participate (against an average for other companies of about 20 per cent). More than 3,500 ideas were submitted, which would have taken months to generate via any conventional process. There were also approximately 12,000 comments and 20,000 votes for and against ideas. These easily exceeded all expectations for engagement.

As important were the qualitative results. Just as MaryKay had hoped, many employees were so enthusiastic that they said this type of ideation event should go on permanently and expressed satisfaction that they were being listened to. The event was also so successful that almost all of the business areas, even those that were initially sceptical, requested to have their own innovation jam sessions.

Electrolux, in addition to capturing more than 3,500 ideas, now has a process in place to catalogue good ideas from employees. And product development teams are now consulting the pool of ideas for general inspiration and insights into consumer preferences as well as for specific ideas to develop.

Critical success factors

The single most important success factor for creating participation was visible backing by senior management. A single email from the Electrolux Group's president and CEO, to all employees urging them to participate, tripled registration within a day. As mentioned already, when the head of one lagging business area called in his management team and told them that iJam was a top priority to accelerate innovation, registration went up ten-fold within two days and wound up reaching the highest sign-up rate (70 per cent) of all of the business areas. Other success factors include:

1. Asking each employee for one hour for innovation. This was a reasonable request from the CEO (who pledged to do the same) and was enough time for employees to engage in the innovation jam. Many employees chose to spend more time as the event was interesting and fun.
2. A well-designed platform and IT framework. Electrolux compared vendors and took steps to modify bandwidth parameters to handle an anticipated increase in load during the event. There were no failures in access to or operation of the site during the 72 hours.
3. Inspiring, multi-pronged communications. Informing people is one thing. Getting them to take time from their other duties to take a desired action is much more difficult. Electrolux used professionally produced videos and posters, cascaded information through PowerPoints in meetings, had ambassadors promote the event via viral "pass-it-on" emails, put on live events and handed out promotional items such as jars of "i-Jam" and fortune cookies.
4. A well-developed rewards and recognition programme. As one executive in North America said, "We are competitive. Just give us something to win. It doesn't have to be much." In this case, a rewards and recognition programme was announced in line with the event's theme of culinary enjoyment. It gave prizes to each day's top collaborators, and to the semi-finalists, finalists and three winners. Rewards included gourmet cookware, gourmet restaurant vouchers and a high-end, catered party for each of the top three winners. Registration jumped in all divisions where the pro-gramme was clearly communicated.
5. Trained innovation coaches to shepherd the ideas through the event. Criteria for choosing innovation coaches were prepared by the project team based on cross-function knowledge, experience and passion for innovation. In another case of senior management backing, the CMO asked each division

head for nominees. The project team then consolidated the nominations from the divisions and announced the innovation coaches for each time zone. "I think they played a pivotal role in fostering meaningful conversation under each idea post", said Li Zhen.

> They posted challenging questions to help the idea owners refine their ideas and other users to contribute to the ideas – they really guided the dialogue and development. Also, as a group, the innovation coaches were the only ones who read through all of the ideas. They provided important input to funnel down ideas from 3,500 to the top 20. They also played the role of ambassadors from the start and generated positive word-of-mouth throughout the divisions.

Lessons learned

Do not underestimate the complexity of a global roll-out, especially when it is a concept completely new to the organization and one that requires people to *take action*, not just be informed. As in a large, external PR event, end-to-end planning is essential, with as much of the material as possible prepared and distributed well in advance.

Inform participating areas of the company at least four to six months ahead of the launch of an initiative of this magnitude in order to get it onto the agendas of major management meetings of top managers, and ideally share plans in time for them to be included in annual communications budgeting. "By the time we really got started, we were only a few days ahead of one business area's top management conference, so we could only get a couple of slides into the communication head's presentation and maybe three minutes of discussion", said Li Zhen.

Do not underestimate obstacles. "The Asia-Pacific business unit kept pushing for more information before we had it ready", Li Zhen explained. "We really underestimated the effort involved in getting communications in English in Singapore ready to go in Chinese in Beijing, for example. We also underestimated how much information people there would want before they got started. We would add at least two extra weeks for translation and distribution next time."

Inform the other communications actors about the entire event from the beginning. "We were so highly focused on just selling the idea and getting cooperation for the sign-up phase that we neglected to fully inform the comms heads that people would need to actually participate with an idea after they signed up", said Li Zhen. "On the one hand, we had to overcome scepticism and getting people signed up was the basis for everything. There was also a lot to explain. So we wanted to keep the focus on the here and now. On the other hand, people had to scramble more than they should have to get people to take the next step."

Compress the time frame. "We were initially going to announce the event four weeks before it started", commented Li Zhen. "But then we realized that we could not keep people's enthusiasm up that long and people would be bored by the concept before we started. So we compressed all of the promotion into two weeks and finished up with eye-catching physical events where possible. On the other hand, I don't think the week between 72 hours and the final judging of the ten ideas was a disadvantage. I think it actually gave us the opportunity to build up momentum to generate a more thorough and transformational organization impact. However, it is actually a challenge for the project team, infrastructure and resources to keep up the momentum within the time span of the two-month innovation jam experience."

Don't count solely on the intranet and other mass communication. "Our intranet is well thought of. Still, fewer than 1,000 people watched the video with the CEO launching the event", Li Zhen reported. "On the other hand, more than 2,000 people responded within 24 hours to his email asking them to register for the event. Person-to-person communication and physical events drove a lot of the enthusiasm for the initial launch."

Clearly communicate from the beginning idea selection criteria and game rules that reward and recognize by level and quality of participation.

Enabled and easy access through portable devices would have been a big help, since people have time to participate when they are outside the office.

Implement effortless login and registration. "We did not have single sign-on, with a direct link from our intranet", Li Zhen explained. "We could not solve the technical obstacles in time. So we had an extra hurdle to participation that took time and resources to overcome."

Be prepared for success. "We underestimated how enthusiastic people would be", commented Li Zhen. "As a result, we did not have enough innovation coaches managing the flow of ideas through the event and evaluating them. They were overloaded, which led to some delays. If we had known we would get such an overwhelming response, we would have trained at least twice as many!"

Want more? See what has been said about this case or get involved and discuss it with the author and other readers on our LinkedIn group, find it by visiting http://www.socialmedia-mba.com *or search for "The Social Media MBA Alumni".*

HR

24 HCL – Social for HR

 This case study will look at how global
IT service provider HCL has managed to
attract the best talent, and engage with every
level of its 90,000 person employee base, through social media. It will offer
examples and best practices that can benefit companies of all sizes.

Executive summary

Overview

Using a combination of innovative bespoke platforms and widely available
networks, HCL has incorporated social media into its core philosophy of
"employees first, customers second" (EFCS). This philosophy partnered with
the power of social media has helped them to engage with employees in
unforeseen ways and has created tangible business benefits.

Key findings

- An employee exchange that has generated ideas worth millions of pounds.
- Hugely effective HR policy which focuses on securing the best young talent
  through social media channels.
- Helped create an engaged, motivated and innovative workforce.

Recommendations

1. Social media is not an experiment, if you are not putting it at the core of your marketing or people strategy, you're planning is not complete.
2. The CEO of the future will be social savvy.
3. It is critical to leverage your strengths in marketing on social media with employee branding and vice versa.
4. From a small business, to a huge business – the barrier to entry for social media is incredibly low. The risk is not committing.

What you need to know

HCL has implemented a flexible and innovative social media led HR policy, which has benefited both staff and company.

The case will discuss HCL's business and how it operates globally, as well as introducing Prithvi Shergill, Chief HR Officer at HCL and the driving force behind the scheme.

The case will also look at the following:

- How HCL's social media strategy is incorporated across all employee bases and hiring practices.
- The overall business environment that HCL operates in.
- The business drivers that led the company to adopt social media policies.
- Issues that HCL had to overcome to ensure the schemes were successful.
- The huge benefits that the company has managed to enjoy and the key factors in its success.
- Lessons for other companies wishing to emulate the social media policies.

Background

Interviewee

Prithvi Shergill oversees the company's many social media initiatives and is a professional with more than 20 years of experience committed to adding value to organizations and enhancing individuals.

In his role as a steward of HCL's employee first, customers second philosophy, Prithvi ensures that the

Prithvi Shergill
Twitter: @hcltech

policies, programmes, processes and practices for people at HCL support individuals. In doing so, employees are encouraged to join, learn, perform, collaborate and grow their diverse contributions and capability, thus increasing the "value zone" created each time they interact with clients.

Prior to joining HCL in April 2012, Prithvi was a partner at Accenture. Since 2004, he has held various responsibilities to enhance functional effectiveness and efficiency, align design and delivery of talent acquisition and management programmes and practices and strengthen strategy development and execution. In addition to leading HR for Accenture's businesses in India, he helped shape the human capital strategy for Accenture in various geographies and supported their technology growth platform as its global talent strategist. He also served as the inclusion and diversity sponsor for Accenture India.

About HCL

As a $4.3 billion global company, HCL Technologies bring IT and engineering services expertise under one roof to solve complex business problems for their clients. Leveraging an extensive global offshore infrastructure and network of offices in 31 countries, HCL aims to provide holistic, multi-service delivery in such industries as financial services, manufacturing, consumer services, public services and healthcare.

A micro-vertical strategy, built on strong domain expertise, ensures that no matter how complex a company's business problem is, HCL can offer a solution that is sustainable and innovation-driven.

That innovation is fuelled by EFCS – a unique management approach that unleashes the creative energies of HCL Technologies' 90,000 plus employees, and puts this collective force to work in the service of customers' business problems.

By engaging HCL employees in a way that allows them to deliver business value – whether it involves enterprise application services, IT infrastructure management, custom application services, engineering and R&D services, business services or enterprise transformation services – HCL turns technology into a distinct competitive advantage for their customers.

The success of HCL's customers' businesses, however, is part of a bigger picture. Sustainability has been and will remain a cornerstone of the global operations. HCL believes business growth can only be sustained when pursuits of profit are balanced with social and environmental imperatives. For example, HCL's impact on the communities where they operate, in the form of local job creation, is a central definition of success.

Their social media strategy

There are two main strands to HCL's use of social media within the HR prism. One is to focus on attracting and hiring top talent to the company through social media channels such as LinkedIn and the other is to use social media as a key pillar in their unique EFCS philosophy – which engages and empowers current employees.

At HCL the recruitment team is directly responsible for hiring through social media. It's a big operation, as the company has an employee base of more than 90,000 people, so it's a constant process to be sourcing the best talent. Recruitment is all about building awareness, consideration and targeting the right set of people. Social media allows the team to do this more effectively than every traditional method available. All recruiters are actively encouraged to engage with candidate groups on various social media.

As well as using social media as a tool for recruitment HCL has harnessed the power of social networks as a force for internal employee motivation, collaboration and inspiration. In January 2011 HCL created its own social media platform to help create strong communication channels with a new generation of workers. Built on a platform of "decoding individuality", MEME, the internal social network, has proved incredibly successful as thousands of employees have embraced it. MEME has a number of the standard applications like network of friends and colleagues, tech forums, posts/comments, pictures, tags, document share and group conversations.

The strategy behind MEME is to improve efficiency, drive employee engagement and create a forum where ideas can be generated, which will help drive the company forward. On all fronts it has proved incredibly successful.

The case

The problem

HCL faced problems that many large companies face – how can a business attract and hire the best talent, then once hired what can be done to ensure those employees are engaged, motivated, productive and result oriented?

The difference was that HCL jumped over these hurdles by asking what the latest generation in the workforce are looking for. Generation Y, or the millennial generation, are those workers who were born between the late 1970s and early 1990s. Generation Y are technology savvy and creative. Not only do they create very strong informal connections, speak their minds and have a digital form of expression but they also despise archaic systems and traditional modes of communication in the workplace.

It was clear to HCL that attracting, inspiring and working with Generation Y would take a great change in thinking. At the same time it was vital to bring more established workers into the fold so that experience and innovation were shared both ways between different generations of workers.

Background

HCL have a large and diverse workforce. They are constantly looking to hire young talent, including a mixture of people in their mid-20s or straight from university. Given this demographic, HCL wanted to use a platform that would be familiar and easy to use for them. Social media was an obvious way of attracting talent and, once hired, keeping those employees engaged in the business and producing at a high level.

EFCS is a core value at HCL and one that stands behind everything members of staff there do. The philosophy survives on trust transparency, culture and collaboration – which are all enabled further through social media.

Social media is not used as an alternative to other engagement tools, but as a vital tool that works alongside more traditional methods. Given the rate of change that technology is pushing upon the business world, using social media to hire staff is not "a nice to have" but a "must have".

For HCL there are four drivers behind the business decision to adopt social media:

- Value system – transparency and openness are key to the success of HCL's EFCS philosophy and social media enables open discussion unlike any-thing before it.
- Collaboration – a business needs to be greater than the sum of its parts. To do this employees need a chance to work together without the restric-tions of managers constantly breathing down their neck.
- Across borders – with a staff of 90,000 across dozens of countries HCL needed a single unifying platform to discuss ideas and issues.
- Demographics – like any innovative technology business HCL needs to bring on and be inspired by the latest generation of talent. Rather than trying to crowbar young staff into an old way of doing things HCL have moved with the Zeitgeist to ensure they get the most from new employees.

The solution

Ultimately HCL realized that to attract the best young talent they would have to communicate with them using channels familiar to them – social media. Once employees are hired it is important to the company to carry on their legacy of collaborative innovation and tackling problems in ways that none of their competitors can.

The most important part of the HCL Technologies' outlook is the unique EFCS philosophy, which, in many ways, turns the traditional management hierarchy upside down. Set up in 2005 by visionary CEO Vineet Nayar, the aim of EFCS is to create trust, grow through transparency and to make managers as accountable to employees as employees are to their bosses; to transfer the responsibility for change and value creation to front-line employees working in the "value zone", where HCL and their customers interact.

It was clear that in order to roll this philosophy out in the most effective way possible HCL would need to create their own social network that mimicked the way other social networks work so employees would be instantly receptive and engaged.

Before the philosophy could be actioned, of course, the employees need to be recruited.

Recruitment

With a constantly growing workforce that is approaching 100,000 people, HCL's HR department is always busy recruiting staff at all levels from senior executives to entry-level administrative roles. HCL follows a well-defined strategy suited for different levels of hiring needs – LinkedIn is the preferred social media channel for sourcing mid to senior level candidates while Facebook and Twitter drive their social recruiting efforts for entry level openings.

HCL's employees use social networking sites to map, validate and reference check executive level candidates. This may include using LinkedIn's validations and references, looking at previous employers and then, once these preliminary checks have been done, reaching out to the candidates to escalate the hire.

HCL is also exploring Facebook as a platform for engaging campus hires by activating e-learning initiatives in the period between the stages when an employee is offered a job and when they start. It's hoped that this should effectively shrink time for new joiners to embark on client projects. Facebook has also proved incredibly popular as a word-of-mouth tool for current employees to use to promote open positions to their friends or family. The old adage of "good people, bring good people" has never been more true. Social media amplifies this and ensures that the best employees are able to attract other high quality people.

MEME

HCL's internal social media network, MEME, was set up in response to the growing need to engage with employees and share the EFCS philosophy. While there was some initial scepticism from senior staff, the employees behind the idea set up a trial run. The sceptics soon realized that in order to yield benefits from close collaboration everyone must look at newer ways to engage these young employees and create an organization of tomorrow.

In HCL's entrepreneurial landscape, where passion and conviction are key, the idea soon kicked off and the positive feedback was immediate.

Very soon employees were forming groups around shared interests and projects. For example, BlogHer, a forum on gender neutrality, was quickly set up and received incredible input from both women and men. The group went on to help frame important changes to some of HCL's HR policies.

At a basic level MEME looks and feels like other social networks with forums, networks for friends and colleagues, posting, tagging, pictures, document sharing and group conversations. It now also has a mobile app so even those employees working flexibly can get involved.

There are four main focuses that have led to MEME's success:

- **Generating ideas worth millions**: there are over three hundred project-specific work groups on MEME that are created to bring together people with different areas of expertise who wouldn't otherwise be able to collaborate. These groups have helped in creating business ideas with benefits of more than $25 million to the company.
- **Improved efficiencies**: one of the most noteworthy achievements of MEME has been its ability to significantly improve employee productivity. MEME users leveraged this platform extremely well by creating a direct interface with various enabling functions like HR, IT help desk and other service desks. Rather than going down the traditional route, employees directly sought answers to their queries in a virtual fashion. For example, the top five pages on MEME are dedicated to resolving HR and recruitment related queries across various business units. Some significant results are:
  - To date over 4,190 HR related queries have been resolved though MEME itself. This has helped the HR team bring down the significant query resolution time by 90 per cent.

- Similarly, over 2,000 queries in the area of IT service desk have been resolved through MEME, saving more than 1,000 person hours.
- **High levels of employee engagement**: MEME is also being used to conduct different employee surveys in the most transparent way possible. For example, HR did an online survey on MEME to gauge employee satisfaction levels and received immense response with 25,871 employees taking part. MEME has also played a key role in promoting other employee-specific initiatives within HCL:
  - For example, EPIC (Employee Passion Indicator Count), an annual survey to help employees understand their passion drivers. EPIC received overwhelming response from 516,555 employees within a one-year period versus 41,403 responses in the previous year. In certain areas, like the USA and Mexico, there was a 100 per cent participation rate from employees.
- **Beyond work**: one of the distinct features of MEME is that the platform is not governed by the organization but by the MEMErs (employees) themselves who drive the communication on the platform. This has resulted in some incredible initiatives. After identifying a popular demand of blood bank requests from across the organization, a virtual blood bank (VBB) was hosted on MEME platform and within a week of its launch around 1,201 employees had used the blood bank.

Resources

HCL has put serious time and resources into both implementing a recruiting programme on social media and building a bespoke social media platform. While it's impossible to put an exact cost on this, the return on investment has been invaluable. Aside from the difficult to quantify elements such as staff morale and motivation, which social media has brought about, there are also more tangible results. MEME has played a huge role in two projects that are already making the company millions.

The value portal is an ideas exchange set up to funnel the innovation of 90,000 employees, especially those at the grassroots level, to collaborate with their managers. They then have the opportunity to lead the implementation of their ideas to deliver value to customers. By bringing together employees and customer employees to share knowledge, best practices and ideas – value portal generated 12,500 ideas, of which 2,242 have already been implemented generating $102 million with a further $148 million in the pipeline. A large part of the collaboration has been enabled through social media sites such as MEME and HCL's open policy towards employees using other platforms.

MAD jam is the *X Factor* of ideas that the value portal creates. Standing for "make a difference jamboree", MAD jam brings together the very best new ideas from throughout the company. Those ideas are then judged by senior people from HCL, and one external judge, an associate partner from McKinsey.

Results

As well as fostering a more collaborative and friendly environment for employees MEME has had some very tangible results.

From its initial start date up to January 2012, MEME user base grew at around 111 per cent (from 28,100 employees in April 2011 to 59,185 employees in January 2012). Within the first four months of use, over 25,000 HCL employees created strong social network connections with each other by creating 521 groups, posting more than 4,300 comments and sharing more than 1,030 photographs. Today MEME engages around 75,000 employees through 2,057 groups, 175 pages and 71,568 posts. Looking at the powerful employee contribution to this platform, it would be right to say that it has succeeded in helping HCL employees meet the challenge of building effective relationships, which are vital to working in large, distributed enterprises.

Not to mention how some of the project groups have helped in creating business ideas that have so far resulted in revenues of more than $25 million for the company.

For the recruitment side, savings start in three ways. Costs of advertisement are much more effective as pay per click is more targeted. Market mapping activities are easier and more accurate. Building referral for candidates or selecting individuals is a quotient on how well you farm your account. These three factors drive considerable cost savings compared to the traditional methods.

Other results that have benefited the company are things like driving referrals among employees. And another lesser known advantage is the ability to "tap" passive job seekers, improve employer branding through social conversations, provide market trends and information and hence reduce the dependency on search firms and networks with similarly focused interest groups.

Critical success factors

1. While at first many leaders within the company were sceptical, one of the most critical success factors has been the buy-in from the very top of the

organization. CEO Vineet Nayar is himself a committed tweeter (@vineet-nayar), and has recognized the power of social media to engage employees with his unique philosophy EFCS.

2. An openness with employees has also been crucial to social media success within HCL. By allowing employees to take ownership of MEME, HCL empowered them to take it in whichever direction they wanted. This resulted in a huge variety of groups that have generated benefits across the company in many different ways, from revenues to HR policies.

Lessons learned

While HCL's social media policies have proven to be a great success, there have been many things the teams have learned along the way.

Shergill explains:

> Ideally there would be two things we would have done differently. One is obvious – start the investment earlier, as this media is definitely here to say and it would be great to be receiving the benefits for a longer time.
>
> The second would have been to take a longer look at how the different platforms blend with each other and found out which is best used for awareness and which is better for outreach. We're starting to see it coming out now but a tool that helped with candidate selection would have been incredible.

In a constantly changing media that is encroaching on more and more of working life, Shergill has some advice for other HR practitioners:

- Social media needs to be at the core of your marketing or people strategy.
- A successful CEO is a social savvy CEO.
- It is critical to leverage your strengths in marketing on social media with employee branding and vice versa.
- Whatever size your business, there is nothing stopping you from using social media – indeed it would be risky not to.

Want more? See what has been said about this case or get involved and discuss it with the author and other readers on our LinkedIn group, find it by visiting http://www.socialmedia-mba.com *or search for "The Social Media MBA Alumni".*

Future

25 Rentokil – Crisis Management

Rentokil Initial

Social media is fluid, fast moving and impossible to predict. Having a robust crisis management strategy in place before commencing with any online activities is essential and empowers employees to respond quickly.

Executive summary

Overview

Speed can often mitigate something potentially damaging, but having clarity on what detractors are saying and where they are commenting about your brand can help steer you through troubled waters. Building a loyal following of promoters can help shout down the detractors but being open and honest is always the best approach.

Key findings

- Immediacy of response can quickly turn a detractor into a promoter.
- Have a robust plan in place to crisis manage.
- Honesty builds trust in your brand.

Recommendations

1. To ensure a consistent brand experience is delivered across the globe, introduce training programmes and develop digital assets that are adaptable for all markets.
2. Profiling existing and prospective customers online and understanding their preferred platforms of business contact will provide insight into best practice.
3. Utilize the knowledge of your employees and empower them to champion your brand.

What you need to know

Published articles on the internet tend to stay out there ad infinitum and can follow you around for a very long time. After a few months of engaging with social media, Rentokil Initial had to crisis manage negative publicity about their strategy. It was a steep learning curve but one from which they learned some important lessons which have been integrated into their social media strategy. Rentokil Initial is a business built upon offering excellent service and its mission statement is "we are the experts". Social media is a natural extension to the traditional methods of delivering expert advice to its customers.

- Social media is not only fast paced it can also be a very noisy place. Understanding the influence and motivation of brand detractors is one of the key factors to crisis management.
- Incorporate a social media strategy that will deliver an educational message to influencers early in the decision cycle.

Background

Interviewee

Alicia Holbrook has worked as the Social Media Manager for Rentokil Initial since October 2010 and is responsible for managing and monitoring global social media activities across all divisions of Rentokil Initial.

Previously she worked as a journalist for IPC Media, including the position of Travel and Lifestyle

Alicia Holbrook
@aliciajharney

Editor for *Golf Monthly*. Alicia has contributed to a number of books and publications across the globe.

About Rentokil

Rentokil Initial is one of the largest business services companies in the world, operating in all the major economies of Europe, North America, Asia Pacific and Africa. They employ some 66,000 colleagues providing a range of services in over 60 countries and have a revenue of £2,544 million per annum.

The origins of the company date back to 1903, when the Initialled Towel Rental Service was established in London. Over the past century Rentokil Initial have made a number of acquisitions, which has enabled growth into other sectors and markets globally. These include three global brands Rentokil, Initial, Ambius and several country- or region-specific brands including Pink (Hygiene Services, Australia), Ehrlich, Presto-X and Western (Pest Control, USA) and Calmic (Hygiene Services, Asia).

In addition, the company operates a number of service specific brands, mainly in the UK. These include: Autograph (Business Catering), Eden (School Catering), Knightsbridge (Manned Guarding) and Perception (Reception Services).

The largest division is Rentokil, a global leader in pest control, operating in over 50 countries and employing local teams to bring expert advice to their residential and commercial customers. Rentokil Initial places a specific emphasis on innovation, health, safety and protection of the environment.

Their social media strategy

The main objectives of Rentokil Initial's social media strategy are enquiry generation and thought leadership, realized by delivering expert advice. Current social media activity focuses largely on the Rentokil blog and Twitter.

Social media activities commenced back in 2009 when deBugged, the Rentokil Pest Control blog, was created in-house on a WordPress platform to enhance search performance and enquiry generation. Twitter, YouTube and Facebook accounts were set up at no cost and a specialist digital agency was appointed to advise on strategy and to support the launch of the blog.

Although Rentokil Initial has a significant budget for online search, less than 15 per cent of this is allocated to social media. There are two employees in the group who dedicate their resources to social media, and part-time resource in some markets.

Ownership of social media sits within the global online team and the two teams work closely together to create projects that will appeal to all markets and boost visitors to country web sites, plus generate sales enquiries. Digital agencies are occasionally employed to generate noise around campaigns but strategy is largely created in-house.

Pest control may not seem an obvious fit in the world of social media where consumers want to publically align themselves with the latest piece of technology, pop band or trainers. Who would want to follow a company who tweets about rodent infestations and the hygiene standards of washrooms? One of the major challenges for Rentokil Initial is that services are often sought as a solution to a problem. Customers may only actively seek out the company when they need urgent help – but the correct advice would have been far more useful earlier in their decision cycle. The company ethos is that prevention is better than cure; Rentokil Initial aims to influence buyers by interacting with customers earlier in the buying cycle.

Whilst social signals are becoming increasingly important for search, the next stage in the social media strategy for Rentokil Initial is to facilitate conversations about industry issues. Sharing the wealth of knowledge that entomologists, biologists, scientists and frontline colleagues, such as cleaners and technicians, hold will only serve to build and strengthen relationships with customers.

Ensuring a consistent brand experience is delivered across the globe, social media training programmes are crucial. Knowledge can be a powerful marketing tool. Profiling existing and prospective customers online and understanding their preferred platforms of contact will provide insight into best practice, enabling Rentokil Initial to leverage their expertise to maximum effect.

Customer service via social platforms has been tested with @CityLink who can receive up to 100 Twitter enquiries a day. This relieves pressure from the call centre and the immediacy of a response can quickly turn a detractor into a promoter.

Overall Rentokil Initial would like to be regarded as the "go to" company for expert advice and information. Whether a customer wants to find out how to clean a stubborn stain off a mat or what's eating their carpet, Rentokil Initial will have the answer, or even better a solution to a problem before the customer realizes they have a problem.

The case

Social media it not only fast paced it can also be a very noisy place. Understanding the influence and motivation of brand detractors is one of the key factors to crisis management. When a crisis rears its ugly head and with no social media monitoring tools in place it is difficult to make a decision on how best to mitigate the damage.

So when a blog entitled "How not to use Twitter, by Rentokil" in March 2010 was published by the influential digital marketing web site *Econsultancy*, Rentokil was slow to respond, which only served to aggravate the problem.

In the same week Ben Goldacre slated a Rentokil press release in his *Bad Science* column. "Rentokil make dodgy claims about imaginary bugs" the headline screamed. "Rentokil have engaged in some seriously surreal PR activity on Twitter during my digging on this story, largely around whether they would give me the information they sent to journalists", wrote Goldacre. "The best bits were when they tried to suggest that they were actually being all open and stuff."

Goldacre had hit the nail on the head. Being open was a cultural challenge for Rentokil. Many of their customers demand confidentiality clauses in their contracts, making it difficult to share information and case studies.

Long gone are the days when news turned into fish and chip wrappers. Online news might stay around for a very long time but it can be steered and managed to protect brand reputation.

Background

In March 2010 Rentokil was still new to social media. A year earlier the company launched deBugged, the pest control blog, and by the end of the year had joined Twitter. A specialist social media agency had been engaged to increase followers. What they didn't tell the client was that they had been using bots to trawl Twitter profiles and follow people who had an interest in relevant topics such as health, hygiene, science or had mentioned a keyword like mice, rat or pest control. There were a handful of Twitter users who upon being followed by @Rentokil tweeted back "Why is @Rentokil following me?" A journalist picked up the story and blogged about it.

The content of the article wasn't overtly damaging and on the whole was balanced, but the heading, which was tweeted 46 times, was. All of the criticism of the Twitter follower issue was generated by social media experts and digital agencies. It was doubtful if any of Rentokil's customers read the piece, or were even aware of it.

The story which journalist Ben Goldacre broke in the same week concerning a story in the *Daily Mail* entitled "The 2000 bugs taking a ride in every train compartment" was based on a hypothetical situation. A press release had been issued, which stated that with optimum breeding conditions and access to food and water a single train compartment could house 1,000 cockroaches, 200 bed bugs, 200 fleas, 500 dust mites and 100 carpet beetles. The *Daily Mail* omitted the part about the "optimum breeding conditions" and the reader was led to believe that every train carriage could be infested. Another social media crisis unfolded and over 50 Rentokil web sites crashed from the strain of traffic.

Hindsight is a great thing but foresight is even better. Both internal communications and the PR agency took the classic line of approach and advised the social media team not to respond and that it would all blow over. Traffic to the blog spiked for a couple of weeks then levelled out, but the blog "Why is @Rentokil following me?" is still out there. At the end of 2010 it was announced by *Econsultancy* as one of the top 25 blogs of 2010.

But, as they say, there is no such thing as bad publicity. Rentokil were invited by *Econsultancy* and a number of other industry publications to write about their learnings in social media.

The solution

Social media sits within the newly created marketing and innovation department for the Rentokil Initial Group, hence providing the key benefit that social strategy is not a silo and keeping the focus on the brand rather than a division. Social strategy can be cascaded to support marketing activities such as new product launches or to drive thought leadership across segments.

Analysis of brand sentiment can be a key driver for marketing and innovation. In the early stages of their social media strategy, Rentokil focused largely on creating content for search to drive enquiry generation. As this became successful and the methodology was proven to increase visitors to the web sites, social strategy evolved to incorporate brand awareness projects including the creation of a game and a pest map.

Other than curating an external flow of communication, listening and engaging with customers should be an important part of a social media strategy. More value can be gained from customer insights, which can be used to empower marketing and innovation decisions. Benchmarking brand sentiment against competitors and analyzing how we can improve our services within relevant business sectors is a valuable piece of insight, which should be driven back into the business. If there is a clear demand for a new service or product this insight can be fed back to the innovation team.

As with any large global company, management and consistency of Rentokil's brand message is crucial to maintain. Rentokil Initial wants their customers to experience the same high levels of service in New York as in Hong Kong. To take social media to the next level would require engagement with local customers and local training sessions with country offices. Social media policies have been cascaded to marketing managers globally and are sighted by every new employee. One challenge is that particular care needs to be taken to ensure customer confidentiality is protected.

Finding the appropriate social media monitoring tool is essential for delivering this strategy. Adopting it for relevant reporting can be time consuming too. It can be very easy to be swamped by information. Deciding which information is relevant to your business and presenting it in a manner that is easily accessible and meaningful to the end users can be a long learning curve. There will undoubtedly be colleagues who don't fully understand social media metrics or the ROI. Training sessions and involving them in social media, such as contributing to a blog or sharing an image on Facebook, will help obtain their buy-in.

Reporting is not only a crucial measure of engagement; it can provide something tangible to stakeholders. Customer questions in black and white can provide hard evidence to the management team that social media is not just a buzz word that isn't applicable to business. Some customers prefer to communicate via Twitter than the phone, plus there are real business benefits such as a saving on call waiting times.

Supported by sophisticated reporting social media can be used to refine marketing strategy. Immediacy is becoming increasingly important and responding quickly to comments or questions is key to avoiding criticism and maintaining support in the fast world of online interaction.

One of the key learning curves for Rentokil Initial is that there is no substitute for one-to-one conversations and using bots for people who list similar interests in their bio is just not enough. Forging relationships on Twitter takes time, and should be done at a local level. With a global company, time zones are an issue. If someone asks you a question you need to be in a position to respond quickly and also have access to the information they are seeking.

Finally, deciding objectives is a key part of being able to measure success. Being open minded will enable the organization to text which type of content customers will find useful. For Rentokil Initial, measuring brand sentiment is an important KPI, particularly in regards to removing detractors offline. Increasing customer engagement should deliver an increase in inbound sales queries.

Results

As a direct result of the problem, Rentokil Initial purchased a software monitoring tool that enables global brand monitoring. Social media policies were written and sent to all global marketing managers with directions to cascade them to their teams. A crisis management strategy was written and shared across the group. The method for responding to queries via social media was reviewed, and an honest and open approach decided upon.

Rentokil took the comments on board and rather than downscaling social media activities they have become more creative and focused on educational content, which wasn't heavily branded.

Critical success factors

Less than a year after the negative *Econsultancy* feature, Rentokil was in the spotlight again, but this time in a more favourable light. *Marketing Week* and *Econsultancy* both published articles applauding Rentokil's innovative use of social media, naming their Scamper Mouse Facebook app as one of the six best examples of branded Facebook apps. For a pest-control company with a budget smaller than a bug to be mentioned alongside brands such as Dove, Nike and Tesco was a huge boost for the organization, who had had a public dressing down.

The ultimate benchmark of trust from senior management came early in 2012 when Rentokil Initial was empowered to live tweets from Investor Days, a seminar which contains sensitive information. Rentokil Initial is possibly the first company to do so.

Lessons learned

Alicia explains:

> Be aware that social media is public. Mistakes and PR disasters are likely to happen at some point to any brand. Make sure you have a plan in place to crisis manage, and road test it by doing a dummy run and examining worst case scenarios. Run your responses by PR if you have

one, or ask colleagues to reflect on your response and try and consider if from different viewpoints – could your words be twisted, quoted out of context or simply misunderstood?

She continues:

Try to be as open and honest as possible. Even if you don't have the information and facts immediately to hand, make sure you acknowledge the person who has contacted you.

Alicia concludes:

Sometimes crisis management feels like playing a game of chess, trying to predict the response to what you are considering posting. I always ask myself – would this comment or photograph damage our brand reputation? If the answer is yes then action is needed. And sometimes you need to decide if a response might make matters worse, in this scenario risk assess the issue and the implications which may unfold once you start to engage in a conversation.

Want more? See what has been said about this case or get involved and discuss it with the author and other readers on our LinkedIn group, find it by visiting http://www.socialmedia-mba.com *or search for "The Social Media MBA Alumni".*

INDEX

Index compiled by Annette Musker

32953011977065